THE GRAIL BIRD

The Rediscovery *of the* Ivory-billed Woodpecker

The
GRAIL BIRD

TIM GALLAGHER

HOUGHTON MIFFLIN COMPANY

BOSTON • NEW YORK • 2006

For information about permission to reproduce
selections from this book, write to Permissions,
Houghton Mifflin Company, 215 Park Avenue South,
New York, New York 10003.

Visit our Web site: www.houghtonmifflinbooks.com.

The Library of Congress has cataloged the hardcover
edition as follows:

Gallagher, Tim.
　　The grail bird : hot on the trail of the ivory-billed
　　woodpecker / by Tim Gallagher
　　　　p. cm.
　　Includes bibliographical references.
　　ISBN 0-618-45693-7
　　　　1. Ivory-billed woodpecker. I. Title.

QL696.P56G35 2005
598.7'2 — dc22　2005042792

ISBN-13: 978-0-618-70941-0 (pbk.)
ISBN-10: 0-618-70941-X (pbk.)

Book design by Melissa Lotfy

Map by Bobby Ray Harrison

Printed in the United States of America

MP 10 9 8 7 6 5 4 3 2 1

For my wife, Rachel,
and my children, Railey, Clara, Jack,
and Gwendolyn

CONTENTS

I wish, kind reader, it were in my power to present to your mind's eye the favorite resort of the Ivory-billed Woodpecker. Would that I could describe the extent of deep morasses, overshadowed by dark cypresses, spreading their sturdy, moss-covered branches, as if to admonish intruding man to pause and reflect on the many difficulties which he must encounter, should he persist in venturing farther into their almost inaccessible recesses, extending for miles before him, here and there the mossy trunk of a fallen and decaying tree, and thousands of creeping and twining plants of numberless species! Would that I could represent to the dangerous nature of the ground, its oozing, spongy, and miry disposition, although covered with a beautiful but treacherous carpeting composed of the richest mosses, flags, and water lilies, no sooner receiving the pressure of the foot that it yields and endangers the very life of the adventurer, whilst here and there, as he approaches an opening that proves merely a lake of black muddy water, his ear is assailed by the dismal croaking of innumerable frogs, the hissing of serpents, or the bellowing of alligators! Would that I could give you an idea of the sultry pestiferous atmosphere that nearly suffocates the intruder during the meridian heat of our dog days in those gloomy and horrible swamps! But the attempt to picture these scenes would be in vain. Nothing short of ocular demonstration can impress any adequate idea of them.

—JOHN JAMES AUDUBON

The Former Realm of the Ivory-bill

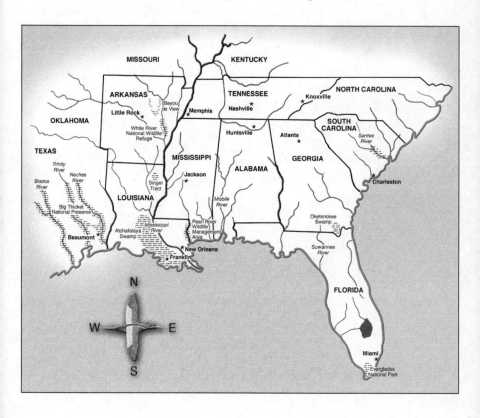

PREFACE

I think I've always been the kind of person who gets caught up in obsessive quests, most of which seem to involve birds. I'm naturally curious, and I love a challenge. I remember for a time in high school I wanted to find out everything there was to know about the Richardson's merlin, a pale subspecies of merlin that breeds only on the wide-open prairies of southern Canada and a few places in the northern United States. I read everything I could find about this small falcon, sometimes traveling to university libraries and digging through ornithological tomes from the nineteenth century. I loved the detective work and the sense of mystery about it.

Finally one summer I talked my friend Steve Nadeau, who owned a small pickup truck, into driving north into Canada with me to search for these birds. It took a couple of days to get there from southern California, where we lived, and we spent several weeks camping out, living on the cheap, trying to figure out where the falcons were.

Of course, by that time the places we visited were nothing at all like what the early ornithologists described. In one case, what had been a wooden stockade surrounded by wilderness was now a thriving city. But Steve and I persevered, and after a couple of weeks we found a pair of the birds nesting in an old crow's nest in a lone stand of trees out on the prairie.

I'll never forget the sense of triumph, the intense joy we felt as we were hiking to those trees — seemingly the thousandth clump of trees we had investigated on the trip — and we suddenly saw the male flying out to investigate, calling as he circled above us. It was so hard to believe, so unimaginable that we had succeeded. If

I weren't hooked on quixotic quests before that moment, I certainly was after it.

That was a lot of journeys ago. I have since taken part in many research projects and expeditions. I have traveled the backcountry of Iceland, roping down lofty cliffs to gyrfalcon nests. I've gone on expeditions to Greenland to study peregrine falcons, gyrfalcons, and other arctic birds — on one trip, traveling north along the west coast of this huge island in an open boat between icebergs as large as buildings. And I once took part in a bowhead whale census off the north slope of Alaska. We camped on the ice, five miles offshore, and used hydrophone arrays to pinpoint each calling whale as well as visual sightings to establish the number of animals migrating past — at the same time as Inuit hunters were paddling among the whales in their sealskin boats, trying to harpoon them.

Ivory-billed woodpeckers have been a longtime obsession with me. I first became interested in them in the early 1970s, when I read a *Life* magazine article about John Dennis's sightings of the species in the Big Thicket of east Texas. Many scientists later discounted his sightings — which seems to be what usually happens when people claim to have seen an ivory-bill. But it was enough to pique my interest and get me started on learning more about the bird.

I was able to control my budding obsession with this bird for many years. I became involved in the peregrine falcon reintroduction effort, which took up most of my time. But every so often this obsession would flare up again, and I would start dreaming about swamps and imagining what it would be like to find an ivory-bill. The bird is so iconic: big, beautiful, mysterious — a symbol of everything that has gone wrong with our relationship to the environment. There is such a sense of finality about extinction. I thought that if someone could just locate an ivory-bill, could prove that this remarkable species still exists, it would be the most hopeful event imaginable: we would have one final chance to get it right, to save this bird and the bottomland swamp forests it needs to survive.

Like many ivory-bill seekers, my passion flared to a fever pitch when a Louisiana turkey hunter emerged from the swamp in the spring of 1999 with a tale about a pair of large woodpeckers with field marks that exactly fit those of the ivory-bill. I think everyone who admires the bird must have breathed a collective sigh of relief: *The ivory-bill is okay; it miraculously survived, and now if we can just maintain enough suitable habitat for it, the species will slowly recover.*

What an amazing thought — and how crushing when no one was able to find the birds during subsequent searches. I think that's what really got me going. I didn't want to give up that dream. I didn't want to accept that the ivory-bill was gone forever. I started looking for people who had had direct experience with the ivory-bill to see if I could glean anything from their knowledge that would help me in my search for this bird. I interviewed dozens of people, a few of whom I felt had definitely seen ivory-bills, many of whom clearly had not. I read every obscure reference to the bird that I could find. It was like my teenage search for the Richardson's merlin magnified a hundredfold. Eventually I hit the swamp myself, exploring potential ivory-bill habitats across the South. What follows is a personal narrative of that journey — one that I am still embarked on.

1

OF PEOPLE
AND PECKERWOODS

I GUESS THIS STORY BEGINS, at least for me, in an old white barn in a field in Ithaca, New York. Nicknamed the Dog Barn, the building has been used for years as a storage area by the Cornell Laboratory of Ornithology, where I work. As I sit here on its upper floor, I gaze at a massive hollow tree stump before me, then at a photograph of an active ivory-billed woodpecker nest. In the picture, which was taken in the mid-1930s by the lab's founder, Arthur A. Allen, an adult male ivory-bill clings to the side of a tree beside its nest hole. It is clear that the stump in front of me was sawed from the same tree shown in the picture. Placing my hand exactly where the bird is sitting in the photograph, I close my eyes. It's an eerie feeling. Right here, on this rough patch of bark, one of the rarest birds on earth — a species that most scientists declared extinct decades ago — clung to this tree and tried, against all odds, to reproduce its kind.

The motion pictures and sounds recorded by Allen during his 1935 expedition are the only universally accepted ones ever made of this species. But I'm getting ahead of myself. To understand and appreciate the ivory-billed woodpecker phenomenon fully, we need to go back to the days of colonial America and trace the history of the birds' relationship with people.

Probably the best place to start is with Mark Catesby, an Englishman who came to this country in 1712 and began working on a natural history of the plants and animals of the North American colonies. Of course the indigenous people already knew ivory-bills well and used their big white bills as items of barter, but the Native Americans' relationship with the birds is known chiefly through the writings of Catesby and a handful of other early naturalists.

Catesby named the bird the "Largest White-bill Wood-pecker" — as accurate a name as any, I guess — and he was apparently the first person to describe the species. I say "apparently" because some believe that Catesby borrowed a number of his species descriptions from the work of John Lawson, an earlier naturalist who ran into a spot of trouble at the hands of the Tuscaroras in 1711. Just a year previously, he had been commissioned to compile a complete natural history of America. Unfortunately, he joined a Swiss adventurer, Baron Christoph von Graffenried, who was trying to cook up some get-rich-quick schemes.

Graffenried convinced Lawson to go with him on an exploratory trip from the Carolinas to Virginia, to see if the Neuse River was a better route than the existing one. The two men and their companions were soon captured by a large party of Tuscaroras, who hated all white men for usurping their land and their hunting rights. The Tuscaroras decided that the unwelcome intruders should be put to death — slowly. But Graffenried, an engaging con man in the Baron von Münchausen mode, convinced them that he was a particular favorite of the Great White Queen in England and that they must release him at once or face the consequences. It must have been a galling moment for Lawson, seeing Graffenried stroll merrily away just before the Indians stuck him and the others full of pitch-pine splinters, which they subsequently set on fire.

John Lawson's untimely demise left the field of North American nature study wide open for Mark Catesby. Catesby had a high time in the colonies, frequently carousing with his good friend William Byrd II of Westover, Virginia. When the two got together, the entertainment was often lavish. One time as they traveled home on a ship, the two "were so merry that Mr. Catesby sang."

The most interesting thing about Catesby's description of the largest white-bill woodpecker is what he says about the Native Americans' relationship with the bird: "The bills of these Birds are much valued by the Cannola Indians, who made Coronets of 'em for their Princes and great warriors, by fixing them round a Wreath, with their points outward. The Northern Indians having none of these birds in their cold country, purchase them off the Southern People at the price of two, and sometimes three, Buckskins a Bill." Apparently ivory-billed woodpeckers have been getting hammered by humans as long as *Homo sapiens* has been present in the New World.

If Mark Catesby did plagiarize John Lawson's work, he eventually received his just reward. Several years after Catesby's *Natural History of Carolina, Florida, and the Bahama Islands* was published, the famed Swedish naturalist Carolus Linnaeus (who invented the modern binomial taxonomic system) lifted freely from the work and formally described and named the bird (which he had never seen), basically claiming its discovery for himself.

Another ivory-bill seeker worth noting is Alexander Wilson, a person I feel close to in a way. A bronze statue of Wilson, about three feet high and set on a white wooden pedestal, sits in an out-of-the-way hallway on the second floor of the Lab of Ornithology's new building. I see him almost every morning as I walk into the upstairs bird observatory to check for waterfowl that have newly arrived on Sapsucker Woods Pond. Like Hamlet contemplating Yorick's skull, Wilson stands in a thoughtful pose, silently regarding a dead bird he holds in his hand — a bird he had no doubt recently blasted with his trusty flintlock musket. You see, like most early ornithologists, Wilson was a confirmed bird whacker. He always went into the field with a gun instead of the binoculars that birders carry today. In the early nineteenth century, many of the birds of North America were not yet known to science, so almost anything held the potential for discovery. Wilson was also a wildlife artist, so he needed specimens to help him draw the birds accurately. But his bird illustrations tend to have a rather lifeless look — not surprisingly, I suppose, since most of them were drawn from dead birds.

Wilson, who immigrated from Scotland, had been a weaver and a would-be poet before fleeing his native land and coming to America. It seems that his political verse offended too many prominent people. He arrived here in 1794 and struggled for a few years as a teacher and surveyor. In a letter to a friend in 1804, he said he intended to make a collection of North American birds, because watching birds had become his chief comfort in life, "a sort of rough Bone that amuses me when sated with dull drudgery." Four years later, he published the first volume of his *American Ornithology* — the first comprehensive account of North American bird life, based on his observations of almost three hundred species.

Despite his bird-killing ways, Wilson had a big heart, which he often wore on his sleeve. I still choke up when I read about the copious tears he shed at the grave of Meriwether Lewis: "That brave soldier, that amiable and excellent man, over whose solitary grave in the wilderness I have since shed tears of affliction, having been cut off in the prime of his life, I hope I shall be pardoned for consecrating this humble note to his memory, until a more able pen shall do better justice to the subject." (Lewis had brought Wilson some newly discovered birds to paint when he returned with William Clark and the Corps of Discovery from their epic exploration of the American West.)

One of Wilson's great yarns involved an ivory-billed woodpecker he shot a few miles from Wilmington, North Carolina. The bird was only slightly injured, so Wilson got the bright idea to keep it as a pet, so he could study it and illustrate it from life at his leisure. The bird had other ideas. Upon its capture, the wood-pecker "uttered a loudly reiterated and most piteous note, exactly resembling the violent crying of a young child, which terrified my horse so as to nearly cost me my life."

Wilson drove his wagon twelve miles south to Wilmington, but as he went down the main street, the ivory-bill started its piti-ful caterwauling again, drawing everyone within earshot ("especially women") to their doors and windows with alarmed looks, as though a small child were being tortured. Ignoring them, he drove on.

When he arrived at an inn, Wilson decided to play a little joke on the landlord and a few bystanders. "The landlord came forward, and a number of other persons who happened to be there, all equally alarmed at what they heard," he wrote. "This was greatly increased by my asking whether he could furnish me with accommodations for myself and my baby. The man looked blank and foolish, while the others stared with still greater astonishment. After diverting myself for a minute or two at their expense, I drew my Woodpecker from under the cover, and a general laugh took place."

A short time later, though, the joke was on Wilson. He left the bird loose in his hotel room while he arranged to have his horse stabled and cared for. When he returned, less than an hour later, the bird had nearly destroyed one wall of the room in its efforts to escape. "He had mounted along the side of the window, nearly as high as the ceiling, a little below which he had begun to break through. The bed was covered with large pieces of plaster; the lath was exposed for at least fifteen inches square, and a hole, large enough to admit the fist, opened to the weather-boards; so that, in less than another hour, he would certainly have succeeded in making his way through."

Wilson needed to go out again, this time to find grubs to feed his unwilling pet. "I wished to preserve his life," he wrote, "[so I went] off in search of suitable food for him." To keep the bird from escaping or further wrecking the wall, he tied a string to its leg and attached the other end to the leg of a beautiful mahogany table. When he returned from his grub hunt, he found another surprise waiting: "As I reascended the stairs, I heard him again hard at work, and on entering, had the mortification to perceive that he had almost entirely ruined the mahogany table to which he was fastened, and on which he had wreaked his whole vengeance."

The ivory-bill died a few days later, much to Alexander Wilson's dismay. "While engaged in taking the drawing, he cut me severely in several places, and, on the whole, displayed such a noble and unconquerable spirit, that I was frequently tempted to restore him to his native woods," he wrote. "He lived with me for three days, but refused all sustenance, and I witnessed his death with regret."

The next in a long line of distinguished ivory-billers was the great man himself, John James Audubon, who saw dozens of the birds on his trips through the South in the early nineteenth century and wrote this colorful description: "I have always imagined, that in the plumage of the beautiful Ivory-billed Woodpecker, there is something very closely allied to the style of colouring of the great Vandyke. The broad extent of its dark glossy body and tail, the large and well-defined white markings and the brilliant yellow of its eye, have never failed to remind me of some of the boldest and noblest productions of that inimitable artist's pencil."

But even during Audubon's life (1785–1851), the ivory-bill had started its perilous downward spiral, owing largely to habitat destruction. This was a bird that thrived in vast tracts of virgin timber, where there were always enough dead and dying trees to attract its favorite grubs. The great trees across the South were being felled en masse to feed an insatiable lumber industry, especially after the Civil War.

Another unfortunate factor in the demise of the ivory-bill and other rare birds in the nineteenth century was the fad of collecting birds. Bird collectors were not an untrained assemblage of backwoods hunters who shot whatever they happened to stumble upon for the dinner table. They were experts and included many prominent ornithologists. They specifically targeted threatened birds — the rarer, the better — to add to their collections, like philatelists chasing a rare postage stamp. And they had enough knowledge of the natural history of these birds and the location of their habitats to significantly harm some species that were already perilously close to extinction.

Mark V. Barrow, Jr., examines this dilemma in *A Passion for Birds,* his excellent history of the early days of the American Ornithologists' Union. Barrow writes, "Faced with the impending extinction of [the Carolina parakeet] and other species, the taxidermist William T. Hornaday's urgent advice reflected the dominant ethos of the culture of collecting: '*Now* is the time to collect.'" So the very rarest birds were the ones most ruthlessly sought.

Even the great ornithologist Frank Chapman, the famed director of ornithology at the American Museum of Natural History, collected some critically rare birds — in his case, Carolina parakeets. He sought the birds in their final stronghold in Florida and finally located a flock in March 1889. He shot three adults and one young parakeet. Then, a couple of days later, he bagged five more specimens. In his journal that night he wrote, "Now we have nine specimens and I shall make no further attempt to secure others, for we have almost exterminated two of the three small flocks which occur here, and far be it from me to deal the final blows. Good luck to you poor doomed creatures, may you live to see many generations of your kind."

But just two days later he found another flock, one he believed was the last in the area, and his noble intentions crumbled. He wrote afterward, "Good resolutions like many other things are much easier to plan than to practice. The parakeets tempted me and I fell; they also fell, six more of them making our total fifteen."

Chapman was later to become a major conservationist and a champion in the fight to save herons, egrets, and other wading birds then being slaughtered by the thousands to decorate women's hats. He was one of the founders of the Audubon Society. Was he perhaps trying to assuage a guilty conscience?

Things were no better for the ivory-billed woodpecker. Even respected scientists, who knew what a devastating effect their actions were having on these species, were not immune to the lure of rare bird specimens and used their intimate knowledge of the birds to hunt them down. An 1890 picture of the renowned ornithologist William Brewster shows him looking like a hillbilly, with a full shaggy beard and a floppy felt hat, sitting on a scow on Florida's Suwannee River with a freshly shot ivory-bill on his lap. Frank Chapman sits a few feet away, gently cradling a double-barreled shotgun.

By 1920, no one had seen any ivory-bills for several years, and many ornithologists believed that the species was extinct. When people did report seeing ivory-bills, they were not believed. The problem is that to the untrained eye, the common pileated woodpecker, another large, crested hammerhead, looks like an ivory-bill. Unless the person reporting was a well-respected ornithologist, he or she might be branded a fool, a liar, or a kook — a situation that, sadly, is even truer today than it was in the early years of the last century.

But then, in the spring of 1924, the bird experienced the first in a series of miraculous resurrections. Arthur Allen and his wife, Elsa, who were traveling in Florida, checked out an alleged ivory-bill sighting and managed to locate an active nest. Allen had no wish to collect the birds. "Since it is our belief that more is to be gained from a study of the living bird than from a series of museum specimens, we refrained from collecting the birds and planned our itinerary so as to spend the greater part of the following month studying them," he wrote. To avoid placing undue stress on the birds, which for all he knew might be the last breeding pair on the planet, he didn't set up camp next to them but stayed in town instead. The word was out, though. One day while he was away, a couple of local collectors shot the pair — legally. And so the ivory-billed woodpecker once more crossed into the nether regions between existence and extinction.

• • •

The next time the ivory-bill reared its beautiful head was in the early 1930s, in a huge tract of virgin timber along Louisiana's Tensas River. Mason Spencer, a country lawyer and state legislator from the wilds of northeastern Louisiana, was visiting the director of the state Department of Wildlife and Fisheries at his headquarters in Baton Rouge. At one point the director asked him how the moonshine was in his area. "One of our game wardens must be drinking it," he said, "because he says he sees ivory-bills there."

"He's right. I've seen them myself," replied Spencer.

Incredulous, the director drew up a collecting permit for Spencer and challenged him to prove it. A short time later, Spencer came back with a freshly shot male ivory-bill and, as legend has it, flung it down on the director's desk.

From there the story returns to Cornell University, where Arthur Allen was still smarting about what had happened in Florida nearly a decade earlier. He had thought he would be able to make the first in-depth natural history study of these birds, but his hopes had been dashed by the bird collectors. If the stories coming out of Louisiana were true — if there really was a small remnant population of ivory-bills hanging on deep in the Louisiana bayou — he might get a chance to study them after all.

And so in 1935 the great Brand–Cornell University–American Museum of Natural History Ornithological Expedition was launched. It was the first scientific expedition of its kind, attempting to record motion pictures and sounds of vanishing birds across the United States. The team included the Cornell professors Arthur Allen and Peter Paul Kellogg, James Tanner, a grad student, and the famed bird artist George Miksch Sutton, who was also an ornithologist and the curator of the Cornell bird collection. One of their primary goals was to check out the Singer Tract, the 81,000-acre virgin forest where Mason had collected the ivory-bill. But was he a reliable witness? Okay, he had managed to bag one bird, but were there really any more out there? It's a good thing Sutton went on the trip; otherwise we would have only dull technical articles published in scientific journals to learn more about the expedition. Sutton was a real life-of-the-party type, a hilarious conversationalist who joked, played the piano, and sang various amusing songs. (I'm sure he and Mark Catesby would have been fast friends.) More than this, he was a wonderful writer. In books such as *Eskimo Year* and *Iceland Summer*, he vividly captured the people, wildlife, and landscapes he experienced. He described what happened on the 1935 ivory-bill expedition in an essay titled "Kints!" in his book *Birds in the Wilderness*, published the following year.

According to Sutton, the first thing the team did was look up Mason Spencer, so they could grill him about the birds. "[Spencer] was good enough to tell us what he knew about the country, to show us big maps, to warn us about the mosquitoes and the dangers of becoming lost, and to put us in touch with friends of his who would help us find the ivory-bills," wrote Sutton. "The talk in Mr. Spencer's office kept us on the edge of our chairs. There could be no doubt that we were in a fearful and wonderful country. We were amazed to learn that mammalogists considered wolves more common in this section of Louisiana than in any other part of the United States."

But the ornithologists still had serious doubts. Sutton finally put it directly: "Mr. Spencer, you're sure the bird you're telling us about isn't the big pileated woodpecker?"

Spencer exploded. "Man alive! These birds I'm tellin' you all about is kints!" he shouted in their faces. "Why, the pileated woodpecker's just a little bird about as big as that." He held his fingers a few inches apart. "A kint's as big as that!" he said, holding his arms wide, like a fisherman describing the one that got away. He glared angrily at them. "Why, man, I've known kints all my life. My pappy showed 'em to me when I was just a kid. I see 'em every fall when I go deer huntin' down aroun' my place on the Tinsaw. They're *big* birds, I tell you, big and black and white; and they fly through the woods like pintail ducks!"

After Spencer's outburst, the members of the team were all believers—not just because of his vehemence, but because his description was so accurate. Ivory-bills do not have the typical bounding flight of the pileated woodpecker. They generally fly away high and straight, with stiff flight feathers, looking very much like a pintail, and their call is a distinctive nasal *kent, kent, kent*—very similar to the local name Spencer used, kint. Sutton and the others couldn't wait to get to the bayou and start searching.

As it turned out, that was not an easy proposition. The cabin owned by Jack Kuhn, the local game warden who would be guiding them, was inaccessible by car. A middle-aged black man met them along the parish road and transferred their luggage and equipment to an old mule-drawn wagon. From there they seemed to step back in time, driving the wagon through the swamp on a flooded trail that Sutton said was practically a lake.

When they finally reached the small cabin, Kuhn was affable and enthusiastic, and he tirelessly slogged through the bayou with them, sometimes through waist-deep water. Woodpeckers were everywhere—pileateds, red-headeds, red-bellieds—and he even showed them what he said were the workings of an ivory-bill in some trees. But a couple of days later they still hadn't seen any of the birds they were looking for, and Kuhn was starting to worry.

"Now, men, by this time I guess you all must be thinkin' that this is a put-up job," he said. "But I want to tell you that the ivory-bills are here. I know it because I've seen 'em myself and I know the man who saw 'em last. He saw 'em right here, right in that very tree, not more than three weeks ago!"

The next day they plunged even deeper into the swamp, walking eastward under the gigantic trees, skirting the hidden pools, poison ivy, and poisonous snakes. To cover more territory they spread out, but they walked in a line in the same direction so they could keep in contact with one another. The vegetation was so thick that they eventually stopped trying to avoid the poison ivy and just plunged boldly ahead. Suddenly Sutton heard Kuhn shouting, but his voice was muffled and indistinct.

When they reached him, Kuhn was practically jumping up and down, his face gleaming with boyish joy. "Right there, men!" he said. "Didn't any of you hear it?" They looked at him blankly. "I heard it plain, several times. Right in that direction!"

He pointed into the distance, but all they heard was the mocking, Woody Woodpecker–like laugh of a pileated woodpecker. Kuhn's face dropped. He motioned them to start again, so they spread out and began walking in the direction from which he had heard the sound. Sutton decided to stick close to him.

When they came to an enormous fallen cypress log, they climbed on top and started walking along its length to get a clearer view of the area. Kuhn suddenly stopped dead in his tracks and whispered hoarsely to Sutton, "There it goes, doc! Did you see it?" Again a blank stare. Frustrated, Kuhn grabbed Sutton by the shoulders and spun him around, almost making them both fall off the log. "It flew from its nest, too, doc!" yelled Kuhn, pointing excitedly. "What do you think of that! A nest! See it? There it is, right up there!"

Sutton had seen a large bird fly from the dead tree, and he could see the huge hole forty feet above the ground — an ivory-billed woodpecker nest. The two men were so overjoyed that they started dancing a "queer jig" on top of the log, laughing giddily and pounding each other on the back, almost falling off several times.

"Jim [Tanner], who by this time had joined us, was beside himself with eagerness to see the nest and bird and with laughing at our capers," wrote Sutton. "And Professor Allen, who had crashed forward like a bear, was laughing too."

It's great to think of those serious academics so beside themselves with joy that they were laughing and dancing in the wilderness. A short time later, two birds returned, providing spectacular views. "The whole experience was like a dream," wrote Sutton. "There we sat in the wild swamp, miles and miles from any highway, with two ivory-billed woodpeckers so close to us that we could see their eyes, their long toes, even their slightly curved claws with our binoculars."

The only member of the team who missed these impromptu festivities was Peter Paul Kellogg, who had gone to town on the day of the discovery. The techno-geek of the group, Kellogg had already been hard at work getting their motion picture and sound-recording equipment ready. The equipment filled a couple of huge vans, which Allen had parked in the yard of the local jail in nearby Tallulah. The inmates got a laugh from seeing the ornithologists load the old mule wagon with their high-tech gear. A few of them told Allen confidentially, "[We] could show [you] more of these 'pecker-woods' if [you] could arrange a leave of absence."

Allen wasted no time in packing up and getting back to the nest site. This time he'd be damned if he let anyone harm the birds. In a letter in the Cornell archives, addressed to the American Museum of Natural History, Allen described how he had tried to avoid disturbing the birds in Florida and how they had ended up getting shot. This time he was coy in all of his letters and telegrams and would not tell anyone exactly where he was. He set up Camp Ephilus — a clever play on the scientific name of the ivory-billed woodpecker, *Campephilus principalis* — within two hundred yards of the nest and kept watch with 24x binoculars throughout the daylight hours, recording the intimate details of the birds' behavior. At the time this was the most in-depth study ever completed on this species.

Although Allen and the others stayed only a couple of weeks, they produced the first motion pictures and sound recordings ever made of the ivory-billed woodpecker. By today's standards, their equipment was primitive. Tape recorders had not yet been invented. (Kellogg would later play a key role in their development.) This was only eight years after the first talking movie debuted, awing film audiences worldwide. Allen and Kellogg's team used the movietone system to record the bird sounds on their trip. In this sound-recording method, vibrations striking the microphone were converted first into electrical impulses and then into light of varying intensity, which was captured on motion-picture film. After the film was developed, the process could be reversed, converting the various undulating light images back into electrical impulses and then into sound. I can't imagine a more convoluted or difficult way to record sound, and yet it worked. And ivory-bill seekers still play tapes and CDs made from those original cuts, hoping to elicit a response from a living ivory-bill.

The motion pictures from the Cornell expedition now seem stiff and jerky, like an old silent movie — which probably only adds to the otherworldly quality of this species, as do the stiff, formalized portraits of ivory-bills painted by Audubon, Wilson, and others who saw the birds in life.

Of course, there was no way the Cornell ornithologists could learn enough about a species like this in the short amount of time they spent at the Singer Tract. "For years it has been obvious that an intensive study of the bird in its natural haunts would be essential to determine its needs before any constructive work for its preservation could be attempted," wrote Allen. "Because of the nature and remoteness of the ivory-bill's habitat the problem offered such difficulties as to make it prohibitive to most ornithologists who have professional obligations of one sort or another."

Allen numbered himself among the group of ornithologists who didn't have time to take part in this kind of intensive study. He led the 1935 expedition during a sabbatical leave. But he knew how vital such work was if the ivory-bill was to be saved. When the National Audubon Society came up with a grant to fund an in-depth study of the species, he recommended Jim Tanner without reservation.

Allen couldn't have made a better choice. Tanner returned alone to the Singer Tract and spent two years, from 1937 to 1939, studying the ivory-bills and trying to find new nesting areas. He stayed in the field for weeks at a time, building up a lengthy report that formed the basis for his Ph.D. dissertation and was later published as a book, *The Ivory-billed Woodpecker*. "I never tired of watching them," he wrote.

In addition to the time he stayed in the Singer Tract, Tanner spent eight months exploring possible ivory-bill areas in other parts of the South and checking out reports. All told, he logged more than 45,000 miles in his aging Model A Ford, visiting the Big Cypress, Apalachicola River bottoms, the Suwanee River area, Jane Green Swamp, Bear Bay, and the Royal Palm Park in Florida. He searched in Georgia's great Okefenokee Wildlife Refuge, the Mobile Delta in Alabama, and the Yazoo Delta in Mississippi. Sometimes he drove, sometimes he took a train or boat, and sometimes he walked, rode a horse, or waded. He was tireless and unstoppable. And he had a knack for engaging local people of all kinds to provide him with clues in his search. A number of people told him of ivory-bill sightings he thought were credible. He checked them all out. Sometimes he found large woodpecker workings on trees; sometimes he found nothing. But in spite of all his travels, the only ivory-billed woodpeckers he ever saw were the ones in the Singer Tract. In his opinion, the only hope of saving the species lay in preserving that ancient forest.

The fight to save the Singer Tract ivory-bills heated up in the early 1940s as logging kicked into high gear. Many hoped that the area could be preserved as a refuge, not just for the ivory-bills but for all the remarkable wildlife that persisted there and for the massive old-growth trees. Some believed it should be a national park. In his report on the ivory-bill, Tanner had made a modest proposal about preserving enough of the original habitat to ensure the survival of a small number of the nearly extinct woodpeckers. But the Chicago Mill and Lumber Company, which owned the logging rights to the land, had no interest in reaching a compromise and apparently speeded up its cutting in response to Tanner's report.

John Baker, the president of the National Audubon Society, appealed to Franklin D. Roosevelt, a personal friend, to intercede on behalf of the Singer Tract ivory-bills. The president told the secretary of the interior to look into it. Baker hoped that the lumber company would sell its right to the trees for a reasonable price, and he obtained a pledge from the governor of Louisiana to put up $200,000 for that purpose. Governor Jones was joined by the governors of Arkansas, Mississippi, and Tennessee in asking that the ivory-bill's habitat be spared.

The lumber company adamantly refused to bargain when its representatives met with Baker and other officials in 1943. The Singer Sewing Machine Company, which owned the land but had sold the logging rights to Chicago Mill, refused to intercede, and all efforts to go through Congress led nowhere.

Baker next sent Richard Pough, an Audubon researcher, to the area to look for more ivory-bills. Pough searched almost every day from December 4, 1943, to January 19, 1944, as enormous trees were felled nearby. He watched in horror as the lumber crew reduced this once beautiful primeval forest to a shattered wasteland. Some of the trees were more than six feet in diameter. He finally located a lone female ivory-bill in an uncut stand surrounded by devastation and told Baker that the remaining trees would soon be felled.

The artist Don Eckelberry, who then worked for the National Audubon Society, went in April 1944 to see if the bird was still around. The stand of trees she had been roosting in had already been cut down, but a local game warden, Jesse Laird, had found another clump of trees where he thought it was staying. The two went looking for the bird. Just before dark they heard her call, and then they saw her hitching up the tree toward her roost hole. In an essay Eckelberry wrote years later called "Search for the Rare Ivory-bill," he described the two weeks he spent in the swamp sketching the bird. It was a discouraging time. To cut the timber, the logging company employed German prisoners of war, who were themselves disgusted with the destruction of the forest. "[The Germans] were incredulous at the waste — only the best wood taken, the rest left in wreckage," wrote Eckelberry. "I watched one tree come screaming down and cared to see no more."

Don Eckelberry's two-week observation and sketching of an ivory-billed woodpecker is the last universally accepted sighting of one of these birds in the United States.

· · ·

From here the story moves to Cuba — as it has done a number of times in the intervening years. A subspecies of the ivory-billed woodpecker had existed in Cuba, although ornithologists believed it had become extinct in the early twentieth century, because so many of the great forests on the island had been clearcut. One interesting thing about Cuba is that the ivory-bill is the only large crested woodpecker found there. Pileated woodpeckers have never lived there, so if you see a large crested woodpecker in Cuba, it pretty much has to be an ivory-bill.

John V. Dennis, who later became a popular bird author, and Davis Crompton, an avid bird watcher from Worcester, Massachusetts, traveled to Cuba in 1948 to check out rumors of possible ivory-bill sightings in the Oriente region. They spent several days exploring stretches of "appropriate" habitat — the kind of places Jim Tanner would certainly have looked at if he had been there. They found nothing. But then Dennis and Crompton decided to search in a devastated area of cutover pines, which Dennis described as being like hell on earth. He told of workers cutting down trees, smoking cigarettes and flipping the butts in the sawdust and cut stumps on the ground, and making no effort to prevent fires, and he mentioned the constant smoke in the background when such fires started. Amazingly, the two men found a breeding pair of ivory-bills in all this chaos and destruction, nesting in a hole in a dead pine. There Dennis snapped the last scientifically accepted photographs ever taken of an ivory-bill, an adult male perched on the side of its nest tree. His article and one of the photographs were published that year in *The Auk*, the venerable journal of the American Ornithologists' Union.

Two years later, in March 1950, Dennis was once again on the trail of the ivory-bill, this time on the Chipola River in northwestern Florida. He and Whitney Eastman, a prominent businessman and well-known bird watcher, were following up on some ivory-billed woodpecker reports from local woodsmen. Dennis bailed out of the search a few days later and then was dismayed to read in the newspaper that Eastman and his party had soon after located a pair of ivory-bills there.

"In spite of a strong wish to believe this report, I found myself in the same camp as the skeptics," wrote Dennis. There is great irony in the fact that he dismissed his colleague's sighting, as I explain later. But the alleged sighting was enough to take him back for another look. Just as the Cornell team had grilled Mason Spencer about his ivory-bill sightings in the 1930s, Dennis cross-examined the man who had guided Whitney Eastman. "No siree," said the man, "this ain't one of them good gods. This here's an ivory-bill for sure." Pileated woodpeckers were often known colloquially as "Good God" birds, because that's what people said when they came across one. The ivory-bills, in contrast, were called "Lord God" birds, because people who saw one were likely to exclaim, "Lord God, what a bird!"

The guide took Dennis deep into the swamp at dusk and left him in a rowboat, partially concealed by cypress trees, close to a huge dead tree where the birds were said to roost. "It was nearly dark when I was startled by the sound so well described as the tooting of a child's tin trumpet," wrote Dennis. "A few blasts came from the darkness beyond the roost tree and then silence . . . This, to my knowledge, was the last time the Chipola offered any evidence of the ivory-bill."

According to Dennis, another well-known ornithologist, Herbert L. Stoddard, also made some credible ivory-bill sightings in the 1950s. One time Stoddard was circling in a small plane over Georgia's Altamaha River during a thunderstorm when he "clearly saw an ivory-bill in flight at a distance of no more than 150 feet." Stoddard was quite familiar with the species and had seen more than a dozen of them as a boy between 1896 and 1900, when he lived in Florida. But he was reluctant to provide location details about his sightings. "Although he was very close-mouthed," wrote Dennis, "it was well known in ornithological circles that Stoddard knew a great deal about the recent whereabouts of the ivory-bill." Dennis mentioned that Stoddard saw a pair of ivory-bills in a beetle-killed spruce near Thomasville, Georgia, probably in 1958.

Stoddard disagreed with Tanner's view that the ivory-bill required large tracts of virgin timber to exist, citing the fact that a taxidermist had shot a pair of the birds in 1924 in a tract that had been cut over in 1904. Stoddard blamed shooters for causing the decline of the species, and perhaps that is why he didn't publicize his sightings. In his 1969 autobiography, he wrote, "I have observed three ivory-bills in the Southeast in the last fifteen years, and while these sightings are several years old, I feel quite confident that the ivory-bill still has a chance to survive."

The naturalist and author John K. Terres sighted a pair of ivory-bills in Florida in 1955, but for fear of being scorned, he kept the sighting a secret for more than thirty years. He and his wife saw the birds fly over them, only twenty feet high. "What I saw I shall remember the rest of my life — ivory white bills, first, then the broad area of white across both the forward and rear parts of their wings," he wrote. "They were not pileated woodpeckers! 'Ivory-bills,' I yelled."

Another tantalizing sighting was made by two Chicago bird watchers, Bedford P. Brown, Jr., and Jeffrey R. Sanders, in the 1950s. They wrote to Dennis that they were driving east of Pensacola, Florida, near Eglin Air Force Base and decided to do some exploring in an area along a stream, "where pine trees merged with creek bottom hardwoods." The two were standing at a narrow bridge when suddenly they heard the distinctive toots of an ivory-bill. Eventually they spotted the birds making the sounds, a pair of the great woodpeckers working on some beetle-infested pine trees, scaling the bark with their huge white bills. "Our entire experience with the birds totaled only about sixteen minutes," wrote Brown. "We have not the slightest doubt in our minds that the birds were correctly identified as ivory-billed woodpeckers. In fact, I would go so far as to say that the unique call note of the ivory-bill would make the identification of the bird a simple matter for me."

Although Dennis searched the area extensively, he didn't find the birds. But he had learned his lesson about being overly skeptical. His conclusion, which he reported to the World Wildlife Fund, was that "the two men in question had had the extremely good fortune to chance upon a pair of ivory-bills foraging in recently beetle-killed pine trees."

In December 1966, Dennis turned his attention to the Big Thicket country of east Texas, a heavily wooded area of some 500,000 acres, containing upland forests of pine and hardwoods and also swamps. Although there had not been a confirmed ivory-billed woodpecker record in the Big Thicket since 1904, he had a good clue. A well-known bird watcher from Beaumont, Texas, Olga Hooks Lloyd, had reported seeing one that April in a swamp along the Neches River, near Steinhagen Reservoir. The area had many dead trees because of flooding. After only two days' searching, Dennis once again heard the mysterious toy-trumpet toots of an ivory-bill. Heavy rain delayed further searching for a few days, but when he finally returned to the bayou, he spotted an ivory-bill flying. "Sweeping majestically from where it apparently had been feeding on the ground, it soon settled upon the trunk of an enormous cypress tree," he wrote.

But the great woodpecker stayed only an instant — not long enough for Dennis even to raise his binoculars. From there the story becomes surreal. Deterred by the chilly black waters of the bayou, Dennis walked back and forth, trying to find a way to get across. It was impossible. Finally he stripped and plunged naked into the dark, forbidding water. When he emerged on the other side, he walked in the direction in which the bird had flown and suddenly stumbled upon her, perched like a vision on a stump, her wings outstretched.

How was his sighting treated by the ornithological community — a report from a person obviously familiar with the ivory-bill, a person who had taken the last accepted pictures of one? It was regarded as a mistake or, worse, a fabrication. Jim Tanner spent a few days exploring the area and saw nothing. He then declared that the habitat was totally unsuitable for ivory-bills, nothing like the virgin forests he had known so well in the Singer Tract. So just as Dennis had at first dismissed his friend Whitney Eastman's ivory-bill rediscovery in Florida, he was scorned as just another know-nothing. In a magazine interview, Jim Tanner said, "Dennis wants to believe he saw something, but he didn't."

The one good thing to come from the sighting is that the possible presence of ivory-bills in the area helped spur the creation of the Big Thicket National Preserve. A bill passed by Congress in October 1974 set aside an 84,550-acre preserve — not bad for an extinct bird. This is not a solid tract but a number of isolated tracts regarded as being of prime importance. Do ivory-bills still exist there? Dennis wrote in 1979, "I am reasonably confident that the ivory-bill still holds on in parts of the Big Thicket." He also mentioned other areas where he thought ivory-bills might be. "Probably the river swamps of southern Louisiana and nearby Mississippi are as likely places as any to look for the ivory-billed woodpecker at the present time," he wrote.

So all you need to do is carry a camera and snap a picture of an ivory-bill, right? Well . . . maybe. One of the most interesting — and controversial — modern sightings took place in 1971 in Louisiana, and two photographs were taken. These were shot with a cheap Kodak Instamatic camera and have some of the typical Bigfoot/Loch Ness monster fuzziness. But the bird depicted was certainly an ivory-billed woodpecker. The story goes something like this: An acquaintance of George Lowery, Jr., the great ornithologist who was then the director of Louisiana State University's Museum of Natural Science, reported seeing an ivory-bill in an area where he trained his hunting dogs, in the Atchafalaya Swamp, west of Baton Rouge. As usual, his report landed on skeptical ears. But the man did not give up. He started taking a pocket camera with him whenever he visited the swamp. On May 22, 1971, he came across a pair of the birds. To avoid scaring them, he took his dogs back to his car and locked them up. Then he began a careful stalk. The female was gone when he returned, but the male was working busily on a hole in a tree, about forty feet up the trunk. He took one picture there and another when it flew to another tree.

Lowery was so impressed that he went to the site several times, searching unsuccessfully for ivory-bills. He believed the man's story, but few other serious ornithologists did. Most declared the pictures a fraud. They insisted that the man had climbed forty feet up a tree, set a stuffed ivory-bill in place, and snapped a picture of it — twice.

It is interesting to note that Robert Bean, then the director of the Louisville Zoo, said he sighted an ivory-bill on November 11, 1975, on a highway about twenty miles west of Baton Rouge — perhaps in the same general area as the one in which the other man had allegedly photographed an ivory-bill. According to Dennis, Bean was driving a truckload of zoo animals across a long bridge in the Atchafalaya Swamp when he saw an ivory-bill fly across the road at eye level, only fifteen feet in front of him. He saw the bird for about five seconds as it cleared the guardrail and landed in a tree at the edge of the swamp, but he couldn't stop on the bridge because of heavy traffic.

The author Michael Harwood wrote in *Audubon* magazine of another intriguing Louisiana sighting that took place in the late 1970s. A hunter had gone to Louisiana State University's Museum of Natural Science during the 1977–78 deer season and presented a provocative tale of an encounter with a possible ivory-bill. He had seen the bird several times while sitting in a deer stand east of Catahoula, in the Atchafalaya Basin. John Morony, Jr., then the collections manager at the museum, told him it was probably a pileated woodpecker. But the man insisted he had seen two different versions of the bird, one that perfectly fit the description of a pileated and another that was bigger and had a large white patch on its back and a big white bill. The man didn't know much about bird identification and assumed that the birds were of the same species but one was male and the other female. Morony went to the deer stand and actually heard a call that sounded like an ivory-bill's. He went back to LSU and began organizing a search team.

Harwood interviewed David Bruce Crider, who was an LSU graduate student when this happened. "At this point, all of us were pretty skeptical," Crider told him. "This old coot had come in with all these stories about ivory-bills, and he didn't even know there was such a thing as a pileated."

Nonetheless, Morony gathered together more than a dozen volunteers and headed into the swamp. According to Crider, they split into five groups to explore different sections of the area. "It was a pretty stinking place to walk," said Crider. "The swales were so deep that the water was over our boot tops."

He and his friend David Hunter tried to get through without getting soaked but finally just plunged into the water. Most of the other parties turned back, but the two pushed on and explored deeply in the area. From time to time they stopped and played a tape of ivory-bill calls — the ones recorded by the 1935 Cornell expedition.

They had been trudging through the swamp since seven o'clock in the morning, and by one-fifteen they were getting disgusted with the whole venture and stopped to take a break. Earlier they had been walking quietly and whispering to avoid disturbing any birds that might be present. But by this time they had pretty much given up and were talking at a normal conversational level. Suddenly a bird call broke in: *kent . . . kent . . . kent-kent.*

"What was that?" one of them said. "An ivory-bill, ha, ha, ha," the other replied. And then they listened more closely. They heard two birds calling back and forth, and they seemed to be only 130 feet or so away. Although the men scanned intently with binoculars, the dense foliage of the trees blocked their view. After listening to the intermittent calls and loud pecking for about eight minutes, they decided to play the ivory-bill tape — and the birds shut up instantly. They tried to get closer to the birds, moving as quietly as possible, but crunching leaves underfoot and briars made it difficult.

"Suddenly we saw this pair of birds flying away from us through the woods," said Crider. "We got a glimpse — it lasted less than a second — of two large black-and-white woodpeckers that seemed to have white secondaries." (One of the most distinctive features on a flying ivory-bill is the white on its wings, which covers all of the secondary flight feathers and part of the innermost primaries, right down to the trailing edge of each wing. A pileated woodpecker has much less white on its wings, and the trailing edge is black.)

Crider and Hunter took a compass reading of the direction in which the birds had flown and took off after them. It wasn't long, though, before they reached a flooded area of the woods and were slogging around in deep water. They tried playing the ivory-bill tape again but heard no response.

By the time they got back to the other searchers (who had seen nothing), most in the group were ready to call it quits and go home. But the news from Crider and Hunter convinced them to stay overnight and try again the next day. They got up at dawn and stayed together for almost two hours, but then people started spreading out. Some even went home. Crider and Hunter toughed it out and eventually relocated the spot where they had seen the mystery birds. They decided not to play the tape, because it had seemed to silence the birds the previous day.

"Between nine and nine-thirty, by some miracle, we heard them again," said Crider. "They were pecking and making the same conversational call . . . I'd say they were three hundred to five hundred yards due east of where we'd heard them before." The two men had earlier decided that if they heard the birds again, they would make a headlong dash in their direction and try to make a positive identification. They quickly found themselves tangled in briar thickets. "While we were fighting that, they must have flown off, because the next time we heard them they seemed to be behind us," said Crider. "We ran in that direction, but we never found them."

Other people searched in the area and occasionally got a fleeting glimpse of something that didn't look quite right for a pileated woodpecker. Researchers later even tried flying aircraft low over the swamp, attempting to flush birds, and one person thought he saw a large, unusually marked woodpecker fly from some trees below. But the strain of the on-the-ground searching — of struggling to move through the dense, forbidding swamp — and the expense of the overflights took their toll. People started losing interest. And so the ivory-billed woodpecker once more receded into memory, not to come back into the national consciousness for more than two decades.

The event that stirred renewed interest in the ivory-bill was a remarkable sighting in the Pearl River area of southeastern Louisiana on April Fool's Day 1999. David Kulivan, an undergraduate in forestry at Louisiana State University, was hunting wild turkeys in the Pearl River Wildlife Management Area, less than an hour's drive from New Orleans. As he sat motionlessly against a tree, dressed from head to foot in camouflage, he suddenly saw two large woodpeckers interacting with each other on a nearby tree. They vocalized continuously, making a sound he had never heard before. Once they came within fifteen yards of him. The remarkable thing is that he had a 35mm camera in his game bag, which he had hoped to use to take a picture of his first turkey. But he was so much in shock, he didn't think to get it out and take some pictures.

Kulivan later said he knew as soon as he saw them that they were something he had never seen before. He described the woodpeckers in minute detail to a biologist at Louisiana State University who interviewed him, even pointing out that the female's black crest (both male and female pileated woodpeckers have red crests) was noticeably recurved forward. He watched the birds for at least ten minutes. One of them, he said, hammered fiercely into the tree, knocking off great chunks of bark.

Perhaps not surprisingly, Kulivan was at first reluctant to share his sighting with anyone. He sat on the story for almost two weeks. Then one day after class he approached a professor, Vernon Wright, and said he needed to talk. He laid out the story before the astonished Wright, who told him to write up his notes immediately.

Wright, who teaches in Louisiana State University's School of Forestry, Wildlife, and Fisheries, has a lot of respect for Kulivan's abilities as well as his honesty. He completely believed his story.

Wright told James Van Remsen, a professor of biology and the curator of birds at LSU's Museum of Natural Science, what Kulivan had reported, and Van Remsen subsequently gave Kulivan the grand interrogation. After he had finished, Van Remsen had no doubts about Kulivan's integrity. Kulivan definitely believed that he had seen an ivory-bill, he said. And his description of the bird was the most detailed and accurate one Van Remsen had ever received.

Kulivan's sighting led to several major searches of the Pearl River area. Zeiss Optics, a major manufacturer of binoculars and scopes for birders, financed a month-long expedition there from mid-January to mid-February of 2002. (The team searched in winter because the conditions are more difficult in spring and summer, when the trees are fully leafed out and numerous mosquitoes and cottonmouths are present. In addition, ivory-bills are relatively silent in summer, according to Jim Tanner.) The hand-picked searchers were all scientists or expert birders. The Cornell Lab of Ornithology sent a team of bioacoustics researchers to hang autonomous recording units (ARUs) in the trees, hoping that they might pick up the ivory-bill's *kent, kent, kent* call or the distinctive *BAM-bam* double-rap signal it makes by pounding its bill against a tree.

The Louisiana Department of Wildlife and Fisheries provided instructions about where to go and how to identify ivory-bills and reminded all would-be woodpecker searchers that they would have to buy a Louisiana hunting license to enter the Pearl River Wildlife Management Area legally. The department also issued a curious warning, noting that it was illegal to play recordings of ivory-bill calls and drumming because it might disturb the birds' nesting activities — an interesting regulation to protect a bird that is supposedly extinct.

This was the backdrop when I began my project. My goal was to find as many people as possible who had taken part in these searches or sightings, and if the sightings seemed credible, to follow up on them myself. In many cases the trail had gone cold — everyone involved in a particular sighting was either dead or difficult to track down. In other cases I did find the people (many of whom were quite elderly) and visited the swamps where they had seen the birds. I also looked at many more recent sightings, as much as possible with an unbiased eye. What happened later was something that I could never have imagined.

2

ME AND BOBBY RAY

To understand what the South means to me, you have to take yourself back to the early 1960s, when my family moved to the United States. Some of my earliest memories from that time are of watching on television as African Americans were attacked by dogs and sprayed with fire hoses during some of the anti-segregation marches in Alabama and Mississippi. My parents and my sisters and I were appalled by the South, with its lynchings, tar-and-featherings, and just plain good-old-boy mayhem. And then a few years later came the movie *Easy Rider*, with those two guys getting blown off their motorcycles by the shotgun-toting rednecks in the pickup truck. This is the tableau against which my paranoia grew.

I think this is one reason I hooked up with Bobby Ray Harrison, a true son of the South. I figured he could show me the ropes and be my southern-dialect translator. It didn't take long to see how much everyone loves Bobby. Wherever we went, he would get into long talks with clerks, people at Taco Bell, you name it — people of every race, ethnic group, and social class.

One of Bobby's favorite lines is "I was twenty-one before I found out 'damn Yankee' is two words." He spends a lot of time telling jokes, often at his own or the South's expense. For instance: "The most popular pickup line in Alabama is 'Hey babe, nice tooth,'" and "Every time someone moves from Alabama to Mississippi, the average IQ goes up in both states."

Bobby is a dyed-in-the-wool ivory-bill chaser with a large den in his home devoted entirely to the bird. The walls are adorned with expensive ivory-bill prints by Guy Coheleach, Julie Zickefoose, John James Audubon, and George Miksch Sutton, and various advertisements, pottery pieces, ceramic whiskey decanters, and other artistic or commercial representations of the bird fill the room. Bobby is constantly trolling on eBay for new ivory-bill knickknacks. When he has extra ones, he sometimes sends them to me. It makes me wonder how many other people across the nation are devoted in various ways to this remarkable bird.

Bobby's day job is teaching art history and photography at Oakwood College, a traditional black college founded in 1896. He has been there more than twenty years and is one of the few Caucasians on the faculty. Popular with students, he is an excellent teacher — not that I've ever taken a class with him, but I've seen him lead a couple of breakout sessions at nature photography conferences. His talks are concise, to the point, and filled with self-deprecating humor. The final slide he showed at a conference in Las Vegas a few years ago was the front page of a newspaper, with a headline about a Bobby Harrison sighting below a picture of him dressed as Elvis Presley.

Bobby is an award-winning wildlife photographer with many impressive credits in national magazines. I first got acquainted with him during the mid-1980s, when I was the managing editor of *WildBird*, though we didn't meet for years. He would call me up all the time to encourage me to buy his photographs or assign him a how-to article, or just to shoot the breeze. It used to bug me at first, this hillbilly with the southern drawl wasting my time. But he grew on me, and by the time we finally met at a North American Nature Photography Association (NANPA) conference a few years later, we were good friends.

Bobby and I were both eventually elected to the NANPA

board of directors, on which we served for three years. In meetings, Bobby had a great ability to simplify the most complicated issue so that it was completely clear what we were voting for or against. He reminded me of a classic southern country lawyer. He would pull his half-frame reading glasses down to the end of his nose and say, "So let me make sure I have this straight. What you're saying is . . ." And he would slow it down. People would have to choose their words carefully and state exactly what they meant. It was brilliant.

Bobby was a great board member. He had been to every annual conference since Roger Tory Peterson organized a get-together at his center in Jamestown, New York. This was before NANPA was created, but the idea was born there. Top photographers such as Frans Lanting, Galen Rowell, Art Wolfe, and others went to the meeting and spoke about how much we all needed an organization dedicated to nature photography. So NANPA was born, and it grew in stature and importance each year.

Come January 2004, Bobby and I had a tough choice to make: do we attend NANPA's big tenth-anniversary conference in Portland, Oregon, or do we skip it and instead go searching for ivory-bills across the South? Our terms on NANPA's board of directors had recently expired, so we didn't have to be there. We chose to look for the birds. We had both been interested in the ivory-billed woodpecker for years. Bobby had bought Jim Tanner's book in the early 1970s and had been doing research and buying ivory-bill knickknacks, paintings, and books ever since. His wife, Norma, once told me, "I've been married to Bobby for over twenty-five years, and he's been chasing that bird the whole time."

Bobby has told me several times how skinny he was when he first met Norma. I guess it's true. One time when I was visiting them, I saw an old newspaper clipping with a picture of Bobby's father and a scrawny teenager with long, thick dark hair and a bushy beard. It turned out to be Bobby. He has changed quite a bit in the intervening quarter-century. He has grown portlier, and his hair has thinned on top. He still has a beard, but he keeps it — and his remaining hair — neatly trimmed.

Soon after Bobby and Norma married, they bought twenty-five acres of forested land outside Huntsville, near the town of Gurley. Bobby started building a house right away, and he has been at it ever since. He designed it and has done most of the construction himself. His father helped at first, but when he suffered a minor stroke and was unable to continue, Bobby had to work on it alone. The problem with building a house by yourself is that you often need a third hand to hold up the other end of a board or help lift heavy objects. To move ahead, Bobby had to jury-rig a block and tackle to hold up large timbers while he put them in place and nailed them. Of course, this meant the entire process took three or four times longer than it would have with an assistant, and it turned into a major engineering project.

Bobby and Norma lived in a tent on their land when he started building the house. He constructed the bedroom first so they would have a solid roof over their heads and an enclosed space during winter, but there was no heat, electricity, or plumbing. They got their water from the tiny creek at the bottom of the hill. Bobby kept building the house bit by bit, after work and on weekends and holidays. By the time their children, Robert and Whitney, were born, he had finished the main structure of the two-story house. It looks great, but it's still a work in progress and may take his entire lifetime to complete. I know he'll never stop working on it. Bobby is doggedly determined to finish everything he starts.

Because of the Marshall Space Center, Huntsville, Alabama, is billed as the "Space Capital of the World," at least by locals (those at Houston and Cape Canaveral might dispute the name). People take their rockets very seriously in Huntsville. One time I was driving into town and called Bobby on my cell phone to get directions to Oakwood College. I was approaching the space center and told him that I could see a huge rocket ship ahead. "Rocket ship!" he shouted. "I'll have you know that that is a Saturn V rocket, the largest launch vehicle ever made, with seven-point-five million pounds of thrust at takeoff." Someone in the background cackled in a high-pitched voice, saying, "*Rocket ship*? Did he say *rocket ship*?" And the whole place exploded in laughter. Recently I sent Bobby a headline from a national newspaper that read, "Private Rocket Ship Breaks Space Barrier," to show that I'm not the only one who uses the proper Buck Rogers terminology for space vehicles.

In an odd coincidence, both my father and Bobby's were at Omaha Beach in Normandy during the D-Day invasion, mine in the British Royal Navy, Bobby's in the U.S. Army. I remember my dad telling me about D-Day and about the American farm boys, many from the rural South, who had sat belowdecks for days, hidden from the German spy planes, waiting for the weather to improve so the invasion could begin. As he ran them ashore in a troop carrier, he held out a tiny shot of rum to each man — many of them were too seasick to think about taking a drink — and said, "Let's go, Yank." And with a pat on the back, they would stagger off through the surf, strafed by German artillery. I sometimes wonder if Bobby's dad was one of the men my father put ashore.

In another coincidence, both of our fathers ran away from home as teenagers. By the time of D-Day, my dad was already a ten-year veteran of the Royal Navy, which he joined at the age of fifteen, and had been on more or less constant combat duty since late 1939, when Britain declared war against Germany. Bobby's father, Ed Harrison, had joined the U.S. Army after Pearl Harbor. He was actually not a son of the South; he was raised in Iowa during the Great Depression, brought up by a stern stepfather after his own father died.

Ed and his older brother, George, used to take a couple of .22 rifles and hunt rabbits and other small game to put meat on the table. One day they were walking across a high trestle railroad bridge to get across a river when a train came chugging around the corner. There was no time to run and the water wasn't deep enough to dive into safely, so the two climbed over the edge and dangled from the trestle, with one hand on a railroad tie and the other grasping a gun. The train shook the trestle so much that Ed had to let go of the gun so he could hold on with both hands. When they retrieved the gun, the stock was broken. Ed's stepfather was furious, and he severely beat him. Ed immediately left home and started riding the rails with the hobos. He never returned. He was sixteen years old. Bobby still has the old .22, its cracked stock held together with black electrical tape.

Bobby's mother, Ophelia Clem (called Jo by her friends), grew up in Ardmore, Tennessee. How she met her husband is one of those classic World War II stories. Ed's army unit was traveling from southern Alabama to the mountains of Tennessee on maneuvers. The men would write their names and addresses on pieces of paper, and whenever they came to a town or city, they would toss the papers to any young women they drove past. Bobby's aunt picked up the piece of paper that Ed threw out and gave it to her sister, Jo. "You should write to him," she said. "He was cute." And Jo did. Ed went to visit her a few times, and then he went AWOL for a few days and they got married. He left for the war in Europe a short time later.

You could say that Bobby and I have a competitive relationship, or at least we tease each other a lot. He's always talking about how over the hill I am (I'm five years older than he is). And I tell him that I know southerners haven't heard yet about some of these modern innovations, like television, radio, and computers. A few years ago we went to the high country at Colorado's Rocky Mountain National Park to photograph elk, picas, and various birds. Bobby was a little overweight and had just recovered from bronchitis, so the ten-thousand-foot altitude really got to him. One day he decided to wait in the car at the trailhead instead of going up on the tundra with me to search for white-tailed ptarmigan. I was gone for several hours. Another photographer was also working there that day, but he and I were miles apart. Bobby talked to several hikers, some who had seen the other photographer and some of whom had seen me, and he got the impression that I had covered fifteen or twenty miles of rugged alpine slopes and come back to the car fresh and ready to keep hiking. I never told him about the other photographer.

Bobby is the kind of guy who does bizarre things that crack me up — like wearing only one contact lens, so he can have one eye for distance and the other for close-up vision, or spitting into his hand and putting the hand to his eye to lubricate his contact lens. "You know, Bobby, they have a special solution you can buy for that," I told him once. "Yeah, but this is just as good and the price is better," he said.

"I don't know what I'd do if they ever stopped making these Dinty Moore beef stew boiler packets," he said to me once when we were camping out in the swamp, searching for ivory-bills. That's one of his favorite foods. Sometimes he will hold a packet next to his face and do a mock television commercial: "Dinty Moore, the food of ivory-bill searchers." He also always brings Starkist tuna lunch packs, which contain a small can of tuna, several crackers, mayonnaise, relish, and a wooden stick to mix the ingredients together. (After eating a few of these with him, I ended up getting hooked on them too.) And he is never without a bag full of beef jerky and another of Snickers and Mounds candy bars, which he frequently hands out to me and anyone else around. He has a huge appetite.

Snakes seem to like Bobby — or at least they want to get close to him. One day he pulled his canoe up next to mine and hung his leg over the gunwale to hold the canoes together. Suddenly a cottonmouth that must have been lurking in a cypress knee rose up right under his leg and reared its head as if it were going to strike. Bobby pulled his leg out of the way just in time, as the snake opened its milk-white mouth wide. Another time a big cottonmouth kept swimming up to his canoe, even though he kept pushing it away with his paddle.

But Bobby's strangest snake encounter took place when we were driving along a high river levee in early spring, just as all the snakes were coming out of hibernation. They seemed to be everywhere we looked. As we were driving along the dusty road above the swamp, we came upon the biggest cottonmouth I've ever seen, with a body as thick around as my upper arm and a huge triangular head.

Now, a cottonmouth is a nasty animal, no matter what my herpetologist friends might say. Unlike the rattlesnakes I grew up with in the West, which will usually go out of their way to avoid you and even give a nice loud warning if you get too close, a cottonmouth won't budge. In fact, it will often move toward you. And it is one scary snake — big, dark, and sinister-looking. The only warning it gives is showing its wide-open white mouth just before it bites.

So we saw this huge cottonmouth, and we both wanted to get out and take a picture of it. We were in a GMC Jimmy sport-utility vehicle that Bobby had borrowed from his wife, since his usual mode of transportation, an aging Safari van with half a million miles on it, was in the shop. When Bobby pulled up, the snake was directly below my door, so I could not get out. As I looked down at it, it reared its head and showed me the white inside its mouth. I pulled back from the window and rolled it halfway up. Bobby got out, went around to my side with his camcorder, and started filming. The snake slithered under the car.

"Can I get out now?" I asked.

"Wait till it moves to the other side," he said. "Okay. You should be able to get out now." I jumped from the SUV.

"Wait a minute! Oh no," Bobby whined, his voice rising to a high tenor. (You always know you're in trouble if the pitch of a southern man's voice goes up.) "It's climbing up in the car!" I looked underneath just in time to see the snake's tail dangle from the engine compartment for an instant and then disappear completely inside.

"What am I going to do? What am I going to tell my wife? It's crawled on up into the car."

"You could take it to a gas station and ask them to change the oil and see what happens," I joked.

"Maybe it'll come out if I start driving," he said. "Keep an eye out and see." I stepped away to give him room.

As he opened the driver's door, he stood well back from the SUV and tried to step into it from several feet away. He looked like a kid trying to get into bed without letting the monsters hiding underneath grab his leg.

Just as he was about to leap, I asked, "You think there's any way it could've gotten all the way inside — through the heater or the gas pedal hole or something?" He hung in midstep for a long moment, and I could see the sweat beading up on his forehead.

"I don't know," he said finally, and in an amazing act of courage, he leaped into the front seat. He put the car into reverse and floored the gas, spinning the tires and hitting me with dirt and grit as he got traction. He went about fifty feet and slammed on the brakes. Nothing. Then he did the same thing in the other direction, driving fast right for me. Again nothing. On the fourth try, I saw the snake's head and the first few inches of its body slip down almost to the ground, but it quickly pulled itself back up.

I started waving at him to move farther back. "Go back, go back," I screamed.

He backed up about a hundred feet, then started forward again. He floored the gas and came screaming toward me at full speed. At the last instant he slammed on the brakes, causing the Jimmy to slide sideways. The cottonmouth shot out from the bottom of the car and flew almost all the way to me. It quickly righted itself and slithered into the long grass at the edge of the levee.

3

JIM AND NANCY

To HEAR NANCY TANNER tell it, the only reason anyone is interested in her is that she was married to the ivory-bill expert Jim Tanner. "If Jim were still here, no one would even want to talk to me," she says. "My only claim to fame is that I haven't died." And whenever someone hands her a copy of Jim's treatise on the bird to sign, she'll write, "Nancy Tanner (Mrs. James T. Tanner)," I guess so people won't forget who she is.

I can say from personal experience that anyone who gets to know Nancy is unlikely ever to forget her. She is a remarkable woman in every way, no matter what she might say to the contrary. The first thing I noticed about her was her accent, which reminds me of Katharine Hepburn's — a kind of patrician-sounding blend of upper-crust British, Boston, and New York dialects, which it turns out is not far from accurate. "I was born in Seattle, Washington, but from the time I was three until I was eleven I lived in England," she told me. Her father was a top executive with a major shipping company, and when he got wind of a plot to kidnap his children, he sent them to live in Britain for their safety. "I came back speaking just like a British child," Nancy said. "But then I was in New York for two years and then in California for four years. Then Boston. Now when I go north, people say, 'Oh, I just love your southern accent.'"

Nancy has vivid blue eyes and white hair that she keeps short. She swims laps most days in a local public pool, but she doesn't go in for leisurely strokes or aquatic aerobics for seniors. She does a powerful freestyle, moving quickly back and forth in the pool like a woman a quarter her age. She is still fit and trim at eighty-seven, and her mind is tack sharp.

I stopped to visit Nancy at her home in Knoxville, Tennessee, in January 2004, on my way south to search old ivory-bill haunts. She lives in an attractive split-level house she and Jim bought in the late 1940s on a mountain outside the city. The house has a splendid view of the Great Smoky Mountains, though it is partially blocked by the tall trees growing across the road. It was quite a chug up there for my car on a steep switchback road that went past houses and cabins. Originally, the Tanners' was one of the few homes on the mountain.

Nancy told me that a magazine writer had come to visit her a couple of days earlier and after interviewing her had asked if he could return the next morning and go birding with her in the Smokies. She thought he just wanted to have a quick look around, so she didn't bother to take warm clothing on their walk, even though it was mid-January. The writer had other ideas. He took her on an interminable trek, stopping every five or ten feet to look at another bird, so she never had a chance to warm up by hiking. "I did have hiking clothes on, but glory Pete, we went as far up as people are allowed to go," she said, laughing. "It was seventeen degrees, and I was freezing."

She was also desperately hungry. After several hours of trudging through the windswept mountains, they finally came down to look for something to eat. By this time it was three in the afternoon, and the first restaurant they got to had closed at two. A restaurant across the street didn't open until six. "We finally found a place to eat, but I haven't been the same since," she explained. She told me all this with laughter and good humor.

I began to wonder, why hadn't she demanded that the writer take her home earlier that morning, when she first became uncomfortably cold and hungry? Why did she have to push herself into a near-life-threatening situation without complaining to this polar-fleece-clad dolt? Then I had a sudden flash of insight about Nancy Tanner. She never says no to any kind of challenge. She had told me many times before that Jim's one fault was that he never realized she might be incapable of wading through swamps, climbing up mountains, and hiking across glaciers. Nancy went with him everywhere — willingly, eagerly. And it had been like that from the start of their relationship.

In 1940, Nancy Sheedy was a recently hired English teacher at Eastern Tennessee State College. She was of average height and trim, with dark red hair, fair skin, and large blue eyes — and she was single. When a tall, handsome biology teacher named Jim Tanner, with a quiet, confident, Gary Cooper–like air, joined the faculty, she was quickly smitten. This was five years after Jim's epic journey across America with the Cornell expedition, when he, Arthur Allen, and the others found the nesting ivory-bills in northeastern Louisiana. And it was after he made his exhaustive study of the birds, from 1937 to 1939. When the opportunity arose for Nancy to join Jim and two other teachers on a trip to Louisiana during the Christmas break, she jumped at it.

Jim drove them all to the edge of the great swamp at the Singer Tract and invited anyone who was willing to accompany him early the next morning when he looked for ivory-bills in his former study area. It was an amazing, enchanted-forest kind of place — dark and forbidding, with trees measuring 7 or 8 feet in diameter rising more than 100 feet in the air; a primeval woodland where bears, panthers, and wolves still roamed.

The next morning, when Jim went to the others' hotel rooms at 4 A.M., Nancy was the only one awake and ready to go. The rest had seen all they wanted of the great swamp forest from the side of the gravel road that ran beside it. "They slept merrily on when Jim came to get us," Nancy explained. She asked if she should

wear waterproof footwear or anything special to go through the
swamp. "Oh, you don't need to wear high boots," he told her.
"You'll be all right."

That first day they trudged more than six miles into the woods
— in the dark. Nancy quickly became soaked as they waded
through the swampy sections. They then had to scramble onto the
higher ridges and make their way through a dense tangle of vegetation. "I'll tell you, plowing through a swamp in the dark is very
difficult," said Nancy. "You sink in the mud; you have to push
through briars and climb over fallen logs." But Jim was completely in his element, charging through or over every obstacle.

Barred owls called loudly in the darkness: *who cooks for you,
who cooks for you all.* At 6:30 the gray light of dawn started to
spread across the swamp. The repetitive calls of brown thrashers
began ringing out, followed shortly by the sweet, melodious songs
of white-throated sparrows, winter wrens, and Carolina wrens.
Then the woodpeckers started up — a cacophony of drum tattoos
and chattering and the wild laughter of pileated woodpeckers. Finally, just as the rosy light of sunrise spread across the high forest
canopy, Jim and Nancy heard from the latest riser. *BAM-bam:* the
unmistakable double rap of an ivory-billed woodpecker echoed
through the woods.

This *BAM-bam* is the characteristic drum of a *Campephilus*
woodpecker, a genus found through much of South and Central
America, with the ivory-bill being the northernmost representa-
tive of the group. "The second part of the double rap is so quick,"
said Nancy, "it sounds like an echo of the first and is nowhere near
as hard." The space between the two parts of the double rap is
only about seventy-five milliseconds, which is so close that some
people hear them as a single rap. But the two separate parts are
clear if you look at a sonogram (a visual representation of a sound
showing its pitch and duration).

You can still hear the double rap if you take a birding tour
to Latin America and locate *Campephilus* species such as pale-
billed, powerful, and Magellanic woodpeckers. But these birds

are at best bland substitutes for the mighty ivory-bill. The only really comparable bird is the imperial woodpecker of Mexico, a near twin of the ivory-bill in appearance but larger and specializing in high-altitude pine forests, not bottomland swamps. Unfortunately, the imperial woodpecker is also believed to be extinct. No one has ever photographed or recorded the voice of an imperial woodpecker, and not one reputable observer has seen one for decades. As far as anyone knows, the birds exist only in specimen cabinets in a handful of museum collections.

Jim and Nancy heard another double rap, followed by some loud, nasal, toy-horn toots, like nothing else Nancy had ever heard: *kent, kent . . . kent, kent . . . kent*. It was December 20, and the trees were bare of leaves, so the sound carried a long way — perhaps a quarter of a mile. They spent the rest of the day searching for the birds' roost holes. "Jim finally found some roost holes that looked fairly new," said Nancy, but they didn't see any ivory-bills that day. They decided to quit searching and go back the next morning.

That second day, December 21, 1940, is one that Nancy will always remember — the day she saw her first ivory-bill. It was also the day she crossed the line and became a confirmed birder. Her blue eyes gleam with excitement as she talks about that morning.

"The next day at dawn we were sitting on some supposedly dry hummocks beside the roost holes, but I was mighty wet," Nancy told me, smiling. The male finally came out of one of the holes — late, as usual; ivory-bills seem to sleep in most days. *BAM-bam:* the huge black-and-white woodpecker struck the trunk of the tree, then hitched up to the topmost limb to preen and stretch. "My heavens, the bird was magnificent," she said. "That glossy black plumage with a gleaming white shield at the bottom, and that spectacular crimson crest."

She heard another *BAM-bam*, and the female came out of her own roost hole and joined her mate. The pair "talked" with each other in a softer, more intimate, and more drawn-out variation of the *kent* call: *key-ennnt, keeey-eeent*. "It was very gentle and not very noisy," said Nancy. The birds preened in the warm morning sun, dazzling her with their immaculate black plumage, which glowed with an almost purple sheen in the sunlight.

"Ivory-bills are beautiful," said Nancy. "They're extremely regal birds, with that long, long, brilliant white bill and the gleaming yellow eyes. Although they're only three inches larger than a pileated woodpecker, they seem much bigger and more impressive."

When Nancy and I were talking, I noticed that she almost always spoke of the birds in the present tense, as though she thought that they definitely still existed. But whenever I asked her opinion about that, she would say that they were probably extinct.

"When they fly, you see the white on the trailing edge of the wing feathers distinctly — much more white than you see on a pileated woodpecker's wings when it flies," she said. "It stands out quite clearly. They fly with their head and neck straight out, like a pintail duck, going fast and straight — they don't undulate. And they make a wooden sound with their wings, because they keep them flat and hit the air. Most artists who paint the ivory-bill have it bent in the wrist, but these birds keep their wings very flat. And their tails are pointed. They are very, very impressive birds, and when they perch on a tree they are quite different from a pileated. They hold their feet far apart, and they lean back on their tails. They really look big."

Nancy tells a story about the time in 1942 that Roger Tory Peterson and Bayard Christy went to the Singer Tract to search for ivory-bills. The two of them heard one calling and began stalking it. "Their hearts were pounding, they were so excited," said Nancy. "And when they saw it, Roger exclaimed, 'That's no puny pileated, that's a whacking big bird!'" They found two female ivory-bills that day, and decades later, Peterson still regarded seeing those birds as the high point of his entire career in ornithology. He wrote of the experience in his 1955 book, *Wild America,* coauthored by the British birder James Fisher: "They did not look as much like pileateds as I had expected; with long recurved crests of blackest jet and gleaming white bills, they seemed unreal birds — downright archaic."

Nancy complains about the way artists often get the ivory-bill wrong. But of course they haven't had a living, breathing bird to work with — only museum specimens. "The study skins are dead-looking," said Nancy. "They seem so shrunken, and the bills have all turned yellow with age. They just look mealy. To see that bird at dawn go up that tree into the sunlight . . . I'll never forget it."

On the wall near the entryway of her home, Nancy has a large framed print of an ivory-bill pair painted by Guy Coheleach, which was presented to Jim when he retired from the University of Tennessee. Later it warped, so he took it to have it rematted and reframed. Coheleach happened to be at the frame shop, and he asked Jim how he liked the painting. To be honest, Jim did not love the picture. He had always looked up to the treetops to see ivory-bills, so he didn't appreciate the eye-level view. And he thought the feet should have been much lighter. But all he said was that the irises of the birds' eyes were not yellow enough. "Oh, well, I'll fix that," said Coheleach. As Nancy explained, "He took out his paints and went *swish, swish* with his brush, painting the birds' eyes bright yellow. So we have the only correct copy of that print."

As Jim and Nancy gazed at the two ivory-bills near the top of the tree, the pair abruptly took off and flew straight and hard through the tall canopy of the forest. "When they do that, they're usually going a half-mile or a mile away," said Nancy. "Sit here and don't move until I get back," Jim told her. Then he raced off after the birds.

Nancy waited. And waited. And waited. "I was probably out there an hour and a half, getting wetter and wetter, sitting on a log," she said. They had waded for miles through the swamp before dawn, sometimes moving through chest-deep water in the dark forest, which had no points of reference. Every direction looked the same to her. At first she was fascinated by her surroundings. She saw some wood ducks and then a couple of bucks with large antlers. But after an hour had passed, she began to get apprehensive. At one point she saw a huge dark animal slinking past. "It looked as tall as a horse," she said. "It turned out to be a wolf on top of a log."

This was wild country, where bears, panthers, wolves, and snakes abounded. She started to wonder about cottonmouths and rattlesnakes, which she knew lived in the swamp. Jim had told her an amusing story about an encounter that Jack Kuhn had had with a timber rattlesnake in these very woods. He had stepped on the snake as he was walking through dense undergrowth, and its loud hiss and rattle had scared him so much, he shot straight up in the air. "He came down on the rattlesnake again and went up and came down and went up and came down," said Nancy. "By this time the snake had had enough and departed."

Now that she was alone in the swamp, the story didn't seem so funny. What if she encountered a rattlesnake? Did Jim say that they hibernate? She couldn't remember. And what if Jim didn't return? "I thought, if he breaks his leg leaping over a log or plowing through the swamp going lickity-split, I'll never find my way out of here," she said, laughing until tears filled her eyes. But just as her fear started to turn to panic, Jim came calmly striding out of the swamp, smiling. She never let on to him that she had been frightened.

The two of them spent the day together in the swamp, and by the time they left for Tennessee, they had seen five different ivory-bills — the adult pair, another adult female, a juvenile female, and a male that Jim had banded as a nestling in 1938. He had nicknamed the bird Sonny Boy, and it was undoubtedly the only ivory-billed woodpecker that has ever been banded.

Nancy once told me the story of when Jim banded Sonny Boy. After he had put the bird back in the nest and was climbing down the tree, Sonny Boy leaped from the cavity and tumbled all the way to the vegetation at the base of the tree. Jim was horrified, fearing that he might have caused the death of one of the rarest birds on earth. He quickly climbed down and picked up the young ivory-bill, which didn't seem any the worse for the experience, just scared and angry. He decided to get some pictures of it before he took it back up to the nest hole. He handed Sonny Boy to Jack Kuhn and started snapping pictures. But he was so nervous, he forgot to focus the camera. When he realized his mistake, he had to start over, this time forcing himself to go through the steps of using the camera — making sure it had film, was focused, and had the correct f/stop and shutter speed. Meanwhile, the bird had climbed up Kuhn's arm and onto the top of his head. When Kuhn tried to remove him, Sonny Boy bit him fiercely on his hand, drawing blood. But the incident turned out to be a fortunate one after all, because the photographs Jim took are the only closeup views of a juvenile ivory-billed woodpecker in existence.

Those first few days in the Singer Tract in 1940 are a blur to Nancy. "I was just madly in love with Jim and didn't care about the birds as much," she said. Even being temporarily abandoned in the swamp didn't cool her ardor. They married the following August. That December they returned one last time to the Singer Tract and stayed two weeks. This was the same month the Japanese attacked Pearl Harbor, and they knew they would soon be separated. Jim was going into the navy as a lieutenant.

Jim wanted them to travel through the woods on horseback that time, so they could cover more territory. "I thought that was simply marvelous," said Nancy. "But I hadn't ridden in about six years, and after a few hours I was ready to carry the horse." She got to see a lot more of the swamp on this visit. They explored some of the best ivory-bill areas — John's Bayou, Mack's Bayou. But they weren't able to visit Greenlea Bend, one of the best areas in the Singer Tract, because logging was under way there.

"Where they were not cutting, there were still many wonderful trees," said Nancy. "Sweet gum, Nuttall's oak, water oak, overcup oak, American elm, green ash, hackberry, red maple. A lot of them were huge: one hundred foot, one hundred fifty foot — beautiful. In some places there was so much canopy, not much could grow on the ground, so it was easy to ride through. In other places, where a tree had fallen, the sun would come through, and lush vegetation would grow."

This brief visit was the last time Jim saw the Singer Tract until 1986, when he attended the dedication ceremony for the Tensas River National Wildlife Refuge visitors' center — long after the bitter controversy in the early 1940s when so many people fought so hard to save this last large tract of virgin bottomland swamp forest, and long after Franklin Roosevelt and the governors of four states tried in vain to stop the cutting. Although a refuge had finally been established, it was way too late. "When he came home from the Tensas dedication, Jim brought back pictures of soybean fields right where we'd seen those ivory-bills," said Nancy. He never returned again.

Jim and Nancy moved to Norfolk, Virginia, in early 1942, shortly before he was to leave for his tour of duty in the navy. "I went with him," she said, "thinking that he might be going to sea for three years or more at any minute." She was pregnant with their first child, David, whose due date was February 14. "Jim was scheduled to leave on the USS *Indianapolis* on that same day," said Nancy. "But the commanding officer said, 'Oh, for heaven's sake, I'll send Bill instead of you, and you can go on the next ship.' As it turned out, David wasn't born until March 12."

Jim could not have known how fortunate he was. On July 29, 1945, a Japanese submarine torpedoed the cruiser *Indianapolis*, sending it to the bottom of the Pacific Ocean. The survivors endured five days in the water before rescuers arrived. Many of them died of thirst and exposure or were attacked by sharks as they bobbed helplessly on the surface in their lifejackets. (You may remember the grisly tale told by the hardbitten old shark hunter in the movie *Jaws*. He was an *Indianapolis* survivor; hence his hatred of sharks.) Of some 1,400 crew members, only 317 survived.

· · ·

The 1935 Brand–Cornell University–American Museum of Natural History Expedition had been one of the best things that ever happened to Jim Tanner. "He was only twenty or twenty-one years old when it started," said Nancy. "He got the chance to go along with these leading ornithologists — Arthur Allen, Peter Paul Kellogg, George Miksch Sutton." All of his talents and strengths came to bear: his intelligence and ingenuity; his ability to survive in the wilderness, stoically enduring physical discomfort and facing any challenge that might arise; and his easygoing nature, the ability to get along with anyone. In some ways he carried the weight of the expedition on his shoulders. "Jim was young — a beginning graduate student — so he was the one who always climbed up the trees or cliffs," said Nancy. "He took the cameras into difficult places on that trip. He held the parabolic mike when they were doing sound recordings. He waded through the swamps, and he cooked the food. He did all the heavy work, because that's why they took him." And he never complained.

A short time after the expedition was completed, John Baker, then the executive director of the National Audubon Society, contacted Arthur Allen and offered a fellowship for someone to study the ivory-bills in the Singer Tract. There was never any question about who should do the study. Allen wrote that Tanner had proved on the expedition that he had "the qualities necessary for a field ornithologist," and he especially praised his adaptability, originality, and willingness to work. "Above all, he had shown a clear mind and superior intelligence," wrote Allen — a ringing endorsement from one of the world's leading ornithologists.

Jim would need all of these qualities and more for this in-depth research project. It was lonely work, with few comforts. In the Singer Tract, he stayed in a small shack with no water or electricity, and when he went on the road to Georgia, Arkansas, Alabama, Florida, the Carolinas, and all the other places where he thought ivory-bills might exist, he usually camped out. He would pull off on a dirt road and find a secluded spot to sleep. Then he would remove the bench seat from his Model A Ford and put it on the ground as a bed, raising one end slightly with rocks so it would slant upward and keep his head higher than his feet. If bad weather threatened, he would erect a tarp over the seat.

He was amazingly frugal. I've seen some of the expense lists he turned in during his travels, and he was definitely living on the cheap. Sometimes the checks would be slow to reach him and his money would run out. Nancy told me of one time when he went to a boat dock looking for work to tide him over. He saw a man scraping barnacles off a hull and offered to help him for a small sum of money. A few days later he helped another man paint his boat. "I suppose these days a young man in that predicament would just call home and get his parents to send money," said Nancy. "But it wasn't like that then."

At one point in the late 1930s, Jim estimated that there might be as many as twenty-four ivory-bills in existence. He had heard seemingly credible reports from several areas in Florida, such as the Apalachicola and Suwanee Rivers and the Big Cypress. Then there was the Santee River in South Carolina and the Altamaha River and Okefenokee Swamp in Georgia, and so many other places. He checked out all these areas and more during the course of his two-year study.

His usual mode of operation when arriving in a new place was to talk to hunters, fishermen, foresters, and other people who knew the local woods. He had an easy way about him. He didn't push people. He would engage in small talk and eventually gently move the conversation toward the local bird life, particularly large woodpeckers. He never led people. If they had seen something, he would let them explain it in their own words.

Nancy gave me a copy of an unpublished manuscript Jim wrote about a trip to the Suwanee River. In it he tells about speaking with some local fishermen in March 1937. The three men had seen his campfire and walked over to talk with him. "Naturally they wanted to know what I was doing there, but with the customary courtesy of backwoods people they introduced themselves first," wrote Jim. They told him that they were intending to go night fishing and have a fish fry. When they asked him what he was up to, he replied, "I am hunting for peckerwoods," which was the colloquial name for woodpeckers. This led to a comical misunderstanding with one of the men. "I noticed that the man who had been the most congenial and talkative had fallen silent and was listening intently, even suspiciously," wrote Jim.

> But suddenly he burst out laughing and said, "By golly, I thought for a minute you really were hunting a peckerwood!" Now it was his turn to explain. A few years before, he said, another stranger had come hunting for a . . . man who had taken to the woods to escape revenge. And while "peckerwood" can mean a bird, it can also mean a man who makes his living in the woods, as a sawhand, turpentiner, or in some other way. My new friend was quite relieved to find that I was not on a manhunt but was after a feathered peckerwood.

I quickly noticed while reading this and another of Jim's unpublished manuscripts that he was an excellent writer. In these pieces he was no longer a scientist writing dry descriptions for a technical journal. He wrote from the heart, bringing the people and places he described vividly to life. Continuing the story of the fishermen, he wrote,

> The men then left my camp to set out their fish lines, and when that was done they built their fire into a roaring blaze because the night was cool. They invited me over to join the party; besides the three men there were four women of varied ages, all roughly dressed and all typical Florida "crackers." While waiting for the fish to bite, we played games around the fire, real old-fashioned games: drop-the-handkerchief, pleased-or-displeased, rush-sheep-rush, and hide-and-seek. It was a gay and friendly party. The ruddy firelight shone on their faces and lighted the surrounding tree trunks on all sides but the one where a great black void marked the river. The fish did not bite, but the people had forehandedly brought some along, and we had a big meal of fried fish,

baked yams, and biscuits. I ate my share, even though I had already had one supper. Then they loaded their truck and near midnight disappeared up the narrow road.

Years later, in 1973, Jim returned to the Suwanee with Nancy and canoed all the way from Branford, Florida, to the Gulf of Mexico, some seventy miles away. They were recreating an expedition that the ornithologists William Brewster and Frank Chapman had taken in a thirty-foot scow in 1890. Those men had collected one ivory-bill and heard the call of another, but eighty-three years later, the Tanners came up blank. The experience of being on the river alone was worth the journey, though. "We camped in solitude each night on the riverbank with no human habitation in sight and listened to the sounds of the swamp," wrote Jim. "During most of the days we were alone in a world of the canoe, the dark water, the forest on both sides, and the sky over all."

This was but one of a number of trips Jim took over the years to try to find out whether the ivory-bill still lived. He had his eyes open and ears alert wherever he went if the habitat looked right, and he hunted for signs of the birds' feeding, roost holes, and nest holes. On one of his most ambitious journeys, he even headed south of the border, deep into Mexico, in search of the ivory-bill's closest cousin, the imperial woodpecker. Before he left he took a crash course in Spanish, hiring a tutor to teach him nearly daily for three months. Then, on a warm day in June 1962, he and his son, David, putted off down the road in an aging Jeep station wagon with a flathead four-cylinder engine. David had just graduated from high school and had the summer off before starting college. They drove all the way to Durango, Mexico, stopping only to eat and sleep and have the Jeep's engine repaired — twice.

For David, it was the adventure of a lifetime. They drove up into the Sierra Madre Occidental, following the tracks of logging trucks leading to the high-altitude forests of pine. Some of the ruts from the trucks were so deep that the Jeep's wheels would drop down into them, bottoming out the vehicle. "We never got stranded," said David, "but it took forever to make any distance."

They found nothing at the first place they checked out — only rumors of sightings five or six years earlier, when the loggers had first moved into the area. The more they traveled around, the more they encountered the same story: the loggers came; the imperials disappeared. Jim later speculated that this wasn't because the habitat was being destroyed. The Mexican division of forestry strictly regulated the logging and didn't allow clear-cutting. Many huge trees remained for foraging and potential roosting and nesting sites. But the logging activities drew an influx of people, many of whom depended on subsistence hunting for their meat. He surmised that the birds were being killed for food.

Using his newly learned Spanish, Jim began talking with people, just as he had done in the South. He found out about a new logging camp in an area of virgin pine forest about a hundred miles away. The camp had been in operation for only a couple of years. Jim and David spoke with the manager of the camp, who arranged to get horses and a guide for them. "He gave Dad a big pistol and a gunbelt to strap on, so we'd be safe, and I got this huge Bowie knife," David told me. "And the guide carried a rifle." The camp manager was concerned about their safety and warned them that some of the locals would do almost anything to steal their horses and belongings, perhaps even kill them. It's just as well that Nancy didn't know about that. "I remember when Jim left for Mexico, he said that if he or David got killed, they'd be buried within twenty-four hours, so don't be surprised. Thanks a lot!" she said.

The man who led them into the high country said he could take them to some imperial woodpeckers. "We were really far from anywhere," said David. "It was cold and windy, with clouds forming to the west of us. But you could look down thousands of feet into the valley and see sunny little villages with no roads leading to them. The people had to ride horses or mules or walk to get there."

Their guide had seen a pair of imperials the year before and said he knew where they nested. They rode with him for three or four days, and he showed them an enormous pine with a couple of cavities that had most likely been chiseled out by an imperial woodpecker. But the birds were not there. Nor were there any recent signs of large-woodpecker activity. "That was the closest I ever got to an imperial woodpecker — one year after the last bird had been there," said David.

Jim Tanner never gave up entirely on the big *Campephilus* woodpeckers. If pressed on it, he would say that the ivory-bill was probably extinct. But right to the end, he would take phone calls from people who thought they had seen one.

Jim Tanner passed away on January 21, 1991. As we talked at her home, Nancy pointed out that the day was the thirteenth anniversary of his death. I could see that she still missed him. Her admiration for him is deep and enduring. She often speaks of him as though he were alive. Their life together ended sadly, a few months after Jim was diagnosed with a brain tumor. The first sign of trouble was some numbness he was experiencing in his left hand and lower arm. He shrugged it off. Maybe he had had a minor stroke or something. But Nancy was worried. She convinced him to have it checked. A CAT scan revealed a tumor, but the doctor wasn't sure whether it was benign or malignant. To find out, he would have to thrust a needle into the tumor and retrieve a tissue sample for a biopsy.

Things could not have gone worse. Just minutes into the procedure, the doctor came running into the waiting room and told Nancy that the needle had punctured a blood vessel, causing a brain hemorrhage. They would have to perform emergency surgery immediately and needed her permission. The surgeon was able to save Jim's life, but he was paralyzed after the operation. Though he lived for several months, he became more and more helpless, eventually losing his ability to speak. Nancy finally had Jim's feeding tube removed, in accordance with his wishes. In some ways she regrets urging him to have the tests performed. But Jim would not have lived more than a few months in any case; the tumor was malignant and rapidly spreading.

Jim Tanner still looms large in the field of ivory-billed woodpecker research. He was the only person who ever studied the species in depth, and his 1942 book is the bible to all who seek this bird, from top ornithologists to crackpots. Whether you agree with his findings about the bird or not, every new theory about the ivory-bill must be measured against and compared to his research, done more than sixty years ago in a piece of primeval swamp forest that no longer exists. And there are plenty of questions to ask. Virtually everything we know about the ivory-bill is based on the meticulously studied population in the Singer Tract.

But what if these birds were an aberration? The ivory-bills in Florida usually roosted and nested in holes in huge cypress trees over water and fed on beetle-infested pine trees, sometimes even on those that had fallen to the ground. But the Singer Tract birds nested only in hardwoods on the drier ground of the second bottoms, and they foraged most often high on the uppermost dying branches of sweet gums and oaks. What if this were not really prime habitat for them? After all, the ivory-bills in Cuba and the imperials in Mexico, like the Florida birds, were pine specialists. What if the Singer Tract ivory-bills had been driven there because most of the large pines across the South had already been logged?

These are the questions I pondered for most of the long night of driving that followed my visit to Nancy in Knoxville. Nancy had invited me to go with her to a church dinner. I was tempted, but I made my apologies and left. I had places to go, far to the west — through Nashville and Memphis and beyond, to the White River of Arkansas, where less than a year earlier a very credible ivory-bill sighting had taken place. Nothing could stop me from racing there to look for the bird.

4

MARY, MARY

ONE OF THE PEOPLE I have come to know in the course of my ivory-bill search is Mary Scott. She is about my age (early fifties) and grew up in my old haunts in Long Beach, California. In fact, we have at least one mutual friend there. She worked for years as a corporate lawyer, and then she left it all behind to chase ghost birds — not just the ivory-billed woodpecker, but also the Bachman's warbler and the Eskimo curlew, neither of which has been positively sighted since the 1960s. She liquidated all her assets, put her money in the bank, and moved into a yurt (one of those huge circular structures used by the nomads of the Russian steppes and Mongolia) that she built behind her parents' house in Long Beach. She became a Web designer, which allowed her to work from home or wherever she happened to be and to have completely flexible hours. She figured she could make it for at least a couple of years on her savings and her diminished income.

Mary has become the quintessential ghost-bird chaser — which is vastly different from a rare-bird chaser. I suspect she wouldn't drive fifty miles to see a bird that is merely a rare or unusual vagrant. It has to be something that is widely believed to be extinct, and few birds fit that description better than an ivory-billed woodpecker. The bird has a kind of glamour — if that's the right word — that the Bachman's warbler, the Eskimo curlew, and even the passenger pigeon lack. It's big. It's beautiful. And its disappearance went hand in hand with the destruction of the most neglected habitat in North America: the vast southern bottomland hardwood forests.

In addition to working on Web sites for other people and companies, Mary created one for herself called birdingamerica.com, which is one of the first sites to come up if you do an Internet search for "ivory-billed woodpecker." The site is full of information about ivory-bills and solicits information from people who think they have seen one. I have interviewed several people who reported their sightings to Mary's site.

Some people, especially scientists, question Mary's credibility, because she doesn't mind associating with clairvoyants, cryptozoologists, and others on the fringe. "Hey, I'm from California," she says, laughing. "I have a high tolerance for this kind of stuff." But she has been an energetic booster of the search effort, and her Web site has been a useful clearinghouse for information on the ivory-bill.

Mary started searching for ivory-bills in February 2000, the season after David Kulivan reported seeing two birds in the Pearl River Wildlife Management Area in southern Louisiana. She spent several days exploring there, which she describes vividly on birdingamerica.com. One of the people that Mary went searching with, a woman from Florida called Cheryl, kept in touch by cell phone with a renowned horse-whisperer (and sometime woodpecker-whisperer), who had occasionally worked for the Olympic equestrian teams. This person told Cheryl that the birds were not extinct: she was in telepathic contact with them, though they were a thousand miles away, and they had let her know that they were willing to be seen by the group of searchers with Cheryl. But apparently Mary and the others offended the ivory-bills in some way during the first couple of days, because no one saw any.

On the third day of the search, Mary got a radio message from Cheryl, who had just had a cell-phone conversation with the woodpecker-whisperer. She said that she had been in touch with the ivory-bills again and that they hated the crackling noise the searchers made as they crunched through the underbrush and dead branches. According to Mary, the woman said that the ivory-bills also "weren't all that pleased with the 'energy' of the group — they thought it was similar to that of the hunters who roamed the area." Mary seemed to take this with a grain of salt. She was willing to try anything that might improve her chances of seeing an ivory-bill, even if it bordered on the absurd. About the woodpecker-whisperer's suggestions, Mary stated dryly, "Not terribly helpful — I would have preferred GPS coordinates!"

On that day Mary went searching with Bob Russell, a long-time ivory-bill searcher from Minnesota, and a couple of others. At one point she walked off by herself, traveling over land dampened by a recent rain, which no doubt muffled the crunching that the ivory-bills had complained about. And she heard the sound of a big woodpecker hammering on a tree nearby as it foraged. She then spotted a huge black-and-white bird flying through the trees, between her and the sun, and got her binoculars on it for an instant as it flew. She saw a patch of white feathers extending from an area of black feathers. She radioed the other searchers, who came running. Mary was in a state of shock. One of the searchers, a man named Paul, asked her about her sighting.

"Paul — who had earlier talked about those lousy witnesses he had interviewed in the Big Thicket [of eastern Texas], the ones who could only say 'Large, dark woodpecker with white on the wings' — asked me where the white was on the wing," said Mary. "I stared at him blankly. He asked me if it was on the leading or trailing edge of the wing. I couldn't imagine what those words meant. He walked away shaking his head."

Another of the searchers, Jim, helped her refocus her mind. He held up his hand and asked her to imagine that his fingers were the flight feathers on the bird's wing. He asked her which of the fingers would be white. She said the first two, at the front of the bird, would be black, and the next two would be white — which corresponds to the wing pattern of an ivory-bill.

But this was at best a fleeting look, like many of the tantalizing glimpses searchers have had from time to time. It was not one to hang your reputation on, and indeed, most ivory-bill chasers probably would not even have mentioned it. You see, the more of these inconclusive sightings a searcher has, the more his or her credibility diminishes. A searcher can easily fall into a boy-who-cried-wolf situation if he ever has a real sighting. This was Mary's first possible sighting. It would not be her last.

Mary's Web site does not report that during that first week of searching in 2000, she also drove north to the Three Rivers Wildlife Management Area with Bob Russell to get a feel for the habitat. "Bob was walking behind me, off to one side, when we both saw a large woodpecker flying straight through the dense second-growth woods," said Mary. They both had their binoculars up and followed the flight of the bird. "After my complete melt-down at the Pearl, I had just one desire," she said. "I wanted to be a good observer of anything I saw."

Mary admits that she had gone to the Pearl River that Febru-ary on a lark. She had no idea whether the ivory-bill existed and certainly didn't expect to find one. Having only recently left her career as a corporate lawyer, she had money and plenty of time on her hands. And because she owned a small amount of property along the Pearl River, she felt that she would be searching in her own back yard. "The chance to join an interesting group of people doing a very interesting thing intrigued me, so I went," she said. "I knew little about the ivory-bill."

After her brief glimpse of the mystery bird, she would not let herself look at a field guide or any pictures or drawings of ivory-bills. She was afraid she might contaminate her recollection of what she had seen. So as she and Bob walked at the Three Rivers WMA, she had not seen a picture of the bird for at least five days.

"The bird took a banking right turn just as it came into my line of sight for the first time," said Mary. "All I saw was the underside of the left wing. I got a clear look and felt satisfied that I had observed the sight clearly." She asked Bob if he had gotten a good view of the bird, and he said no. But he would be the first to admit that his eyes are not great. Bob is at his best as an ear birder and knows the songs and calls of all the birds anyone is likely to encounter anywhere in the East. Mary said, "The bird's wing had white on the front and back edges, with a central black band — *a perfect pileated woodpecker underwing.*" Bob gave her a quizzical look, and then they walked back to the car. When they got there, Bob wanted to discuss her sighting. He handed her a *National Geographic Field Guide to the Birds of North America* and convinced her to look at the page with the ivory-billed and pileated woodpeckers, since their searching was over.

"My eye went right to the illustrations of the underwings of the birds," said Mary. "I had described the underwing of an ivory-bill." By this time Bob was convinced Mary was wrong. He was tired, his feet hurt, and this hyperactive, excitable woman whom he barely knew was bursting with excitement at her second supposed ivory-bill sighting in less than a week. He pleaded exhaustion and said he had to return to New Orleans. He would not be back.

Mary flew home the next morning, but as soon as she got there, she made reservations to fly back to Louisiana the following weekend. She was hooked. "It was the underwing I saw at Three Rivers that made me a true searcher, and it's the reason I studied the bird so deeply," she said. But that second sighting killed her credibility with a lot of people. No one can just go out looking and find an ivory-bill like that, they thought, much less two of them. "So what can I say?" said Mary. "I'm a lucky birder. The first time I walked down to my pond when I moved to Arizona, a rufous-backed robin sat up in the perfect morning light on an unobstructed branch and posed for me to take a picture."

Mary returned to the Pearl River and Three Rivers area and searched the swamps alone from dawn to dusk for three days. She saw nothing, but she reported her earlier sighting to Jeff Basham, the son of the renowned birder Benton Basham, and he camped out in the area. According to Mary, he reported seeing a large woodpecker with a recurved crest at first light, when it was too early to distinguish colors well. He felt certain that he had seen a female ivory-bill.

Mary became obsessed with the bird. She was absolutely determined to keep searching until she found one and documented its existence. For the next three years she lived and breathed the ivory-billed woodpecker. She read everything she could find. She developed a lecture and slide show and took it on the road to nature centers and Audubon chapters. She visited the South again and again and again, slogging alone through dense, trackless swamps, where cottonmouths and quicksand abound. And she carried a camcorder constantly, like a permanent appendage, everywhere she searched.

Mary met some interesting characters along the way — such as Kenn Duke, a middle-aged Louisiana man who claimed to have seen ivory-billed woodpeckers when he was growing up along Gum Creek in the southeastern part of the state. He contacted Mary through her Web site, and they arranged to meet on one of her trips. He lived in Baton Rouge but planned to go home to the town of Pearl River to watch the annual Mardi Gras parade with his family.

Mary was supposed to meet Duke on a Sunday morning, but after searching all day Saturday on the Pearl River, she decided to see if she could find Gum Creek and have a look around by herself. She followed a dirt road to a dead end where the creek spilled into the West Pearl, and as darkness fell, she struggled to turn her car around. Then a car pulled up behind her. After a second of panic, she saw that a woman was driving, and she went up to the window of the other car and asked the driver if this was Gum Creek. The woman, who introduced herself as Judy, didn't know, but invited Mary back to her house to ask her husband, Lucky. She said he had hunted and fished in the area all his life. At the house, Lucky confirmed that she had indeed been on Gum Creek and spoke with her about the local woodpeckers.

"He kept telling me that the birds I was looking for were everywhere, but he kept describing pileateds," said Mary. He called them "Good God" birds. Mary tried her best to explain to him that the birds she was looking for were similar but had some important differences, but she didn't want to tell him what the differences were or lead him in any way. If he had seen an ivory-bill, she wanted him to describe it in his own words. He seemed in a daze as he puzzled over what she was asking. "He had that look like he was reaching really, really deep," said Mary. "And then it was like a light bulb suddenly went on over his head. 'Oh, you mean those ones with the big white patches halfway down the back on both sides?'" And she just wanted to shake him: "Yes, yes, the ones with the big white patches on their backs!"

The next morning at about ten o'clock, Mary had her rendezvous with Duke. He arrived in a pickup truck with his wife and children. A National Rifle Association bumper sticker on the back of his truck read MY PRESIDENT IS CHARLTON HESTON. He was Mary's polar opposite in every way. While he liked guns, NASCAR, and right-wing politics, she was a pinko liberal environmentalist. While he was round and sluggish, she was thin and hyper. What they had in common was an overpowering interest in the ivory-billed woodpecker. Duke claimed that when Hurricane Camille struck in 1969, many trees had been knocked down along Gum Creek. Dozens of woodpeckers had subsequently moved into the area to exploit the disaster and consume all the insect larvae and grubs that the dead and dying trees attracted.

"There were many pileated woodpeckers, which some of the locals call 'laughing jackasses' because of their call," he told her. Then he talked about other, similar woodpeckers he had seen there — ones that had white on their backs and their flight feathers. "I looked them up in some bird book and ID'ed them as ivory-billed woodpeckers. The white triangle on the back and their bright red crest matched perfectly." He didn't read far enough in the field guide to find out that the species was supposed to be extinct.

Growing up, Duke had spent hours watching the big woodpeckers that lived in the woods within walking distance of his home. He made fascinating observations about them, commenting on how much more graceful they were in the air than pileateds, with much more "smooth gliding and less pumping." He estimated that six pairs of pileated woodpeckers and two pairs of ivory-bills lived in the woods along that stretch of Gum Creek. "Both types could really tear up a tree, with wood chips flying like some Woody Woodpecker cartoon," he said. "They both made large holes, which I assume were nests. Both males and females spent much time going in and out. I never saw any young of either kind."

Duke went off to college at Louisiana State University, but he returned home regularly to hunt along Gum Creek. And he always saw the big woodpeckers, pileateds as well as ivory-bills. Then he read that the ivory-bill was extinct, so he went to LSU's Museum of Natural Science and told someone there about the birds he was seeing. "All I got was, 'Sorry, kid, you saw a pileated,'" he said. "No," he replied in frustration. "I've watched them for hours on end, year after year." He was told that it was impossible; the birds were extinct. He left a message, but no one ever contacted him. He had made most of his sightings from September to February in the years from 1969 to 1990, when his mother moved away. This was the first time he had been back since then.

It was a warm day as Mary walked through the woods with Duke, and few birds were singing. The two of them crossed back and forth over the creek on fallen logs. Mature stands of pine as well as sweet gum, black gum, and bay rose up around them. He showed her long-dead trees with cavities dug deep into their trunks and said that this was where he had seen the ivory-bills. After Hurricane Camille, the place had been like a Sam's Club for woodpeckers, he told her.

Mary looked around in awe, imagining what it had been like

when the birds were there — completely convinced by his story but filled with despair. The ivory-bills had probably moved on in the decade since he had last visited the place, looking for other areas where natural disasters had struck. Groping for something to say, she said it must have been amazing to see the black crests on the females. "No," he told her. "What was really remarkable was the white. When they'd land on a tree, there'd be this brilliant white. There's not much white in the forest. It really stood out. It was beautiful."

I later talked with James Van Remsen, the curator of birds at LSU's Museum of Natural Science, about Duke's sightings, and he believed the report. The story made a lot of sense, and Duke's observations seemed accurate. Van Remsen felt terrible that someone at the museum had turned Duke away and ignored his sightings. "I don't know who he spoke to," he said. "It may have been a grad student — it's hard to say. I hope it wasn't me."

So is there any chance that a couple of ivory-bills might still linger along Gum Creek? It isn't likely. The area was clear-cut not long after Mary's visit.

Mary's quest was far from over after that first season of searching. She continued to look in several different southern states and to present lectures to increase public awareness about the ivory-bill. Then, in March 2003, she hooked up once again with Bob Russell and two other searchers and went to Arkansas's White River National Wildlife Refuge. When they arrived there after a three-hour drive, they went to one of the more promising areas of forest, with large second-growth timber and one area of remnant old-growth forest. Bob stopped the car, and he and the other two in front got out and walked along the dirt road ahead of the car to stretch their legs. Mary was sitting in the back seat, and as she stepped out, the door blocked her way to the front, so she started strolling in the other direction, past the rear of the car. All of them were in a daze after being cooped up for so long. Mary suddenly noticed a large woodpecker rising from near the forest floor. But this time it didn't vanish immediately into the thick woods. It flew up and landed on a broad tree trunk and hung there, in good light.

"I had an unobstructed view," she said. "It was huge, and I got a really good look at it. It couldn't have been anything but an ivory-billed woodpecker." She started calling out the field marks to the others as she watched it in her binoculars.

"In all the drawings that I've ever seen of an ivory-billed wood-pecker on a tree, the white patch on the back is shown as one big triangle with the wings pulled back together," she explained. "On this bird, I was seeing a dark line down the middle of its back, so it looked like two white triangles. I'd never seen that in a drawing — I'd never even considered it. So I was shouting, 'It has a dark line down its back!'"

By the time everyone else got there, the bird had flown away, and Mary was left with only a memory. Her camcorder was on the back seat of the car. "It was so bizarre," she said. "I never go anywhere without my camera in my hand. But we'd been in the car for three hours, and it was the moment where you get out of the car and stretch before you start searching. So I had my binoculars around my neck, but no camera."

The bird was facing the tree, so she couldn't see its bill, but she did see all of the other ivory-bill field marks. As she watched, it fell sideways from the tree and glided without flapping. "The wingspan was enormous," she said, "and the white on the wings when they opened was incredible. It had a huge white band on the trailing edge. But it never flapped." She saw it fly for about ten feet, and then it was gone. It headed across the bayou to the old-growth forest.

Mary sketched it in her date book but didn't write down any detailed notes. "I had drawn it," she said, "and it is indelible in my brain. What was totally interesting to me was that it had an elon-gated neck and a very distinct head, neck, and shoulders. It was elegantly proportioned."

What did the others think of her sighting? Bob Russell said,

"You can't always see an ivory-bill, Mary," and climbed back into the car in disgust. The others followed.

"I couldn't get them to go back," said Mary. "I mean, they wanted to drive around and take pictures of mansions behind barbed wire fences in fields. They wanted to see if they could find another form of fried okra. I was so frustrated. I couldn't even believe it. I couldn't get these people to search."

Mary felt crushed by their response. She has nothing but respect for Bob's abilities as a birder and was discouraged because she couldn't get him to keep searching there that day. "He's so amazing," she said. "He doesn't just know every song — he knows every call note of every bird in North America. It's unbelievable birding with him. I've been with him when he hears the call note of a bird migrating in flight a half-mile above your head. He's extraordinary. His ears are extraordinary."

A couple of days later, just before leaving for home, Bob, Mary, and the others finally returned to the area where she said she had seen the bird. It was then that Bob heard a birdcall unlike any he had ever heard in his forty-plus years of birding — a call very much like the tin-horn toot of an ivory-bill. "He still will not say, 'I heard an ivory-bill,'" says Mary. "He doesn't want to be thought of as a nut case. But he will say that he heard something that sounded like the bird and that it did not sound like any other bird in North America."

No one else heard the call. The group had spread out, each person taking a zone, and they were scattered throughout the area. The place where Bob heard the call was not far from where Mary had seen the bird, and the call came from the direction in which the bird had flown.

The story of the call Bob Russell heard was so compelling — even though he would not identify it as an ivory-bill — that the Cornell Lab of Ornithology put up three autonomous recording units in the area, hoping to record this unusual sound. Unfortunately, the units were not in place until summer, a time when ivory-bills are mostly silent, and the results were inconclusive.

What of Mary's sighting? It went unmentioned and was

known only through rumors. And on her Web site, which contained voluminous, detailed reports about everything else she did, Mary was curiously silent. Only one paragraph mentions the trip to Arkansas at all: "There's some beautiful habitat down there. Lots of trees, lots of woodpeckers, but we weren't able to verify the existence of ivory-bills this time out! (No Bachman's warblers either.) We're undaunted and planning to continue our searches. Thanks for all your good wishes!" And that was it. She stopped adding to her site.

I spent months trying to get in touch with Mary, but she didn't answer my e-mails or the phone messages I left. Then one day she called me out of the blue and spilled her story. She said that she had been silent because she didn't see how anything good for the birds could come out of her sighting. "Can you imagine the horror of that story getting out?" she said. "I could have gone back for two weeks and tried to shoot a video of the bird. I didn't want to. Every scenario I ran through my mind came up negative. I could just see that place swarming with idiots in boats — such an ugly vision. And birders are the worst. Given the remoteness of that place, there's no way you could secure the area.

"The bird is such an icon," she said. "People's sense of loss is huge. And yet the bird doesn't know any of this. It's doing its thing, just being a bird. Extinction is our loss."

Mary said she has no regrets that she didn't get a videotape of the bird. "I wouldn't have been able to do the right thing with it," she said. "I would have played the video back for the others; phone calls would have been made; the damage would have been done."

Asked why she had finally told me about the sighting, she said this was not something she could bear on her shoulders alone. "It's a huge burden, and I'm not capable of carrying it myself," she said. "I hope you have the smartness to do the right thing. If Cornell gets verification, the only appropriate thing to do would be to try to secure the adjoining tract of forest. But if you make the sighting known, you doom the bird. So far, we've shown as a species that we're incapable of doing the right thing."

5

WHITE RIVER REVISITED

$\mathcal{T}$HE MORNING I WAS TO LEAVE my home in Freeville in January 2004, a blizzard came blasting through, blowing snow sideways and causing whiteouts up and down the highway. Cars lay in ditches, their embarrassed drivers standing outside stamping their feet and shivering as they called for help on their cell phones. Tow trucks with flashing blue lights trolled up and down the highway, looking for customers. And I paced back and forth in my front room, wondering when the snowstorm would end. I had to meet Bobby in Arkansas, and it was a long, long way from upstate New York.

I waited until almost ten o'clock to see if the storm would blow over. No way. It was only getting worse. *What the hell,* I finally thought. *How bad can it be? At least I'm heading south. If I can just get to the interstate, I can drive slowly for a state or two, watching the season progress toward spring before my eyes, like a time-lapse sequence of a flower blooming, and then I'll be home free, blasting down those dry southern roadways to my rendezvous at White River.* I figured in Virginia or Maryland I would get out of this damn snow. The only catch was getting to Interstate 81. Should I drive north through Cortland, going out of my way but traveling on a better road? Or should I go south through the hills and intercept the interstate at Marathon?

I drove south. Big mistake. In the places with open pasture-land, high winds roared through unabated, with no trees or obstructions of any kind to block them, causing long stretches with near-zero visibility. Snowdrifts formed right in the road, which was okay in the places where a lot of people were driving — at least I could follow their tracks. But when I turned off the main road at Harford and drove up into the hills, I was blazing my own trail. I guess everyone else in that area had enough sense to stay home.

The worst part was when I came to a high, open hilltop with no trees or fencerows to guide me. I was driving slower than I could walk, feeling my way over the hill, fearful I might go off the road into a hidden ditch at any moment. It was just like the Arctic — the way it looked *and* the bird life. I kept catching glimpses of snow buntings in that barren, white, windswept field. How at home they must have felt. And a rough-legged hawk hung high overhead in the wind.

And then I was finally out of it, dropping down from the hills into Marathon, past the statue of the Union soldier, now white with snow, standing tall in the center of town. It would not be the last Civil War monument I would see on this trip. By the time I quit driving, around midnight, I had blown past the Gettysburg battlefield (ghostly in the stark white snow), where some 51,000 combatants had met their fate. I would have loved to stop there, as well as at the many other Civil War battlefields — Shiloh, Vicksburg — I would pass on my trek through the South, but there was just no time.

When I finally felt I could drive no farther, I pulled in to a hotel in a tiny burg called Kodak not far from Knoxville, Tennessee. I had a nice Henry Higgins moment as I booked the room. (I once played the lead in a community theater production of *My Fair Lady*, so I already had some experience as Professor Higgins.) I noticed the night clerk had a slight accent.

"You haven't always lived in America, have you?" I asked.

"No," he said.

"Are you originally from Scandinavia?"

He nodded.

"Denmark?" I asked.

"Yes," he said, beaming. "That's amazing. I've lived here for thirty years. How did you know I was from Denmark?" I told him I'd been to Greenland a couple of times and had met some Danes there. He was so excited he brought out the other clerk, an Indian woman, and told her all about it. Luckily, he didn't ask me what part of India she was from.

It would be another day and a half before I met up with Bobby. I had a few people to see en route. We planned to meet at the headquarters of the White River National Wildlife Refuge. Our dream was to return to the spot where Mary Scott had seen her ivory-bill and, I'll admit, to try to find the bird ourselves. Not much to ask for.

Of course, shortly after I had interviewed Mary, I had had a long talk with Bob Russell. Let's say he was less than enthusiastic about the credibility of her sighting.

"I don't know," he said. "I've been on three trips with her, and she's seen ivory-bills on all three trips, so no, I don't believe her. Not that I think she's lying, but she has such a rich imagination."

I told him I had heard about her earlier glimpses and had been dubious, but this last one . . . "Either she saw it or she's lying or she's crazy," I said. I must admit, I had come to believe strongly in her sighting. The fact that she clammed up after being such an avid and vociferous booster of the whole ivory-bill search effort seemed compelling to me. She acted like a person who had had an epiphany.

"You know, Tim," said Bob, "she's a very bright woman and a good friend of mine. But we were in the car — four of us — and we came to this area at White River and jumped out of the car, because it looked like really good habitat. So she's scanning the woods away from the bayou, and suddenly she says, 'There it is!

There it is! I think I have something!' And then pretty soon it's 'I have an ivory-bill.' We made a beeline right for where she saw it. I was maybe a hundred yards away, and what came out of the woods was a red-headed woodpecker."

A red-headed woodpecker does have a white lower back like an ivory-bill, but it's tiny in comparison — slightly smaller than an American robin. Mary had told me that she saw more red-headed woodpeckers at White River that day than she had seen in her entire life, so it was possible that she and Bob saw different birds. Mary had stressed that the bird she saw — at close range, through binoculars — seemed to have a black vertical line running down the middle of its lower back, which she hadn't expected. An ivory-bill does have a black back, which could look like a vertical black line if the bird was not holding its wings tightly together in back. But the rump and lower back of a red-headed woodpecker are white, so no black line would show there, no matter how the wings were positioned.

"How could she mistake a red-head for an ivory-bill?" I asked.

"You know — you've been traveling," he said. "You just get out of the car. You don't have your sizes down yet. You see a red-headed woodpecker at a distance — the big flashes of white. You may not see the size of the bird. You may just see the flashes of white."

"God, they're so tiny, though," I said.

"Yeah, I don't know how you would mistake one for an ivory-bill," he said. "But maybe that's the explanation. I was right there, and I didn't see anything else come out. Mary was focused on one part of the woods, which was really dense, and on either side it was more open. The red-headed came out of there and nothing else that I could see."

"But didn't you hear a call later?" I asked.

"Yeah," he said. "I heard something about a mile and a half south of there that sent shivers up my spine. It wasn't a classic ivory-bill call — it wasn't the *toot-toot* — but it was something in the same realm."

"Was it a series of toots or what?"

"It was a really loud call," he said. "It was on the order of a toot, but it was louder than the Cornell recordings."

"You know, I've never really thought that much of those recordings," I said. "I don't think they show the typical call of the bird — the loud toot that Audubon, Tanner, and all the others described. The Cornell tapes are two birds, close together, interacting with each other. I can't see those calls going a quarter-mile or more like they say."

"You're right," he said. "The birds [in the Cornell film] come in and there's kind of a little, soft conversation back and forth. I don't see how that would carry. This thing I heard, it was loud. You know it was carrying."

Like Mary with her sighting, Bob was the only witness to the loud call. The others had gone off into the woods. He decided to hang back and move more slowly. "Everyone is always crashing into the woods and not seeing anything," he said. "I was going to maintain my silence and wait."

When everyone got back together, they returned to the place where he had heard the call. But no one saw or heard anything else noteworthy.

It was actually Bob's report of the unusual call that caught the interest of the Lab of Ornithology, not Mary's sighting. Before I left for Arkansas, I spoke with Kurt Fristrup, the assistant director of the lab's bioacoustics research program. He was the one who had placed the three autonomous recording units at that site the previous summer and later brought them back to Cornell for analysis. Kurt is a longtime innovator in using sound to census wildlife populations remotely. He has worked on projects that detect whale vocalizations in the deep sea and elephant calls in the African forest as well as the sounds of birds and insects. An avid amateur tennis player in his early fifties, Kurt is tall and lean, with red hair. He has been at the lab for ten years.

One of his most interesting recent projects involved attaching recording devices to weather balloons and floating them high above the rugged terrain at Fort Hood, a military base in Texas, to take a census of rare golden-cheeked warblers and black-capped vireos. The ruggedness of the area wasn't the only thing that prevented ornithologists from searching on foot; unexploded ordnance from years of bombardment during various war games and military exercises littered the ground or lay hidden in the brush. Kurt and his assistants released the balloons upwind of the target area and retrieved them miles away, in safer territory. The sensitive microphones the balloons carried picked up the songs and calls of the birds vocalizing far below.

Kurt had installed the ARUs at White River on his way to Fort Hood and picked them up on a subsequent trip there. He left them in place for much of the summer. The sound researchers did not find anything conclusive during the sound analysis — no *kent* calls — although there is an interesting double-rap sound on one tape. But the absence of an identifiable call does not prove that ivory-bills were not present. ARUs pick up sounds emitted within only one hundred yards or so, unless it is something particularly loud, like a gunshot. According to the scientific literature, ivory-bills are not known to call while they're flying, so one of these birds would have to land fairly close to the ARU for its calls to be recorded.

The White River refuge is huge, ranging from three to ten miles wide and extending for ninety river miles. At some 160,000 acres, it includes one of the largest remaining bottomland hardwood forests in the entire Mississippi River drainage. And we had three ARUs. A few little tin-horn toots could easily have been missed.

Another problem is that ivory-bills are relatively quiet in summer, when the ARUs were in place. According to Jim Tanner, "Work in summer is practically a waste of time, because of the dense vegetation, silent birds, and depressing heat." He said winter and early spring were the only good seasons for investigating ivory-bill habitats. "Leaves are then off the trees, allowing good visibility and hearing, the birds are quite active and noisy, and the cooler weather makes work in the woods pleasant."

It's too bad Jim didn't take his own advice. He made two brief visits to the White River in the summer of 1938, on June 17 and 18 and August 1 through 6. "Ivory-bills were once recorded from this area," he wrote, "and there are a few virgin tracts of sweet gum and oak timber but too small and scattered to make really good ivory-bill territory; I found no indications of the birds still being there." I can't help wondering if he would have had better luck searching in the winter. But of course winter was also the best time to work at his primary study site in the Singer Tract.

Kurt gave me GPS coordinates for the locations where he had set up the ARUs, and he told me to look up the refuge biologist, Richard Hines, who had been helpful. "It's worth going there just to see a big bottomland forest like that," said Kurt. "But watch out for cottonmouths. I've never seen so many in my life."

I kept trying to call Bobby on his cell phone as I drove to White River, but I got no response — just his voice mail, which I knew was a bottomless pit that didn't reach him for days. He told me that it's as if the message is in a big pipe and has to shrink down to fit through a tiny hole before it can reach him. I was dubious about this explanation, but it did take an amazingly long time for him to get messages — sometimes several days. It usually didn't matter. Bobby is the kind of guy who always has his cell phone nearby and switched on. I've reached him while he is driving cross-country and while he's in line at Taco Bell or McDonald's, and even a couple of times when he was teaching in a classroom. It seems that he will stop in the middle of a lecture and talk on the phone, at least if the topic is the ivory-billed woodpecker.

I wondered what was going on. Maybe the half-million miles he had logged with his van had started to take their toll. Maybe the old Safari had died somewhere along the road between Huntsville and St. Charles. I didn't know. But when I pulled into the parking lot at the refuge headquarters, I saw his aging white camper van, sitting low on its tired leaf springs.

Bobby was inside taking a nap, so I banged on the side of the van hard and barked like a southern sheriff: "Y'all cain't sleep here! It's against the law!" He jumped up with his eyes wide and started digging frantically for something beside him.

"Hey, Bobby, it's me, Tim," I said. He came up a moment later with a clear plastic bag full of candy bars. As I opened the door, he tossed me a Snickers.

"How you doing?" he said, smiling broadly.

"Great," I said. "But I couldn't get you on your cell phone."

It turned out that cell-phone reception was almost nonexistent in this area. In fact, almost every modern convenience was nonexistent here.

After our quick-energy candy bar break, we walked into the refuge headquarters to look for Richard Hines. The only person we saw was a dark-haired woman in her early twenties, dressed in a tan U.S. Fish and Wildlife Service shirt and khaki pants. We introduced ourselves, and I told her I was supposed to meet with Richard. She said he was somewhere out in the refuge and might not be back for hours.

Bobby asked her about herself, and she said her name was Elizabeth and she was originally from Georgia.

"Oh, good," he said. Then he nodded toward me. "You know, Tim's a Yankee. He's from New York!" They both laughed.

"Is there anyone else we can talk to?" I asked.

"Well, there's the refuge manager," she said. "Larry Mallard."

"What?" I asked. "You mean like mallard duck?"

"Yes."

Bobby made a perfect mallard quack in the background, and we started laughing hysterically. By this time we were giddy — too much driving, not enough sleep — so it didn't take much to tip us over. But it must have been infectious. Elizabeth was laughing too.

Finally she said she would go and get him. As she was walking toward the hallway, she turned and looked back at us with a serious expression on her face. "Now don't you dare laugh," she said. Bobby quacked, and we all broke up again.

Larry Mallard came out a few minutes later. Elizabeth glanced at us sternly, and we looked down, trying not to smirk. Bobby didn't quack. Mallard was a stocky middle-aged man with glasses and a mustache and a no-nonsense attitude. He knew all about the possible ivory-bill sightings but didn't give them any credence. "If there were ivory-bills out there, someone would have seen them by now," he said. I told him that was probably true, but I was trying to follow up on as many sightings as possible. This one was particularly interesting because it was so recent.

Mallard took us over to a large wall map and pointed out the extent of the refuge. He said it had been established in 1935, largely as a waterfowl refuge, though now it was managed for all kinds of wildlife: white-tailed deer, bears, wild turkeys, and of course the waterfowl (there was an amazing number and diversity of ducks). The staff did a lot of hands-on habitat management — controlling beavers and raccoons and thinning the forest, creating gaps and trying to vary the height of the canopy to provide habitat for the maximum number of species. Mallard said they would go through the forest and paint a colored slash on trees that were slated for cutting. "I like to feel that I'm painting a landscape," he said.

Then he said something intriguing. He mentioned a kayaker who had gotten permission to explore the refuge. The man had spent days floating through the forest, camping out at night along the way.

"Do people go kayaking or canoeing here a lot?" I asked him.

"No," he said. "Hardly ever."

"What a great way to search a place like this," I said.

To kill some time while we waited for Richard, we went to have lunch at the St. Charles Community Store, a combination gas station, restaurant, grocery, and general store we had seen about a mile from the refuge headquarters. It's the kind of place where hunters hang out, dressed head to foot in camouflage, filling up on greasy food before hitting the marshes. It's open at 4 A.M. every day of duck season. But the food is good — mostly simple fare, like hamburgers and fries, but the place has a great catfish fry at least once a week.

After we had eaten, we decided to look around and see if there was any more to the town of St. Charles. From Highway 1, all you can see is the community store. We followed a road toward the river and suddenly found ourselves in small-town America — only it was a small town that had died on the vine. An elderly man at the store told us, "The town has a population of one hundred and seventy-five, give or take." We passed a deserted brick building with busted-out windows that had once been a high school. We saw an old duck club and a few houses, and then we turned onto the broad main street, completely empty of traffic. Smack in the middle of the road, a massive stone monolith rose up before us. I couldn't believe that some drunk driving home one night hadn't run into it with his pickup truck yet. Or maybe someone had, but it was so huge and heavy that he hadn't made a mark on it. It was impressive. The monument honored the men who had died fighting on the banks of the broad White River. According to a brass plaque near the water's edge, "the deadliest shot of the Civil War" was fired right here. The Confederate battery had been fighting off an attack by the Union gunboat *Mound City* when one of their artillery shells pierced the ship's steam drum. More than one hundred Union sailors were scalded to death. Only twenty-six crewmen survived. But the rebel victory was short-lived. Other federal forces attacked by land and seized the fort. A grain silo now rises where the proud Confederate battery once stood.

We finally hooked up with Richard, a career wildlife biologist in his early fifties. Originally from Kentucky, he had been at the White River National Wildlife Refuge for about four years. He lived with his wife, Pam, and a teenage son in St. Charles; his other son was in the Coast Guard. He said he would be glad to take us out with him the next day while he was working on his waterfowl counts. He would show us more of the refuge and take us where the ARUs had been installed — and where Mary's sighting and Bob's sounding had taken place.

David Luneau, who had been one of the researchers on the Zeiss ivory-bill search team in early 2002, had also been doing some searching at White River. I visited him in his office at the University of Arkansas at Little Rock the day before I met Bobby at the refuge. David went there frequently and had found a tree with some interesting stripped bark. He saved some pieces of the bark and showed me pictures of the exposed wood and the lateral grooves cut into it, possibly made by a large woodpecker's bill prying sideways to strip off the bark, or at least that's what he hoped. David was so intrigued by this that he set up a remote camera, hoping to get a picture of the mystery bark-peeler in action. Richard had helped him install the camera and kept an eye on it for the several months David had it there. But somehow, whatever was peeling the bark came back and peeled more without triggering the camera. The problem might have been that the setup was designed for photographing deer, so hunters could see how big the bucks were that frequented a given area. Maybe it took a larger animal than a woodpecker to trigger the remote sensor.

We made arrangements to meet Richard early the next morning at the general store. Before we left, Bobby and I asked him about the local lodging situation. St. Charles had nothing. A nearby town had a small hotel, but he advised us against staying there. He told us some duck hunters had checked in recently and been unable to sleep, because their Labrador retriever kept them up all night chasing mice or other vermin around the room. We ended up driving to Stuttgart, almost all the way to Little Rock. And then it was nearly impossible to find a room. It was the last weekend of duck season, and hunters were packed into every hotel and motel. The prices were outrageous — at least for the South, where I was getting used to paying thirty dollars a night for a room.

We finally found a place with a vacancy and went in to book a room.

"You duck hunters?" the woman asked.

"Why?" I asked. "Does it cost less if you're a duck hunter?"

"No," she said. "It costs more."

I smiled. "Then we're definitely not."

· · ·

We were still driving two vehicles. Even though we were going back to the same place the next morning, Bobby didn't want to leave his van unattended at White River. He had brought some expensive camera equipment and other gear. We moved a lot of it into the room and then went looking for a restaurant. We must have driven around for an hour or more before returning to the McDonald's we had passed near our room. It made me wish we had just slept in our cars so we could have eaten at the community store again. It was catfish night.

The next morning also made me wish we had slept somewhere closer to St. Charles. It took about an hour and a half to get there, driving in the dark on farm roads with many ninety-degree turns along the way, and Bobby's big van did not corner well. We took advantage of the community store again for bacon and eggs and coffee. It was a happening place at 5 A.M., though I felt a little conspicuous without a full suit of camo. Richard finally pulled up in a U.S. Fish and Wildlife Service truck with his wife, Pam, and we climbed inside.

Pam was lively and enthusiastic. She wanted to hear all about ivory-billed woodpeckers and peppered us with questions as we drove along the big levee, high above the swamp. Below us in the water-filled "borrow pits" — from which the Corps of Engineers had "borrowed" the dirt to create the levee — we saw hundreds and hundreds of migratory ducks: northern pintails, American wigeon, mallards, shovelers, gadwalls, and more.

Richard was taking his monthly rough count of the refuge's waterfowl population. "I get a quick estimate of what we've got on the place," he said. "I have certain areas I look at — it gives me an idea from month to month of what we've got." Amazingly, Richard is the only biologist employed by the refuge — one man covering 160,000 acres — and he has no assistants. "I'm it as far as biology goes," he said.

He is also a great guide. He knows a lot about the entire countryside — its history and people as well as its wildlife. Like many I've met in the South, he feels that the North raped the former Confederate states after the Civil War, at least in terms of their natural resources. Before the war, the South was a land of vast woodlands and bottomland swamp forest, largely untouched by the ax. Wildlife abounded: wolves, bears, panthers — and ivory-billed woodpeckers.

"Everything was overrun as soon as the war was over," he said. "The carpetbaggers came in and set up governments and basically ran everything. They tried to break up the plantations. Everything was disrupted. Things probably would have been better if Lincoln had lived. But Andrew Johnson, he hated the South."

"But he was from the South himself, wasn't he?" I asked.

"From east Tennessee," said Richard. "But east Tennessee never went Confederate. It was Republican. If you had a Republican county, it remained true to the North."

As we drove along the high levee, a great expanse of forest spread out to the west of us. But to the east, a vast open plain of plowed fields stretched as far as you could see. I knew at one time this whole area had been an old-growth bottomland hardwood forest, hundreds of miles wide, stretching all the way to the Gulf.

"A lot of the country — the land, the forests, the coal mines — became owned by big corporations from someplace else," Richard explained. "The Ford Motor Company bought up maybe thirty, forty, or fifty thousand acres of Kentucky forest to supply the wood-spoke wheels for their Model Ts. Steel companies owned thousands of acres of land that they strip-mined for coal to send back to Pittsburgh to fire up their foundries. And of course the Singer Sewing Machine Company, out of Chicago, owned the Tensas tract in Louisiana. A lot of logs were being cut and hauled back to Chicago to provide wood for sewing machine cabinets. Where I grew up in western Kentucky, this one company owned the coal mine. And they paid you in coal company scrip, not cash. You could only spend it — guess where? At the company store. It was like the old song, 'I owe my soul to the company store.' This went on up through the twenties, thirties, and even the forties. A lot of the same kind of thing was going on in this part of the world with logging."

Richard talked animatedly as he drove with one hand on the wheel. Occasionally he would stop to count the ducks on some of the water-covered areas below. I had heard a lot of this before — and it was hard to dispute it. Some terrible things had been done to the pristine lands of the South, some of them perhaps out of spite, and an amazing number of people are still angry about it almost a century and a half later. One thing I had never heard before, though, was about the significant destruction of bottomland hardwood forest and swamp that had taken place much more recently.

According to Richard, during the late 1960s and early 1970s the price of soybeans rose astronomically, perhaps in response to a boom in the vegetarian and health food markets. "The price of soybeans went up to ten dollars a bushel," he said. "The price right now runs between five and seven dollars a bushel in 2004 money, and a farmer can make a profit at that price. Can you imagine getting ten dollars a bushel in 1969? Gas was twenty-five cents a gallon back then."

"Yeah, I remember," I said. "And the minimum wage was a buck and a quarter an hour."

"The farmers cleared every square inch of property anywhere they could," he said. "They stuck tiles in the ground and drained the swamps. Anyplace they could get a crop of soybeans in, they were doing it. They literally had bulldozers working twenty-four hours a day clearing bottomland forest — pushing it out. It was more cost-effective to roll a thirty-six-inch-diameter tree into a brush pile and burn it. There was no time to cut it and haul the log out, because you could make more money on soybeans. They would bulldoze the woods up into long windrows and set fire to them while they were planting beans down the edge. That's when a lot of that country east of the levee was cleared — not only here, but all up and down the whole Mississippi Valley and the Green River bottoms of Kentucky where I grew up. I mean, anyplace they could get a crop of soybeans in, they were doing it. It took its toll."

Richard looked away in disgust. "You know, I can remember

land selling for fifty or sixty bucks an acre," he said. "You could buy a D8 dozer, put a guy on it, clear out the woods, and then start growing forty bushels of soybeans to the acre at ten dollars a whack. Big money."

A few minutes later we came to a dirt road that ran down off the levee. Richard pulled up the truck to a gated fence and got out to unlock it. We then drove a couple of miles into the refuge. To the left of us stood a tract of nice second-growth forest, with quite a few large trees. It may not have been cut for a century. On the right side, across the bayou, it was even better, an area of old-growth forest — but how to get there? Bobby and I hadn't brought a canoe. We were mostly just scouting at this point, but it looked promising over there.

The day had turned dark by then, and a storm was threatening. Richard turned left onto another dirt road and drove about a mile to the tree where David had set up his remote camera. We all climbed out of the truck and went over to examine the peeled bark. The tree was only about ten or twelve feet into the woods. It was intriguing: some fairly tight bark had been scaled away, revealing distinct horizontal grooves in the wood underneath, unlike anything I had seen in the Northeast, or indeed anywhere. But it was all fairly close to the ground, which made me wonder whether it might have been caused by a mammal of some kind rather than a bird.

We got back in the truck and returned the way we had come. "Kurt put up one of the ARUs right over in there," said Richard, pointing into the woods.

"Is this where Bob Russell heard the bird?" I asked.

"A little bit farther down," he said.

"And what about Mary? Where'd she see the bird?"

"That was back near where we first turned left," he said.

Bobby spotted another tree with patches of stripped bark as we were driving along. "You see that?" he said. "Say, can we stop and take a look at that, Richard?"

We all clambered out again and jumped across a muddy ditch

to get to the tree. It had fresh woodpecker work on the bark about eight feet up. By this time there was a light drizzle, but we decided to spread out a little and walk through the woods. Both Bobby and I had camcorders in our hands and cameras hanging around our necks. I spotted another tree a couple of hundred feet away that also had woodpecker workings. The fresh excavations showed up amazingly well in the dark, wet forest. And the bare wood had distinct lateral grooves cut into it. At the base of the tree, freshly peeled strips of bark — some of them six inches, eight inches, or more in length — lay scattered in the mud. I picked up a few to take with me.

Bobby found another tree with stripped bark nearby and tried to videotape it, holding the camcorder in one hand, pressed against his face, as his other hand pulled at the bark. He talked loudly as he worked, like a surgeon describing the procedure during an operation. "I am pulling against this bark with all my might, and I can barely budge it," he said. "Notice my fingers in these grooves. They are approximately one quarter to three eighths of an inch deep." He was oblivious of anything going on around him. I think an ivory-bill could have flown past and rapped on his head and he wouldn't have noticed. I started video-taping him as he shot his video and talked to the tree. I showed it to my wife a few weeks later, and she shook her head. "You guys are just a bunch of Sasquatch chasers," she said.

A minute later we heard Pam's high-pitched voice echoing through the woods. "Over here," she said. "I found another one." Sure enough, she had another tree with peeled bark and lateral grooves. Pam was completely hooked on the search. She kept run-ning ahead. "I've got another one. I've got another one," she would say, and then she would run deeper into the woods. By this time the rain was coming down in sheets, pouring down the backs of our necks and giving us chills.

"Damn," I said to Bobby. "If only the weather was better. I'd re-ally love to search this area thoroughly. But an ivory-bill would probably stay in its hole on a day like this."

He nodded. "You're right," he said.

Richard and Pam came walking back toward us. "Any idea what the weather will be like for the next day or so?" I asked.

"Probably a lot more of this," Richard said.

As we walked toward the road, Pam called out, "Say, you want to take this tree back to New York with you?" I looked behind me. She was pushing and pulling on a ten-foot stub, trying to get it to fall over.

"No thanks," I said. "I don't think it'll fit in my truck."

As we drove back to the levee, it looked like the start of monsoon season. Vast sheets of rainwater poured from the skies into the already sodden swamp. The four of us retreated all the way to the warmth and security of the community store, many muddy miles away. The camo people were there in force, hunkered over steaming cups of coffee, rainwater still dripping off their bill caps, while the cooking crew slaved tirelessly to produce enough burgers and fries.

We ordered some food and sat down together at one of the tables. "You know, Bobby, I think we should head for the old Singer Tract now," I said. "We can't afford to sit here for a couple of days waiting for a break in the weather. Even if it's raining there, we can still check out the visitors' center. I want to see the mounted ivory-bills they have there. They used to be at the Lab of Ornithology years ago, you know." Bobby nodded and started working on his second cheeseburger.

"Do you know how long it'll take to drive there, Richard?" I asked.

"The Tensas refuge?" he said. "I don't know. Maybe four or five hours." He called over to a man at another table. "You just got back from the Tensas, didn't you?" he asked. "How long did it take to get there?"

"I think you could do it in four hours," the man replied. I asked him the best route, and he said we should drive east into Mississippi, then turn south on Highway 61, and finally cut back west into Louisiana at Tallulah, which was only about ten miles from the refuge. I thanked him.

Richard and Pam finished eating their meals, and Bobby insisted on paying for them. "That's the least I can do after all you've done for us," he said. Richard thanked him and said to be sure and look him up if we came back to White River; he would be more than glad to help us out.

A few minutes later I made my second big mistake of the trip. I let Bobby talk me into taking one of his shortcuts. He had pulled out a map and was studying it as I drank another cup of coffee.

"You know, that's ridiculous," he said.

"What?"

"Driving into Mississippi to get to Louisiana," he said. "Look how much shorter it is if you go this way, down through Arkansas. It looks like it's only about a hundred and fifty miles. There's no way it should take that long to get there."

"I don't know, Bobby," I said. "These guys live here. They ought to know the best way to get someplace like that."

Ten minutes later we filled up on gas and started down the highway, southbound. I was supposed to follow Bobby, since we figured his vehicle was more likely to break down than mine, so I could stop and help him if it did. Besides, he had the route emblazoned on his mind. I was sleepy and really didn't know where I was going, so I was glad to leave the thinking to someone else.

By this time it was already dark, and the rain was coming down harder than ever. I hung a couple of hundred feet behind Bobby, so I'd have time to take evasive action if his transmission dropped out in the middle of the road.

We drove into the teeth of the storm, sometimes traveling on tiny farm roads through empty fields. I had my windshield wipers going full blast but still could barely see anything. Every so often a big truck would go past the other way on the tiny two-lane road, splashing muddy water all over my car and completely obliterating my vision. In some places the water pooled up three or four inches deep on the roadway. *Great shortcut,* I thought. And I began imagining Highway 61: wide open, well drained, brightly lit, with plenty of places to stop for coffee along the way. Here there was nothing but darkness and mud.

Then I saw a fork in the road up ahead and a green sign with TALLULAH written in big block letters and an arrow pointing to the right. I wondered why Bobby hadn't put on his turn signal yet. *They probably don't work,* I thought. *I know this has to be the right way.* And then he blew right past the junction and continued to the left. *So should I turn here,* I wondered, *or follow Bobby, trying to get his attention? Turn here or follow Bobby?* I turned, thinking I could easily call him on the cell phone. I struggled to switch on the map light and then my phone. The "no service" message blinked on its screen.

6

A PARADISE ON EARTH

I DECIDED TO KEEP DRIVING to Tallulah and let Bobby fend for himself. The rain still poured down profusely like a biblical deluge, and I knew the shoulders of the road would be way too muddy to risk turning around. As I reached the outskirts of town, I saw a huge well-lit compound with high chainlink fences topped with wicked coils of razor wire. It was obviously a prison. I wondered if this was the same place where the Cornell expedition had parked their big sound mobile in 1935. I thought about driving closer to the fence, near the big lights, so I could try to call Bobby again. But then I thought it might be suspicious. I figured with my luck, I would get arrested and end up busting rocks on a Louisiana chain gang for six months.

Farther up the road, I entered the main part of Tallulah, which is not much of a place. Boasting only some 12,000 inhabitants, it lies in the heart of Madison Parish, one of the poorest parishes in Louisiana. The closest large city is Vicksburg, Mississippi, about thirty miles east along the interstate, which we would have been traveling on if we hadn't used Bobby's shortcut. Which reminded me: where was Bobby, and how would I ever find him? At least I was getting a signal on my cell phone now, but Bobby was still floating somewhere in the vast netherworld between cell towers, and I couldn't reach him. What should I do?

As I stared down the highway, I noticed some brightly lit gas stations and stores up ahead at the edge of the interstate, screaming for business. And then I saw it: a gleaming golden McDonald's. I smiled and drove into its parking lot and sat there waiting.

Forty minutes later, Bobby came chugging into the parking lot. "I thought I'd see you here," I said as we walked inside. He told me his van windows were all fogged up and he had driven right past the turnoff. He went about fifteen miles before he figured out he was lost and came back to the junction.

After pigging out on bad burgers, we got a room at a cheap motel and quickly fell into a deep, exhausted sleep with lots of snoring.

The next morning was beautiful. The storm had completely blown past, the air was fresh, and the sun shone down brightly through a clear blue sky. After breakfast we got directions to the Tensas River National Wildlife Refuge from a waitress in the restaurant. It didn't sound easy, but we were eager to make the pilgrimage. The Singer Tract was something we had both dreamed of visiting for years. It was such an important part of the ivory-bill saga — the last known stronghold of the species in the United States. And we couldn't help thinking that maybe, somehow, a pair or two of ivory-bills might still be hanging around there. Anything seemed possible.

We hit the road immediately after breakfast, me following Bobby's van in my Toyota 4Runner. A short distance out of town we turned left, went across some railroad tracks on a small overpass, and started driving slowly along a muddy gravel road through vast agricultural fields. The deluge from the night before had played havoc with the road. Awash in several places, it seemed barely passable. We hadn't gone far when we reached a badly flooded section, where it looked like the road disappeared into a lake. Bobby stopped at the edge of the water to mull over his options. After pausing for a couple of minutes and maybe munching a Snickers bar or two, he just went for it, easing his muddy van into the water like an old river barge. The water was deep — easily above the tops of his tires in places. If he got stuck in soft mud or his van's ignition got wet, I knew it would be bad, really bad, and he knew it too. After watching in dull amazement as he drove a couple of hundred yards without getting stuck, I let out a deep sigh, threw my Toyota into low four-wheel drive, and plunged in after him.

Although my 4Runner has fairly good ground clearance, the water was amazingly deep in places. If I went too fast, trying to catch up with Bobby, the water would push up into a wave and come washing back across my hood, lapping against the windshield. *Not good,* I thought. *Not good.* I completely lost sight of Bobby for a while, which made me wonder whether he might have hit a soft spot or hole and sunk out of sight. But finally I spotted him on the far shore, waiting for me to catch up.

We continued on through more open fields, some with adjacent second-growth woodlots, and more expanses of pooled-up rainwater. Finally we got into some more extensive woods and spotted a muddy stream winding through the trees to the right of the road. *So this is the Tensas River,* I thought. A few minutes later we suddenly hit a beautifully paved blacktop road, and a half-mile or so after that we reached the refuge headquarters.

We had photocopied some maps of the Singer Tract from Jim Tanner's book and were trying to orient ourselves. But it was hard to imagine what the place had been like in the 1930s. We saw nothing that compared with Tanner's descriptions. We drove on, to a section next to a huge field where the Tensas River wound along in slow, lazy loops.

"Look at this," said Bobby. "This must be Greenlea Bend."

"No way," I said. Tanner described Greenlea Bend as beautiful, one of the best sections of old-growth woods in the entire Singer Tract. In the early 1940s, he had written a letter about it to John Baker: "Greenlea Bend is small compared with the entire tract, but it is the gem of it all; it is the part that I would rather see preserved than any other."

We rechecked the map and then noticed a sign up ahead,

identifying the place as Greenlea Bend. It was now a flat field with no trees. We stood stunned for several minutes, watching a northern harrier — a hawk of open meadows and marshlands, never seen in woodlands — coursing back and forth low, searching for small rodents and other prey. At one edge of the field, beside the river, stood an ancient stub riddled with woodpecker drillings. I wondered how many ivory-billed woodpeckers had clung to the side of this tree in decades past. Bobby put his hand on the old tree, feeling the texture of the bleached gray wood and examining the holes bored in it so long ago. "You know, those workings in the trees at White River were probably nothing," he said sadly. "Probably just pileateds."

We were both depressed as hell, and we didn't talk much on the way to the visitors' center. This had to be the low point of our entire search for ivory-bills. There was something irrepressibly gloomy about being in what had once been such a remarkable place — a paradise on earth, as one person I talked with had put it — and seeing how much it had changed, how ordinary it looked. What possible chance could there be that any ivory-bills still existed here or anyplace else?

The doors were locked at the visitors' center. A sign said that it was closed on Sundays, which was of course the day we had come. We hung around for a while, hoping that someone might show up, and we finally got lucky. A U.S. Fish and Wildlife Service truck pulled up in the parking lot outside, and a young man in a uniform stepped out. I went over and asked if there was any way we could take a peek at the ivory-billed woodpecker exhibit. He said the visitors' center was closed and he couldn't let anyone inside. I pressed the issue, saying that I had come all the way from Cornell University in New York and that our researchers had done all the groundbreaking work on ivory-bills back in the 1930s and this was the only day I could be here, and so on. He finally loosened up. "Okay," he said. "You can look at them for a few minutes."

He unlocked the front door and held it open as we walked inside. "The ivory-bills are over here," he said, leading us to a glassed-in diorama bathed in darkness. "Wait here a minute." He went off somewhere to try light switches. We could hear him clicking them as lights went on and off everywhere around us — everywhere except in the diorama. "I'm sorry," he said finally. "I don't know where the light switch is for that." He walked to his office and left us standing beside the glass. Through the darkness, we could just make out the shapes of a wolf and a panther, and then we saw two ivory-billed woodpeckers clinging to the trunk of a tree. The heavy symbolism of gazing into the darkness at these ghosts of the southern swamps only added to our sense of gloom.

"Let's go," I said grimly, and we stepped back outside into the sunshine. We strolled through the woods on a boardwalk behind the center. And it was nice — a thick swamp forest of tupelos and other trees, ankle-deep in water. Some trees had pileated woodpecker workings on them, but none of them were anything you could conceivably call large. This was nothing at all like the Singer Tract had been. These woods had grown up since the 1940s, when the trees had been clear-cut, and it would take several lifetimes more for them to return to their former state. Even though we had never before stood in this place, our sense of loss and grief over the things that no longer existed here was profound. We knew we would never be able to experience a primeval bottomland swamp forest.

As Bobby and I walked farther through the woods, we came to a plaque commemorating a cypress tree that had been planted by descendants of President Theodore Roosevelt. He had hunted bear in these woods in 1907 and greatly admired the place. Roosevelt was in awe of the ancient forest with its enormous trees. He wrote, "In stature, in towering majesty, they are unsurpassed by any trees of our eastern forests; lordlier kings of the green-leaved world are not to be found until we reach the sequoias and redwoods of the Sierras."

Roosevelt was a keen bird watcher and said that finding ivory-bills was the high point of his visit to Louisiana. "The most notable birds and those which most interested me were the great ivory-billed woodpeckers," he wrote. "Of these I saw three, all of them in groves of giant cypress; their brilliant white bills contrasted finely with the black of their general plumage. They were noisy but wary, and they seemed to me to set off the wildness of the swamp as much as any of the beasts of the chase."

I felt sick in the pit of my stomach as I gazed around me at what had been the old Singer Tract — heartsick about this place, which had been so extraordinary at one time. Where were the great trees towering skyward above us? Where were the wolves and the panthers? And where were the ivory-bills? Gone forever? Such a waste; such a tragedy.

"The Singer Tract is . . . unique in that every form of animal native to the region, except those now extinct, is still living there," wrote Jim Tanner. "Deer and wild turkey are abundant; wolves, including black individuals, bear, and panther are present; big alligators still swim in the lakes; and smaller animals and birds are everywhere abundant . . . This forest affords an excellent example, and is the last remaining large stand, of the primeval forest that once covered all the bottomlands of the Mississippi Delta."

For anyone who knew the great bottomland forests along the Tensas River as they used to be, this place would be unrecognizable, a wan shadow of its former glory. I spoke with several people who had spent time in the Singer Tract before it was cut — most notably Richard Pough, the famed conservationist. My wife and I spent several days in the spring of 2003 at his home on Martha's Vineyard, off the coast of Massachusetts. Although he was ninety-nine years old at the time of our visit, he had the booming voice of a much younger man. You could still catch a glimpse of his powerful charisma, which he had used successfully throughout much of the twentieth century to get people to preserve huge tracts of land.

I love the story of how Dick went to an area near Kempton, Pennsylvania, in the early 1930s to find out why hunters there had sent a phenomenal number of dead goshawks to collect a state bounty. He drove from Philadelphia one weekend to make inquiries. He asked a local farmer where he could go to shoot hawks and was given directions to a rocky lookout called Hawk Mountain by locals. When he got there, he saw more than fifty men with shotguns lined up on the ridge top, shooting at migrating hawks as they flew past. The carnage was incredible, with dead and dying hawks littering the ground far below.

Dick went back later with his brother Harold, and together they gathered several hundred dead hawks and took pictures of them. He showed the photographs to dozens of people and took every opportunity to present lectures about the destruction of these raptors. One of his talks in New York City attracted the interest of Rosalie Edge, a wealthy philanthropist. She leased 1,400 acres in the key hawk-killing area, hired a warden to keep out shooters, and set up a public sanctuary. She eventually bought the land and deeded it to the Hawk Mountain Sanctuary Association, and it is now one of the top bird-watching attractions in North America.

Dick worked for the National Audubon Society from 1938 to 1948, and during that time he wrote a bird field guide, which sold more than a million copies. In the late autumn of 1943, John Baker asked him to visit the Singer Tract to search for ivory-bills. This was shortly before Baker was to meet with the CEO of the Chicago Mill and Lumber Company, which was logging the tract. Baker was trying to get the logging halted for the benefit of the ivory-bills. He wanted Dick to confirm the presence of the birds "so that no one could say there weren't any down there." But the messages Dick sent to Baker were depressing. "It is sickening to see what a waste a lumber company can make of what was a beautiful forest," he wrote. "I watched them cutting the last stand of the finest sweet gum on Monday. One log was six feet in diameter at the butt." He did finally locate one lone female ivory-bill roosting in a dead snag in a small section of standing forest. He sent a telegram to Baker: "I have been able to locate only a single female and feel reasonably sure there are no other birds here." Soon after he sent an urgent message: "I really fear the area will be cut any day."

Not only did the Chicago Mill and Lumber Company fail to halt its logging of the Singer Tract, there is some evidence that the rate of tree cutting was speeded up in response to the Audubon Society's efforts. This had a profound effect on Dick, and he spent most of the rest of his career trying to figure out how to buy up land in key areas to preserve it for wildlife. In the early 1950s, he became a prominent leader of a small group called the Ecologists Union and radically changed its direction. Renaming it the Nature Conservancy (TNC), he pushed the organization to start saving land as its primary mission. He served as TNC's president from 1952 to 1956, during which time the group acquired its first tract of land — a sixty-acre stretch of the Mianus River gorge on the border between New York and Connecticut. He also formed the Land Preservation Fund, which is still TNC's most important conservation tool. He practically invented the idea of buying up vital pieces of land to preserve wildlife habitat.

Dick seemed to know everyone. He was a close friend of Charles and Anne Morrow Lindbergh and helped set up the Lindbergh Foundation, a group dedicated to furthering a balance between technological advancement and environmental preservation. He sometimes stayed with Aldo Leopold, the famed wildlife ecologist, in his tarpaper shack near Barabou, Wisconsin, where Leopold wrote his renowned collection of essays, *A Sand County Almanac*. Dick seemed prescient at times in the causes he championed. Nearly two decades before his friend Rachel Carson warned the world about the dangers of DDT in her best-selling book *Silent Spring*, Dick spoke out against the harmful effects of this pesticide. In a 1945 article in *The New Yorker*, he declared, "If DDT should ever be used widely and without care, we would have a country without freshwater fish, serpents, frogs, and most of the birds we have now."

I'll never forget sitting with Dick in his living room, having long talks about his life and the conservation work he had accomplished. It wasn't easy for him. Sometimes the weight of nearly a century of life exhausted him and he could no longer speak. But at other times, especially when we were talking about ivory-bills, he would fill with excitement, and the years seemed to fall away. I think in some ways he took the destruction of the Singer Tract as a personal failure — something he was unable to stop despite his best efforts — and it drove him to find creative new ways to save wild lands. In an article in *Audubon* magazine, Frank Graham, Jr., wrote of him, "Pough was a wheeler-dealer developer turned inside-out, reaching for great swatches of land not to exploit but to retire in perpetuity."

Shortly before we left to catch the ferry back to the mainland from Martha's Vineyard, Dick told us that he did not expect to live to be one hundred. He died just two months later. But what an amazing impact his life had on the world.

Another man I interviewed about life in the old Singer Tract was Gene Laird, who had grown up there in the 1930s and 1940s in a log cabin without electricity or running water. His father, Jesse Laird, was a local game warden and assisted Jim Tanner with his fieldwork in 1939. Gene and his boyhood friends lived like Tom Sawyer and Huck Finn in those golden days, which now seem so remote.

"I don't remember if I was born in that log cabin or not, but when I got old enough to remember anything, that's where we lived," said Gene. "It was close to the bridge across the Tensas River, just before you get to where the refuge headquarters are now. But of course there wasn't any road there back then."

He and his father kept several head of cattle and some hogs, and as soon as he was old enough to ride a horse, he would accompany his father, helping to care for the livestock. "We grazed cattle in the woods," he said. "Where the trees were big, it was open underneath — not much undergrowth, especially on the ridges — so you could see a quarter-mile or more through the woods."

Gene went to school all the way through seventh grade in a one-room schoolhouse several miles from home. There, older children were taught side by side with five-year-olds. "Oh, man, I remember one older boy, when he sat in his seat, his knees were higher than the desk," he said, laughing. "I had one teacher — could she wield that stick. I mean, she'd knock the dust off your pants in a minute."

Gene told me a lot about Jack Kuhn, who had shown the Singer Tract ivory-bills to Jim Tanner and the other Cornell expedition members in 1935 and had also assisted Jim with his research in 1937 and 1938. Jim had often praised Jack Kuhn's abilities. He said he was the finest woodsman he had ever known, and he trusted Kuhn's observations implicitly. But Gene pointed out some of the more humorous aspects of Kuhn's personality. "He had a Model T Ford, and in the summertime he'd drive it around in the woods," he said. "The woods were open enough that he could just meander down through the trees. That was something to see. He could drive all the way from Highway 80 to Sharkey Road, just meandering down through the ridges and places, jumping over the logs, limbs, and things."

"He never got stuck out there?" I asked.

"Yeah," said Gene. "He'd get stuck, and what he'd do, he'd just leave his car until the water dried up the next spring. Then he'd carry a gallon of gas back and crank his car and drive it out."

"Guess he didn't need his car too much, huh?" I asked.

"Didn't everybody have one back then," he said. "Horseback was the mode of transportation, especially in the woods."

"Were there many wolves?" I asked.

"Yeah," he said. "We had lots of wolves. Didn't have any coyotes then, though. Coyotes didn't come into this country until after I was grown."

Gene remembered seeing ivory-bills in the woods near where he lived. "I saw three, I guess, in my lifetime — a pair and a young bird," he told me. Asked what was most memorable about the birds, he said the *kent* call and the rap. He didn't consider the white bill to be that prominent. "It wasn't really an outstanding feature as far as I'm concerned," he said. "I mean, you had to be pretty close to really see that beak." But the way they rapped on a tree — two rapid-fire pops — was unique. "The bird would land on a tree and immediately do a couple of loud knocks," he said. "Then there'd be a pause, and he'd do it again. I remember that." He told me the pair he had watched seemed to favor ash trees. "We had these ash flats, we called them," he said. "The ash was dying, and that's what they lived on. They'd peel the bark off and get the grubs and bugs out from under the bark."

One of Gene Laird's best friends in those days was Billy Fought. They have known each other since they were young boys. Billy's father had moved Billy and his little brother Bobby to the Singer Tract a short time after their mother died. They lived in the logging camp and had little or no supervision.

I later had a couple of long talks with Billy about the old days. He told me his father had been the engineer on the small railroad engine the logging company used to take cut trees out of the woods. "At that time they had what they called a steel camp," he said. "They would go and build a camp in the woods. This was on a gravel track called Sharkey Road — the one and only road that penetrated the Singer Tract." He said that they would run small spur railroads deep into the woods so they could haul the massive logs to the sawmill in Tallulah.

"After my mother passed away, we went down to live with my grandfather for a while, but things didn't work out," he said. "Daddy made arrangements for another family, some real nice people, to take my youngest brother and my sister. They raised them and were wonderful parents to them. When we got on the bus coming back — at that point Daddy didn't have a car — Daddy was telling my brother Bobby and me, 'Boys, you'll like this. There's wolves down there and bear and panther.' And sure enough, everything proved out. At that time there were quite a few wolves right around the camp."

Gene Laird and his father lived on the other side of John's

Bayou from the lumber camp where Billy and Bobby stayed. "The wolves would come right up to Gene's house," said Billy. "I've been there when they attacked their dogs at night. They cut up several pretty bad, but I don't know that they killed any of them. The dogs would get under the house. They'd stay close."

Although Billy never actually saw a panther, he did find their tracks and have a couple of close encounters with them. One night he went frog-hunting with a friend in John's Bayou. They stood on opposite banks of the bayou from each other, searching for frogs, when his friend suddenly said, "Be still! Be still!"

"I didn't know what was going on," said Billy. "I thought maybe he had seen a snake, but we saw snakes all the time, so that shouldn't have excited him."

Later, when they got back together, his friend told him that a panther had put its front paws over a huge downed log and was looking down at him. His flashlight had reflected in its eyes, and he had been chilled by its predatory gaze.

Another time a panther broke into the hog pen at the logging camp, raising a deafening ruckus from the pigs and waking everyone up. But by the time the loggers came running out, the panther was long gone.

One of the most memorable experiences Billy and his brother had in the Singer Tract was when they met the famed bird artist Don Eckelberry, who was sent there in April 1944 by the National Audubon Society to observe and sketch the lone female ivory-bill that Dick Pough had found a few months earlier. Logging had been proceeding at a fever pitch in the Singer Tract, and as far as anyone knew, this was the last ivory-bill in the area, or perhaps anywhere. Eckelberry was in his early twenties, only ten years or so older than the boys. He saw them playing on the bridge over John's Bayou one afternoon and invited them to visit the ivory-bill's roost hole with him. He told them what a rare bird it was and said that they might never have another chance to see one. Of course they jumped at the chance. Before they left, Eckelberry asked the boys if they thought their parents would mind if they went with him. "No sir," Billy assured him. "We don't ask anyone before we go in these woods. We just go anywhere we want."

They slogged about half a mile into the woods, wading through knee-deep water and mud in several places. It was late April, and there had been a lot of rain. They finally reached the roost tree and sat on a downed log. And then they waited . . . and waited . . . and waited. Eckelberry sketched constantly on a pad to kill time and amuse the boys. He drew pictures of trees, a couple of wolves, a squirrel, and a portrait of seven-year-old Bobby, which Bobby still has. Later, as the boys became restless, he urged them to settle down. "Now, you know this is my last chance to see this," he said. "Please be quiet now. Be still and quiet." So they hunkered down on the log and sat watching as the light began to dim.

Finally the great bird flew in, landed on the trunk of a nearby tree, and did a double rap. Then, just as promptly, it flew away. "We waited a little while, and it lit on another tree, just watching," Billy said. The bird stayed for a few minutes, hitching nervously around the trunk of the tree, her yellow eyes gleaming, before flying off again. She came back once more and this time climbed into her roost hole. They saw her pop her head out for a second, then pull it back in. It was getting late, so they decided to go home.

"It was almost dark then," said Billy. "We went back to the gravel road and walked on to the logging camp. Don must have gone back to Mr. Jesse's house. As far as I know, that was the last time Don saw the ivory-bill. He had told us it would be his last chance to see it, and he wanted to put it to bed."

A week or so later, Gene Laird rode his horse to where Billy, Bobby, and Don had seen the bird, but the old snag the bird had been roosting in had blown over in a windstorm. No one ever saw the bird again. "I don't know where she went after that, whether she perished in the tree or what," Gene said. I asked him if he had gone back to the area again in the last twenty years or so, after a lot of second-growth forest had grown in some places.

"No," he said. "I haven't been back to that spot. It's all been cleared. It's in farmland."

"Yeah," I said. "I went to Greenlea Bend, and it's completely gone too. It's just a field."

"A lot of it's gone," he said. "I'm sorry we didn't have cameras and things to record all that. I just didn't think it would ever be important. You know, one time when I was a kid I was cleaning out behind the shack where Don Eckelberry stayed. I found a cardboard box full of his sketches. When Don was sitting there waiting for that bird all day long, he'd sketch whatever came through the woods, whether it be a wolf, a turkey, or whatever. And he'd just toss the sketches away. I didn't even realize what they were."

"Probably be worth a lot of money now, huh?" I asked.

"Oh boy," he said, laughing. "And I burned them for trash."

I asked him how he felt about the Singer Tract being logged. "It ruined my life, if you want to know the truth about it," he said. "It takes hardwoods so long to grow. It'll never be the same. I wish my kids could have seen it."

As I thought about the old Singer Tract, I remembered a paragraph I read in an unpublished essay by Jim Tanner that Nancy had given me:

> We—the woodpeckers, Jack Kuhn, and I—lived in the forest, and I came to know it well. It was a bottomland forest of oaks, sweet gum, wild pecan, hackberry, and several other kinds of trees covering over a hundred square miles. At the time of my living there almost all of this was virgin swamp timber, a beautiful forest with many big trees. A few small cotton plantations had once been cleared and cultivated, but had long since been abandoned to and reclaimed by the forest. The primitiveness of the area was its greatest charm. All the animals that had ever lived there in the memory of man, excepting the Carolina parakeet and the passenger pigeon, still lived there. The hand of man had been laid so lightly on the

deeper woods and its inhabitants that it took an experienced eye to see the traces that had been made. The naturalness of the area became more real and impressive the longer I lived and the more I learned in the forest.

Jim Tanner had at first hoped that the entire Singer Tract would be preserved "in its entirety and wildness for all time" as a national park or wilderness. By the end, he would have been happy if just a few small reserves could have been set aside for the ivory-bills, side by side with logging areas. But even that proved impossible to accomplish.

Bobby and I spent a few more hours searching the woods along the banks of the Tensas River and then decided to head south. We retraced our drive along the gravel road and pooled-up rainwater, which had receded a lot since morning. The farther we got from the ghost forest of the old Singer Tract, the better we felt. We were on an adventure again — on our way to the great Atchafalaya Basin, which still held out hope for ivory-bill chasers. It was incredibly vast, and although it had been largely clear-cut in the early twentieth century, it was now well forested. If a few of these birds had held on somewhere through the bad years, had somehow passed through the bottleneck, it seemed reasonable to assume that they might be living in a place like this, and perhaps increasing in numbers. From time to time people had reported seeing ivory-bills fly right across Interstate 10 on the stretch between Baton Rouge and Lafayette. We were eager to explore the area. Best of all, I had the name and phone number of a person who might be able to help us finally clear up an old mystery about who took the supposed ivory-bill snapshots in 1971.

7

THE BOXER

*W*HEN GEORGE LOWERY arrived at the annual meeting of the American Ornithologists' Union in the summer of 1971, he carried with him something sure to astound everyone present. At least, that's what he thought. He had two pictures — just low-quality snapshots, really, but each one clearly showed an adult male ivory-bill clinging to the side of a tree. What's more, they had been taken just that spring. The white borders around the small square pictures had "May 1971" printed along the side. If authentic, they would be the only pictures of the ivory-bill taken in the United States since Jim Tanner photographed the Singer Tract birds in the 1930s, and indeed, the only ones taken anywhere since John Dennis photographed the species in Cuba in 1948. At last someone had come forward with tangible physical evidence of the continued existence of the ivory-bill. Or had he?

Lowery's pictures were met with immediate withering skepticism by most of the other ornithologists. The photos showed two different trees, but the posture of the bird in them was too similar. You couldn't see its bill or feet. Somehow, it just didn't look right. And yet the question remained: why would someone go to all the trouble of climbing fifty or sixty feet up two different trees to fake these pictures — particularly since the man who took them wanted to remain anonymous?

The attitude of his colleagues was very perplexing to Lowery. He had always been well respected by the ornithological community. He had been the president of the American Ornithologists' Union from 1959 to 1961 and was the director of the Louisiana State University Museum of Natural Science, which had been created largely as a result of his efforts. To all who knew him, he seemed the perfect southern gentleman, someone who would never even think of telling a lie. He put his entire reputation on the line in support of this anonymous photographer. In a 1972 letter to Jim Tanner, he wrote,

> I must tell you that several people expressed the opinion that the bird in the photographs is a mounted specimen that was tacked on the side of a tree. This is pure hogwash. I know the man in question extremely well and I am sure that he would not pull something like that. In the first place, where would he have got the mounted specimen? Why would he have two photographs of the bird way up on two separate trees, both of considerable diameter and not subject to being shinnied? Also, assuming he might have had a mounted bird to photograph, why didn't he get a better picture of it?

It was a heartbreaking experience for Lowery to have his word doubted. Part of the problem was that he refused to divulge the man's identity or even where the picture was taken, except to say that it was somewhere in the vast Atchafalaya Basin, west of Baton Rouge. "I have told no one where the observation and photographs were made," wrote Lowery. "You know what would happen if the information became general knowledge. There would be two hundred amateur bird watchers on planes from all corners of the United States descending on the area tomorrow. And I think that would be the worst possible development so far as the birds themselves are concerned."

Lowery began to regret that he had ever mentioned the sighting. "I wish now that I had said nothing about these birds [and] had not shown the photographs to anyone," he wrote. "It would have been better if I had waited until I had actually seen or heard the birds myself. Then I could have said something on my own authority rather than on a secondhand basis. A lot of people seem to want to doubt the record, and perhaps it is only human nature for them to do so. If they can't see an ivory-bill they do not want to believe that anyone else has done so."

And so this remarkable sighting faded into the lore of the ivory-bill. George Lowery passed away a few years later, in January 1978, of complications from diabetes and circulatory problems. He was sixty-four years old. He left behind a mystery: who took the ivory-bill pictures, and why did the man want to remain anonymous? A lot has been written over the years about these photographs, where they might have been taken, and the identity of the photographer, but until now nothing concrete had emerged. The only tangible evidence from this sighting remained the two old photographs, which lay safe in a vault at the Academy of Natural Sciences in Philadelphia. But even the people at VIREO (Visual Resources for Ornithology), the academy's photographic archive, had no idea who had taken them. Some people said it was "the Chief," an elderly Choctaw who went to the LSU museum in the late 1970s with a story about another ivory-bill sighting. But no one seemed to know for sure. I even tracked down John Morony, who had been the collections manager at the LSU museum when the Chief announced his sighting. He couldn't remember the man's name. Was the Chief the person who took the pictures? He didn't know.

This was something I desperately wanted to explore. I wanted to find the person who had taken those pictures and look him in the eye as I questioned him about them. I wanted to determine his truthfulness for myself. I had already seen the pictures, small, square snapshots badly yellowing along the white borders. They had obviously been taken with a cheap camera. They were fuzzy.

One of them was really dark. But there could be no doubt: the bird in the pictures was an ivory-bill — whether alive or dead, I couldn't say, but it looked good.

I had been following a number of clues as I tried to figure out the photographer's identity, but my big break came by chance when I was visiting David Luneau in his office at the University of Arkansas at Little Rock. David had been one of the members of the Zeiss Optics team who spent a month searching for ivory-bills in Louisiana's Pearl River Wildlife Management Area in early 2002, in response to David Kulivan's alleged sighting there on April 1, 1999. He has been an avid ivory-bill enthusiast for years and was one of the most optimistic members of the search team. As I sat in his office, he pulled out plastic bags full of peeled bark and told me about some of the interesting woodpecker workings he had seen in eastern Arkansas. We discussed several credible ivory-bill reports from the 1960s and 1970s, and then we started talking about the Chief. David told me that his brother, Guy — another ivory-bill seeker — knew who the Chief was and had met him briefly the year before. David said his name was Fielding Lewis, and he lived somewhere in the Atchafalaya Basin.

Later that day I did an Internet search and found Lewis's phone number. I wasn't sure exactly what I would say to him. I wasn't even positive that he was the one who had taken the pictures, but I figured I would call him up and speak as though I knew he was the mystery photographer, to see how he responded. "I'm Tim Gallagher from Cornell University," I told him. "I'm interviewing everyone I can find who has reported seeing an ivory-billed woodpecker. I'd like to talk with you about the pictures you gave to George Lowery in 1971." And he just said, "Sure. I'll be glad to see you."

We made arrangements to meet the next day after lunch. He said he lived in the woods and it would be hard to find his place, so he suggested that we meet in the parking lot of a Cajun restaurant in town so I could follow him home. My wife, Rachel, was appalled when I told her about this on the phone that night. "Don't do it," she said. "You don't know anything about him. A lot of strange people live out in the swamp. Anything could happen."

"I know, but this guy is someone I really need to talk to," I said. "And besides, Bobby will be there too."

But it *was* a little strange. I had no idea what Fielding Lewis would be like. I pictured an aging swamp rat, with long, stringy gray hair, his skin baked and cracked from years of living deep in the backwoods, far from civilized society. And I did feel a little sick at the thought of going to his house or shack or whatever it was. But at least he had a telephone. How bad could things be?

Bobby and I pulled into Franklin, Louisiana, two hours earlier than the proposed meeting time. For some reason I thought it would take much longer to get there. We ate an early lunch but still had a lot of time to kill, so I thought, *What the heck, I'll call him now and see if we can get together earlier.* A woman answered the phone when I called. I explained that I had a meeting with Mr. Lewis but had arrived early and wanted to see if we could get together sooner.

"He's not home right now," she said. "He went to his office."

I must have paused for about five seconds, stunned by what she had just told me. The idea of this man working in an office did not fit my fantasy image of him at all. "His office?" I said. "What does he do?"

"What does he *do*? What do you mean, *what does he do*?" she said, in a high-pitched, annoyed voice, apparently offended by what I had asked.

"I . . . I don't know," I said. "I mean . . . I didn't know he would have an office. I've never actually met him. I just wondered what he does."

"Well, he does all kinds of things," she said.

I could see Bobby smirking as I stammered on the phone. The woman finally suggested that I call Lewis at his office, and she gave me his number. I phoned him right away and told him we were in the Wal-Mart parking lot. "Wal-Mart parking lot?" he said in a deep Louisiana drawl. "I'll never find you there. Go to the restaurant, and I'll meet you in ten minutes. They know me there."

At this point I didn't know what to expect. My visions of the old swamp rat were quickly fading away, and somehow I missed that image. But what would this guy really look like? An old duffer in a lime-green polyester leisure suit? And what *did* he do? Sell real estate? Run a business of some kind? We were so eager to find out, we didn't go into the restaurant. Instead we sat in the parking lot, peering at every car that came driving down the road, trying to figure out whether the person inside was the Chief.

And then we saw it: a shiny white Chrysler New Yorker driven by a portly man in his seventies, smoking one of the biggest cigars I've ever seen. If this was the mystery man, then all the people who thought the ivory-bill picture-taker and the Chief were one and the same were dead wrong. He didn't look a bit like a Native American. His hair, graying now, was combed back and looked as if it had been blond.

"Are you Mr. Lewis?" I asked as he stepped out of the car. He nodded, and we shook hands. He seemed like a character from Tennessee Williams — like Big Daddy, or maybe a southern lawyer or politician. Or . . . and then it struck me: like Mason Spencer, the guy who had blasted the ivory-bill in the Singer Tract in the 1930s, the guy who had told Doc Allen and the others all about the birds when they went there in 1935. This man was exactly how I would have pictured Spencer.

He invited us to follow him to his office, about a mile away. As he drove down the road ahead of us, I noticed that the lettering on the frame around his license plate read, "Louisiana Boxing Commission."

I asked him about it when we got to his office. "I've been chairman of the state boxing commission for twenty years," he said. "But I'm just getting ready to get off. We got a new governor, and I don't think she's going to reappoint me."

"Oh, she doesn't approve of you?" said Bobby.

"That's right," he said, laughing. He puffed on his cigar as he unlocked the door. When we went inside, the room reeked of stale tobacco smoke, and each ashtray held two or three big cigar butts. A large 1940s cigarette poster with a sexy Hollywood starlet hung on the wall near his desk, and framed pictures of various boxers, trainers, and fight promoters stood prominently on top of every piece of furniture. One that caught my eye was a picture of Cassius Clay as a teenager (long before he changed his name to Muhammad Ali), with his trainer. It was signed, "To Fielding Lewis, from Angelo Dundee (I'm the one on the right)."

Lewis looked at a picture of another fighter and smiled. "Sweet Willie Pastrano," he said. "He was a good friend of mine — a light heavyweight champ. Angelo Dundee trained them both. Willie was going up fast. Ali was only eighteen, just starting out. Willie taught him all that footwork."

"Were you ever a boxer?" I asked.

"I've boxed since I was seven years old," he said. "We used to have high school boxing teams, and I fought when I was in the air force. I had nineteen wins and no losses in the air force. At first we were scared of those boys from Brooklyn, New York. Until we fought 'em and beat the shit out of them." He laughed loudly, then clicked his lighter and puffed on his cigar, trying to get it going again.

Fielding went on and on like this. He was a great talker, and everything he said was interesting and funny. He told us all about growing up in the Mayberry-like town of Franklin, with its trim white wooden houses and picket fences. Only in this case, unlike Sheriff Taylor, the police chief didn't mind carrying a loaded gun — and using it.

"The chief of police was a big fat guy with a snub-nosed revolver on a fifty-two-inch belt," he said. "If you came in here and the town didn't want you here anymore, he'd run you to the bus station and say, 'Get your ass on that bus and never come back again.' And he'd shoot somebody about once a week — shoot 'em in the leg. It was bad. We'd be playing in my grandma's front yard, half a block off Main Street, and you'd hear *bam!* 'Oh, shit! The chief's shot somebody.' We'd run up and there'd be someone on the sidewalk bleeding with a bullet in their foot or their leg, because they did something he didn't like."

Bobby laughed hard at the story. "That's really funny," he said. "You know, when my dad turned sixteen he started hoboing across the country, riding the rails, back in the Depression. But he said he would never come South. He was *afraid* to come South."

Then Fielding told us about a man he had once seen playing baseball on a bush-league team that came to town. Despite a pronounced limp, the man was a superb player — a gifted fielder and hitter. After the game, Fielding walked over to compliment him. "Say, you're a fine ballplayer," he said. The man frowned. "Yeah. I coulda been in the majors if that damn chief of police hadn'ta shot me in the foot three times."

For a time in the 1970s, Fielding was a newspaperman. "This guy came here from Kansas City," he said. "He had three hundred dollars, and he took over a local newspaper. But he wouldn't pay his bills. Everyone wanted to run his ass out of town. The chief of police finally took him down and put him on a bus. One of the guys said, 'Let's keep the paper after he's gone.' We never saw him again, so I became the editor and publisher."

He pointed to an eight-by-ten color picture of a pretty woman in her early twenties with long dark hair, sitting on a log and cradling a huge double-barreled shotgun. "She worked for me back then," he said. "She was the city editor."

Fielding told us he was also the author of a book titled *Tales of a Louisiana Duck Hunter*. He pulled a couple of copies of it from a cardboard box beside his desk and inscribed them to us. (I read it later, when I got home, and it is wonderful — full of stories about the colorful characters he has known and about his favorite Labrador retrievers. It even has a chapter about ivory-bills, though it doesn't mention the pictures he took.)

I asked Fielding if he was still a duck hunter. "No," he said. "The last dog I had, when it died, it almost killed me. I quit hunting ducks, and I quit keeping dogs. I missed that dog so much, I just didn't want to go out anymore."

As Bobby and I flipped through the pages of the book, looking at the pictures of the local forests and swamps, the conversation finally started moving in the direction of the ivory-billed wood-pecker. We had already been with Fielding for an hour or more, and we were both eager to hear about his sightings and the photo-graphs. He finally pulled out a quadrangle map of the area and laid it across his desk. Bobby and I leaned over it as if we were poring over a treasure map — and I guess we were.

"I remember the first time I saw one," he said, pointing at the map. "We were driving just about here and one flew across the road." He paused and started clicking his lighter to fire up his cigar again. "I was in my '53 Jeep pickup truck with John Richard, a good hunter." As the two of them drove through a section of cy-press swamp, a large bird caught their eyes, flying low less than forty feet in front of them. "Look at that son of a bitch!" yelled Fielding. "What is that?" "I don't know," John replied. "It looked like a pileated, but it's not."

"I knew it wasn't any pileated," Fielding told us. "What the hell. I already knew that bird. We called them log gods. This bird was bigger and had a powerful flight, more like a duck. And it had too much white on its wings and in the wrong places for a pileated."

John Richard suggested that Fielding talk to Charles Lobdell, a biology teacher at Franklin High School. After Fielding de-scribed the bird to him, Lobdell said, "It sounds to me like some-thing that's not supposed to be there — an ivory-bill." He urged Fielding to tell George Lowery at Louisiana State University. "He told me that Dr. Lowery was one of the top ornithologists in the world and had written the book *Louisiana Birds*," said Fielding.

When Fielding contacted Lowery, Lowery was polite but somewhat skeptical; he had heard too many reports of ivory-bills that turned out to be pileated woodpeckers. He thanked Fielding for his report and invited him to visit the museum the next time he was in Baton Rouge. He also encouraged him to try to get a picture of the bird if he ever saw it again. And that's just what Fielding did.

"I was training a retriever on an oil company right-of-way that ran through the swamp when I saw the ivory-bills fly over and then dive down into the trees," he said. "I put the dog back in the trailer, picked up my camera, and went back in there to see them."

At this point Bobby and I were leaning forward, wide-eyed, hanging on every word. Fielding took a long drag from his cigar for effect and blew out a choking cloud of gray smoke that completely enveloped us.

"The female took off, but the male stayed," he said. "I had a little two-bit camera for taking pictures of my dogs, so I put it on top of my head like this and I walked straight toward the bird to see how close I could get."

Fielding stood up and mimed holding a camera on top of his head, then walked slowly and deliberately across his office. Why he put the camera on his head, I have no idea, unless he thought it would somehow be less threatening to the bird.

"I just started snapping pictures," he said. "I think I got two or three pictures. I sent 'em to Dr. Lowery, and he got all excited. He called me right up and said, 'I'm coming.'"

Lowery and his wife, Jean, came the next day and walked into the swamp with Fielding. "First thing I remember hearing is this loud *wuk-wuk-wuk-wuk-wuk-wuk-wuk*," said Fielding. "Dr. Lowery looked at me to see what I was going to say."

"You didn't say anything," Lowery said after a minute.

"No," said Fielding.

"Why not? You heard that, didn't you?"

"I know, but that's a pileated."

"Oh, shit," said Lowery, laughing. "Now I know you know what you're talking about."

As they walked together, Lowery told Fielding that an ivory-bill roost hole tends to be more oval than a pileated's, which is usually fairly round. Fielding pointed out a round hole. Then they walked a little farther and found an oval hole with big fresh wood chips on the ground underneath it. Lowery speculated that the birds were building a nest. He asked Fielding if he would come back every day and pick up the chips.

"After a few days, I couldn't find any more chips," said Fielding. "The birds had left. We looked quite a few more times. I almost stepped on a cottonmouth once when we were walking down the trail. Dr. Lowery was real cautious after that and told his wife to stay behind us. Sometimes he'd have to stop and drink orange juice. He had diabetes really bad."

Lowery wrote about his experiences with Fielding in a letter to Jim Tanner:

> Jean and I have made several trips with him to the places where he has seen the bird on more than one occasion and so far we have had no luck at all. The first attempt was a few days after he made the photographs in late May last year. I was not discouraged by not seeing or hearing the birds because I remember so vividly spending one whole week in the Singer Tract back in 1934, when there were quite a few ivory-bills in those woods, without seeing or hearing one. But, as you will recall, the following winter we had no difficulty locating four in a matter of a few hours on Christmas morning. I believe ivory-bills are more vociferous and easier to find in the winter when the leaves are off the trees.

Fielding stared off wistfully at times as he spoke about George Lowery. "He was a nice guy," he said. "One of the nicest men I ever met in my life. He came down here a lot. He got to be a friend of the family. I've got pictures of him holding my granddaughter." Fielding slowly exhaled, emitting a cloud of smoke, then ground out his cigar in the ashtray.

I decided to hit him with the big question: "Did you know that those pictures you took caused a huge controversy with ornithologists and that some of them think the bird was taxidermied?"

He was stunned for a second and then started bellowing with

laughter. "Now where the hell would I get a stuffed ivory-bill?" he said. "Shit! I've only ever seen the ones that Wildlife and Fish used to have in the Natural Resources building, and they were scrubby-looking."

"I know," said Bobby. "I'm a bird photographer. When I saw your photographs, the bird looked so good, I said, 'That's a live freaking bird.' All these skins I've seen, they look so raggedy."

"They look like they shrank," said Fielding. "The stuffing seems to make the skin loose."

"And they're ratty," said Bobby. "You can always tell a taxidermied bird, because it doesn't clean its feathers. The one in your photographs is a preened bird — a bird that's taken care of itself."

When Fielding saw what an appreciative audience he had, he bombarded us with ivory-bill stories. For instance, one time he was hunting ducks with a friend, and as they entered the swamp on a trail, a pair flew past close to them.

"Goddammit! Look at that!" he shouted. "Those are ivory-billed woodpeckers."

"What the hell do you know about ivory-billed woodpeckers?" said his friend.

"I've been looking for them."

"How you know that's what those were?"

"Because of the white bill and red topnot."

"But one of them didn't have a red topnot."

"That's right. That's the female," said Fielding.

"You're full of shit," his friend said.

"Well, if you don't believe me, I can't help that."

Bobby and I started grilling him about the details of his sightings. How did the birds fly? Did their wings make any sound as they flew? Did he ever hear them call when they were flying? He said he had never heard them call in flight. And when he imitated their calls for us, they sounded perfect.

"When you heard the ivory-bill call, what would you say about the volume?" said Bobby.

"One time when we were crawling through the myrtle bushes, he was loud — *kent-kent, kent* — because he was just on the other side of the bushes," he said. "When we got over there, we saw a big old tree that had fallen into the water, and all the limbs were sticking up. I would assume that's where he was."

"But you didn't see the bird that time?" I asked.

"No."

"What about when you heard them knock on wood, what did it sound like?" said Bobby.

"Real loud," said Fielding. "*POP-pop. POP-pop.*"

Fielding told us about a time when he took some people from the state wildlife and fisheries department out to the swamp. "I was showing them that virgin timber," he said. "They looked around and saw a few pileateds. One of the guys said, 'I did my thesis on the pileated woodpecker.' And while we were talking: *kent, kent, kent.* 'What's that?' he said. I said, 'I think it's what you're looking for, but I ain't going to tell you anything.' He looked at me like I was crazy, and he never said anything else after that."

By this time Bobby and I were hunched over the big map, taking copious notes and trying to write down as much information as we could. Then we saw that Fielding had a copy machine.

"Is that working?" asked Bobby.

"It's not working well," said Fielding. "You can try. Sometimes it does. Sometimes it doesn't."

Bobby struggled to balance the huge map on top of it. The machine would only make eight-and-a-half-by-eleven copies, so we needed to copy the map in several different positions and tape the sections together. It was tough. Bobby seemed to be having an impossible time lining the map up correctly. He would get it where he thought it should be and hit the button, and a section five miles from the place we were interested in would come out.

"Pull that side up a little," said Bobby. "Okay, I think that'll do it."

Ch-chung: a piece of map even farther from where we wanted to be printed out.

"I'm off," said Bobby.

"You're way off," I said.

"How could I be so far off?"

"Well, I know you people in Alabama don't get much chance to work with such high-tech equipment," I said.

We got everything lined up, but the copies were too pale. I cranked the copier to the darkest setting.

"It must need a new ink cartridge," I said.

"In Alabama, we'd know that it needs more toner," Bobby said.

We finally produced some copies that were almost readable. I taped them together carefully and started writing Fielding's information on them. He told us about how after he had been bitten by the ivory-bill bug, he started talking to everyone he could find who had seen an ivory-bill in the area. There was the old hunter in the 1950s who was sitting on a log in the swamp when one flew by. "He said he knew what it was because he was from north Louisiana, where they'd had a lot of them in the old days," said Fielding. And then there was the man, also in the 1950s, who had seen an ivory-bill fly across the road between Franklin and Morgan City. Fielding took these sightings and several more recent ivory-bill reports from other people and started pinpointing them on his quadrangle map. He circled all of them, and right in the center was a six-hundred-acre stand of virgin timber in an area of the swamp that was difficult to reach. It was right in the general area where he had seen most of his ivory-bills. "They say they have a range of five or six miles," he said. "All of these sightings are within five miles of that area. I believe that's where they're nesting."

He pointed at the map. "This is the wildest place," he said. "No telling what you'll see in there — cougar, bear. I talked to a trapper once who'd seen ivory-bills in there." Fielding also told us about a conversation he had had years earlier with Wilbur Cole, a man he had gone to high school with.

"Hell, I see them every day," said Wilbur.

"Where?" said Fielding.

"Back in the swamp where that virgin timber is. I fish back there."

"You mean in the middle of that swamp?"

"No, just a little east of there. Where all those bears are."

"Yeah. I know the place," said Fielding. "How often you see them?"

"Almost every time I go fishing. A big black-and-white bird with a white beak."

"Well," said Fielding, "you know what you're talking about."

Wilbur had not gone out fishing since the early 1990s. According to Fielding, he had contracted a lung disease and rarely left his home anymore. But he had been seeing the ivory-bills right up to the time he stopped going to the swamp. Fielding's last sighting had been in 1987.

As we were getting ready to leave later that day, Fielding confessed that he had once almost taken the opportunity to get undeniable proof that the ivory-bills were there. Fortunately, he hadn't. "I came out of the swamp one day when I was hunting wood ducks, and a pair of ivory-bills flew across in front of me, then lit in a tree. They were about forty yards away, and I had a three-inch magnum twelve-gauge loaded with number six. I was about to shoot. Then I thought, *I better not do that. Dr. Lowery'll kick my ass.*" He laughed loudly, rocking back in the chair and puffing on his cigar, filling the room with smoke.

We said goodbye and stepped into the warm, clean air of southern Louisiana. We reeked of cigar smoke for days.

8

THE LSU CONNECTION

$\mathcal{B}$Y THE TIME we had left Fielding Lewis, Bobby and I were so excited about the possibility of seeing an ivory-bill that we couldn't stand it. We stopped at a Taco Bell briefly to replenish Bobby's sagging strength with beef burritos and Mountain Dew. We also spread our map out on a table, holding the corners down with our soft-drink cups.

"Looks like we can drive right to the oil company gate," said Bobby.

"Yeah," I said. "And if it's open, we can drive all the way to the edge of the bayou."

A few minutes later we were headed down the road, me following Bobby's van as usual. Fielding's directions were confusing, and we had to talk with each other on our cell phones and even stop a couple of times to compare notes before we found the place.

"This has to be it," said Bobby. "It's about the right distance, and it's got a gate with a chain."

"Yeah, this is definitely it," I said. "And the gate's open."

"But what if the oil company workers lock it while we're inside?" asked Bobby.

"Well, let's leave one car here and drive the other inside," I said. "If your van gets locked up in there, we can come back tomorrow morning to get it."

"I was thinking that we should drive your car inside," he said.

After some discussion, we compromised: we left both our vehicles at the gate and went all the way to the bayou on foot—about a two-mile walk. It was nice country, dense woods and swamp interspersed with small areas of open water. Wading birds strode past at the edge of the marsh. A barred owl sat on a branch, peering nonchalantly down at us. We were tense with anticipation at the thought of seeing an ivory-bill, as though we could just stroll down a road through a swamp for a couple of hours and see such a sought-after prize, which so many people had struggled for so long to find. But then again, why not? We both believed Fielding's stories about his ivory-bill sightings, and if they were truly accurate, maybe we *would* see an ivory-bill. And we were ready. We each had a palm-sized camcorder strapped to our right hand, like a gunslinger with his trusty six-shooter.

A shadow crossed over us. "What's that?" I cried out, spinning around with my camcorder raised. A red-shouldered hawk circled low above us, its high-pitched scream echoing through the swamp.

We laughed and continued down the road. Finally the road turned and a stretch of muddy bayou blocked our way forward. Ahead we could see massive cypress trees, but most of them were pale gray and bare, obviously long dead. We both wondered what could have killed them. Through our binoculars we could see holes in a few of them, perhaps large enough to accommodate pileated or ivory-billed woodpeckers. We could also see dense hardwoods on the higher ground ahead, but it would be tough getting there without a canoe. We walked along the edge of the bayou, trying to see if there was a good place to cross. In the end, I decided to try wading through it. I was wearing knee-high boots and had found a stout limb to use as a staff, but I got mired in mud just a foot or two from shore, and the water was already within an inch of my boot tops. It was all I could do to get to the side without falling over into the muck (which I've done plenty of times before, and I don't like it).

I was sorry I had left my chest waders in my car, but we didn't have time before dark to go back and get them — and I think even those would not have been enough for the bayou. The really frustrating thing was that we couldn't stay another day or two and check it out. Bobby was driving all the way to Tennessee to pick up his daughter, Whitney, at boarding school. And I was planning to spend the next couple of days interviewing people at Louisiana State University, which has been a hub for ivory-bill rumors and research for years. As the sun set behind the trees, we made our way back to our cars. On the way up the road, a bobcat blasted from cover and ran across in front of us.

"This is a great place," I said to Bobby.

"It really is," he said.

Before we left the area, we stopped for another meal. Bobby took a road map inside with him.

"What do you need that for?" I asked. "We can just drive right up 90 to Lafayette and then shoot back to Baton Rouge on 10. It's interstate highway all the way."

"Yeah, but it would take us out of our way," he said. "I just want to see if there's a better route." He gazed at the map as I sat back in my chair, sipping a cup of coffee. "Look at this," he said. "We can just cut across here, and it's a straight shot to Baton Rouge. See how much farther it is if we go to Lafayette?"

Now, I don't know why I was so easy. Maybe I was tired. Maybe I had a bad case of ivory-bill fever and wasn't really thinking about the drive to Baton Rouge. But twenty minutes later I once again found myself following Bobby in the dark on a narrow country road. If that wasn't enough to trigger a déjà vu reaction, the cloudburst that followed should have. And that was before we even got to the detour and the bumper-to-bumper traffic and were funneled off into the hinterlands of southern Louisiana. I felt like Gene Wilder in the movie *Silver Streak*, when he is thrown off a fast-moving train for the third or fourth time.

· · ·

I woke up early the next morning in a cheap motel on the out-skirts of Baton Rouge. It had been a tough trip from the swamp, taking two or three times as long as it would have if we had driven on the highways. But it had been worse for Bobby. At least I could go right to sleep. Bobby looked like a zombie, and he still had to drive to Portland, Tennessee — about seven hours away — to pick up Whitney, and then drive almost four more hours to get home. He said if he got tired, he would stop somewhere in the boon-docks of Mississippi and take a nap in his van. It sounded awful, so I didn't hammer him about his shortcut.

I had an appointment that morning to meet James Van Rem-sen (called Van by his friends), who is the curator of birds at Lou-isiana State University's Museum of Natural Science. I had met him when he visited the Lab of Ornithology, and we had several mutual friends, but I had never had a long talk with him about ivory-bills. Over the years, Van has become an unofficial reposi-tory of ivory-billed woodpecker sightings and lore, so I was eager to visit him. Getting to LSU involved driving through morning rush-hour traffic, and then I had to figure out how to find the mu-seum in the maze of a campus. But I finally got there and parked behind the building.

Van gave me a cup of coffee, and I followed him to his office. He is of medium height and in his mid-fifties, with receding brown hair and a goatee. He reminds me of someone you might see playing a standup bass in a smoke-filled jazz club. He seemed slightly bored. Maybe it was too early in the morning. But his en-thusiasm quickly built as we talked about ivory-bills.

I first asked him about the Atchafalaya Basin, which over the years has been the source of so many tantalizing stories and ru-mors of ivory-bill sightings.

"It's all been cut over in the past, of course — well, almost all of it," he said. "In my opinion, the last believable record of an ivory-billed woodpecker came from an area in the southern Atchafalaya that was never logged. The trees were finally killed by saltwater intrusion."

My ears pricked up when he said this. I thought of the area

Bobby and I had visited the day before and all the dead old-growth cypresses we had seen. "So you think that place is pretty well shot?" I asked.

"Yes, unfortunately," he said. "I was trying to think if I could put you in touch with the guy who photographed the birds there in the 1970s, but I think he still wants to remain anonymous."

Then it all came together. He was talking about Fielding Lewis and his secret ivory-bill spot. "To tell you the truth, I've already interviewed him," I said. "He was really a character."

"He *is* a character," said Van, his eyes lighting up. "So what do you make of him?"

"I believe his story," I said. "I think those photos are real."

"Oh, good," he said. "So do I. I'm a hundred percent sure they're real."

"He completely convinced me," I said. "I looked him in the eye and told him that a lot of people were sure he had faked those pictures. He didn't even blink. 'Now where the hell would I get a stuffed ivory-bill?' he said."

Van nodded enthusiastically. "I've talked with him on the phone a couple of times," he said. "He even offered to take me out there at one point in the 1970s. I'm not a detective, but I deal with a lot of bird sighting verifications, and every instinct tells me this guy is perfectly legitimate. He had no motive, and he definitely did not want anyone going in there."

We talked about the problems people had with the two photographs — that the birds had a similar posture in both pictures and that the bill was not visible. I had seen the pictures before but had never had a chance to study them closely. Van told me that he was using the pictures in a PowerPoint presentation he had been giving to bird groups, and he offered to show them to me on his computer. A few minutes later he had the photographs side by side on the monitor.

"In my opinion, the bird has a slightly different posture in the two pictures," he said. "Its body axis is leaning this way in that one and the other way in this one. It's actually twisted."

"And it's not as if woodpeckers have a lot of different body attitudes," I said. "I remember when I sent out a request for sap-sucker photos once for *Living Bird*, most of them looked almost exactly the same."

"That's right," he said. "A woodpecker is the opposite of, say, a great egret, which has this huge range of flexibility. Woodpeckers — bark-foraging birds in general — have pretty much a single posture. It's part of the program. They're constrained by their morphology. They prop their tail against a tree; they hold on like this; there's a little bit of play this way — they can look right, they can look left. Their plumage is hard and compact and sleek. So I wouldn't expect them to look much different from picture to picture."

We turned to the topic of the bird's bill, which was not visible in either photograph. This had been a great sticking point with many of the ornithologists who attacked the veracity of the pictures. Many suggested that the ivory-bill was a taxidermied mount and its bill had been lost.

"Well, yeah," said Van. "It could have been anything, but it looks like a live bird to me. It's just facing away from the photographer. It's unfortunate that you can't see the bill. These same people say you can't see the feet, but the feet are in the shadows, and ivory-billed woodpecker feet are the same color as bark."

Of course, the biggest problem with Fielding's pictures is that he took them with a Kodak Instamatic, which gives them their fuzziness. It's really hard to see detail even if you enhance the images, which Van had already done. One of the pictures is particularly bad, with the bird in dark shadow.

But why would someone want to go to so much trouble to fake these pictures anyway? This would have involved climbing up a tall tree, carefully attaching a stuffed ivory-bill, climbing down, taking the picture, then climbing back up to retrieve the bird — twice. The bird is clearly on two different trees in the two pictures.

"Sure, it's possible that someone could be that clever and devious," said Van. "But why would he want to bamboozle George Lowery, of all the people in the world?"

"Yeah," I said. "Fielding told me that George Lowery was one of the nicest people he'd ever met. They became friends."

"And there's absolutely no motive," said Van. "There's anti-motive. There's just no way that these are not real."

I told Van that I had visited the area where Fielding had supposedly seen the ivory-billed woodpecker and taken a brief look around, but that I would really need a canoe, chest waders, and plenty of time to check it adequately.

"I don't think it used to be quite as swampy there as it is now," he said. "I'm pretty sure that rising water levels and incursion through the years have made that place wetter than it used to be. But it still might be worth taking a look."

I asked him if he thought that the saltwater incursion had killed an enormous number of trees, providing a bounty of food for these birds. As noted, the ivory-bill has been described by some as a nomadic "disaster species" that shows up in areas with a lot of recently killed trees.

"With the benefit of hindsight, that's probably why they were there," said Van. "One of the things we've thought about doing is killing some trees in a large area, basically creating a birdfeeder for ivory-bills. Actually, if we ever did find a population of ivory-billed woodpeckers, it would be the easiest bird in the world to manage from an ecological standpoint. One thing people are good at is killing trees. You could make unlimited food available for ivory-bills and at least solve that part of the problem."

In Van's opinion, the lower reaches of the major river drainages of the South were probably the last stronghold of the ivory-billed woodpecker. Here trees grow fast and live a short, hard life, he told me. They face flooding, lightning strikes, beetle kills, hurricanes. For the ivory-bill, things couldn't be better. "I'm sure ivory-billed woodpeckers couldn't care less if they're in some majestic pristine forest," said Van. "They just want to eat." He doesn't think it's a coincidence that so many of the more believable sighting reports have come from these areas. He pointed out that pileated woodpeckers are essentially everywhere: "If people were randomly mistaking pileated woodpeckers for ivory-bills, then the distribution of sightings would be more even than it is." The most credible sightings Van has encountered have come from the Atchafalaya Basin, the Pearl River, and the Sabine River.

"The Sabine River is in the same general region as the Big Thicket, where John Dennis saw those birds in the 1960s, which I also believe were real," said Van.

"It's hard to imagine him being wrong about those east Texas sightings," I said. "He had seen those ivory-bills in Cuba in the late 1940s, so he knew what they looked like and sounded like. It's amazing how strongly some people came out against those sightings. He was really persecuted."

"What happened to John Dennis is one reason I didn't want to go and see an ivory-billed woodpecker when I was offered the chance in '78," he said. "There's so much abuse heaped on people who claim to have seen them. Fielding Lewis was willing to take me out to look for them. I basically declined because I didn't want—"

"Because it would reflect badly on you?" I interrupted.

"Well, it would be like reporting a Bigfoot," he said.

"I know," I said. "The crypto-zoologists are all over this now. They have presentations about ivory-billed woodpeckers running side by side with people showing plaster casts of Sasquatch footprints."

"Oh yeah," he said. "It's embarrassing. I remember I told David Kulivan when he had that sighting at the Pearl River, 'If you go public with this, lots of people are going to put you in the same category as those who claim to have seen UFOs and Bigfoot.' So there's that danger. I just didn't want to deal with it. Besides, it was on private land, and no one was planning to log it."

"Do you ever regret now that you didn't go out with Fielding Lewis?" I asked.

"Yeah, in hindsight, I do," he said. "But I knew that my seeing them was not going to have a positive effect on the survival of the ivory-billed woodpeckers, and it could potentially backfire on them. So I think I did the right thing — but another side of me would like to have gone out there just to see them."

"Do you think someone might try to kill the birds?" I asked.

"People are afraid that the feds are going to come in and confiscate their land, which they're not going to do," he said. "We have the same problem here with red-cockaded woodpeckers. We know darn well that there are people who are going to shoot those birds if they find them on their land. It's paranoia."

"Something similar happened with the condors in California," I said. "Several of them disappeared in the winter of 1984–85. Four of the five wild breeding pairs were lost. Right after that they brought them all into captivity."

"Oh, really?" Van said.

"Although it was never covered in the news, a lot of condor researchers privately said that some ranchers or local hunters probably came out and blasted the birds in the winter when no one was watching," I said. "I guess they were sick of all the land-use restrictions."

"Well, if they're like that in California, you can imagine what they'd be like here," he said. "I would love to have seen an ivory-bill, but then what? I couldn't go public with it. I couldn't tell anyone. I knew I'd be hounded constantly."

We started talking about the Pearl River, which I was planning to explore in a few days. It would have been great if birds had been found there, Van told me, because the area is not private property. It is all public land — both federal and state — so controlling what goes on there for the benefit of the birds would have been easy. And the area seemed like excellent habitat. "Everyone who went searching there after the Kulivan sighting thought it looked good — at least according to their worldview," he said. "Of course, they were never in the old Singer Tract or anything like that, but compared to anything they had seen, it was great. Lots of big trees, the perfect hydrology — seasonal flooding but not permanent flooding. And it's relatively remote." The only problem was that they didn't find any ivory-bills.

"In retrospect, what do you think of David Kulivan's sighting?" I asked.

"I don't know," he said. "I really don't. I believed him at the time, and I still want to believe him. But I think we can say with almost one hundred percent certainty that there were no ivory-billed woodpeckers in the Pearl River and Boque Chitto wildlife management areas during the search in 2002. They could not have escaped us. We covered every inch of that area with ace black-belt birders, and we had the listening devices."

"So do you think he made it up?" I asked.

"Well, I've probably received about two hundred reports of ivory-billed woodpeckers over the years," he said. "Most of them I can dismiss as pileated woodpeckers right away or after a little bit of probing. There are about half a dozen reports where I think, *Boy, I would like to have been there and seen what they were look-ing at.* And then there's David Kulivan's sighting, which is in a completely different category. That's why all the hullaba-loo. It's so detailed. And he described the calls. No one had ever been able to give me any kind of cogent description of what the bird sounded like. He was up close. And he was doing exactly the kind of thing that would allow up-close viewing — sitting quietly, dressed in camo. At first he was reluctant to come forward, be-cause he knew people wouldn't believe him. And when he finally did come forward, I wouldn't say we put him under the bare-light-bulb-and-water torture, but with our collective experience dealing with bird sighting verification, he came out smelling re-ally clean to some of our most skeptical people. This is evidenced by the fact that essentially the entire museum staff went out there as soon as they heard about it. This was hot on the trail, in late April and early May of 1999."

Of course, no training course exists to teach people how to rec-ognize fraudulent or erroneous sightings, but Van and the others who first spoke with Kulivan had years of experience in evaluat-ing rare bird sightings. "I know David Kulivan is honest," said Van. "I know he saw birds that he thought were ivory-billed woodpeckers. I've talked to the guy and to all kinds of people, and there's just no way he made this up."

If Kulivan was perfectly honest about his sighting, as Van believes, there are two possible explanations for why no one was able to locate the ivory-bill pair again, Van told me. "Maybe he had a legitimate sighting, but the birds are now dead or have moved from the area," he said. "The only other possibility is that he was as close as he's ever been to a pileated woodpecker, and he just didn't think about it at the time. This would explain why a couple of weeks later he might think back on it and say to himself, 'You know, those might have been ivory-bills.' Then you fill in the blanks. These *ex post facto* reconstructions do happen sometimes in bird watching."

Some of the people who do not find Kulivan's sighting credible say that it was too good. His description of the birds' calls is essentially the same as one published in a field guide. Van doesn't take that as conclusive evidence one way or another. "I think if he were a sophisticated birder, he would have altered his description slightly from what he saw in the book," he said. "I mean, he probably saw the description and didn't think anything about using that as a description. So it just goes back and forth, and frankly, at this point I don't know what to make of it, except to say that there were no ivory-billed woodpeckers at the Pearl River or Boque Chitto during the Zeiss team search in January and February of 2002."

Ivory-bill skeptics often point out that there are so many birders in the United States, it would be virtually impossible for this species to exist under the radar screen; someone would surely have stumbled upon one by now. The problem I see with that equation is that probably 95 percent of birders never get off the wildlife refuge boardwalk. Van agrees. "Birders are not going to find themselves in good ivory-billed woodpecker habitat," he said. "There's no point in it. The habitat is not that interesting in terms of vagrants or unusual birds. There are a few decent breeding birds, like the Swainson's warbler and the swallow-tailed kite, but you don't have to go a mile into virgin timber to see either of those. So there's no incentive for the people with great birding skills to go where the ivory-bills might still be. You know, hunters and fishermen are the only people who are ever going to be in a position to find an ivory-bill."

At this point, I asked him the big question: "Do you believe there are any living ivory-billed woodpeckers left anywhere?"

"I'd say that hope is fading fast," he said. "I hope they're out there. I give it a slim chance — a five percent chance that there are some birds left."

One thing that greatly bothered Van is the fact that soon, as those who actually saw the bird pass away, we will lose our living link with the ivory-billed woodpecker. Just in the past few years we've lost Roger Tory Peterson, Don Eckelberry, John Dennis, and Richard Pough. "The number of people who have actually seen an ivory-billed woodpecker is down to two or three," said Van. "We're about to lose that contact. Pretty sad."

When I finished interviewing Van, he showed me the ivory-billed woodpecker specimens. The museum has several, a couple of which are taxidermied mounts. I'm always disappointed by ivory-bill study skins. They barely convey an idea of what the living bird was really like. We have two of them in the Cornell collection, and I saw more than sixty when I visited the Museum of Comparative Zoology at Harvard. Somehow they always seem drab and shrunken. Their feathers have in most cases gone a century or more without being preened, and it shows. Their bills have invariably turned a dull brownish yellow, like old piano keys. To look at them, you would never know why this species was named the ivory-billed woodpecker. One mounted specimen in a museum case at LSU has had its bill painted with pearly white nail polish to make it more closely resemble a live ivory-bill, but it just looks weird.

I spent another two days in Baton Rouge, interviewing people who had been involved in some of the earlier searches in this area.

Especially interesting was Laurie Binford, who had been a graduate student of George Lowery's through most of the 1960s. I
arranged to meet him at LSU the morning after I spoke with Van.
We sat down in an out-of-the-way section of the museum, between rows of specimen cabinets, and had a long talk about ivory-
bills and the people who have chased them over the years.

I was eager to find out more about George Lowery. What was
he like? And why were Fielding Lewis's photographs rejected?

"The best way I can describe George Lowery is that he was
your typical southern gentleman," said Laurie. "He was always
thinking and doing the right thing, and he was very helpful to his
graduate students. He had a one-track mind about birds." He
smiled. "People used to say there's one thing you can be sure of
about George Lowery: you get into a conversation with him, and
the third sentence will be about birds."

Lowery was extremely interested in the ivory-billed woodpecker, and because he was in Louisiana, he received numerous
sighting reports. He usually sent graduate students to check them
out. On one of these chases, a man took Laurie deep into the great
Atchafalaya Swamp in a pirogue (a traditional Cajun boat) with a
motor mounted in back. As far as he could see in every direction,
there was nothing but huge cypress trees and water, and it all
looked the same. "It wasn't half an hour till he was lost," said Laurie, laughing. "He didn't know where the hell he was. And then he
tried to slow the boat down and instead hit the accelerator, so we
ran into a great cypress tree. At that point, I couldn't get out of
there soon enough."

One of the most interesting searches Laurie went on took
place in March 1962 at what was left of the Singer Tract. A man
who owned a hunting camp and lodge beside the Tensas River
told Lowery that he had ivory-bills on his property. This was almost twenty years after the last one had been seen there, so Lowery had his doubts and at first didn't act on the report. But the
man called again and told him that one day he had been up in a
deer stand and had seen an ivory-bill land on a distant tree. He

said he knew no one would believe him unless he could produce one of the birds, so he took a shot at it and missed. This got Lowery's attention. He sent Laurie and three other graduate students there the next weekend to see if they could find the birds.

"We stayed at the lodge and got up at the crack of dawn," said Laurie. "Our technique was to walk along for about a hundred yards and then just stop and listen."

All of the students had listened repeatedly to the 1935 Cornell recording of ivory-bill vocalizations and knew what to listen for. At one point they heard a tooting call, but it somehow didn't sound right — too weak, too tinny. They tracked it down and found a blue jay. Later they heard a similar noise, but it too was somehow not right. They tracked that down and found a northern flicker. "That was very interesting," said Laurie. "The blue jay and the flicker must have learned these calls, but how long before? They don't live very long."

Then, finally, as the students made their way through the woods, they heard a distinct series of calls that were identical to the recording. "We estimated the bird was maybe two or three hundred feet away," he said. The four of them spread out and made a skirmish line, then headed toward the sound, trying to stay even with each other. That proved to be impossible in the dense thickets. "Stuart got ahead of everyone else, and he's the only one who saw anything. He said this huge bird took off from a log and flew away. There were fresh woodpecker workings on the log — very fresh. They were almost warm," Laurie said, laughing again. "So that's the closest I ever got to an ivory-bill. We were as sure as we could be without actually seeing it that the bird was an ivory-bill," he added. "But that was the problem. We didn't see it."

According to Laurie, this was near where Jim Tanner had worked in the 1930s. In fact, the students saw the shack where he had stayed. But this was nothing like the place Jim had known. Except for a few large cypress trees, it was all second-growth forest, and most of the trees stood only fifty feet high or less. "Our feeling was, if there are any ivory-bills left, they've got to be in this stuff," he said. "There's nothing else."

A lot of people were searching for ivory-bills in those days, Laurie told me. One of them was Lester Short, of the American Museum of Natural History. "He had the idea that you could fly an airplane over these forests and see ivory-bills, because from the top their big white secondaries would be so obvious," he said. "He actually came down here and flew over the Atchafalaya and also the Big Thicket in Texas. He concluded that there were no ivory-bills, because he hadn't seen any." Laurie then asked Short how many pileated woodpeckers he had seen on his overflights, and he replied, "None." "Well, it's pretty obvious if you can't see a common bird like a pileated, what are your chances of seeing an ivory-bill?" said Laurie.

Laurie and the other graduate students also made a trek to the Big Thicket soon after John Dennis reported seeing ivory-bills there. "We had no idea what we'd find," he said. "It turned out to be a vast forest, but all young, scrubby stuff. We drove around for a day or two and concluded it was pretty lousy habitat. We saw the spot where Dennis claimed to have seen a bird. It was right on the road."

I asked him why so many people had doubted John Dennis's story. "I don't know," he said. "I think they thought he wanted to prove that there were ivory-bills and maybe was a little over-zealous."

I was especially interested in hearing more about the Fielding Lewis photographs. Laurie said he had been at the annual meeting of the AOU in 1971, when Lowery passed them around for other ornithologists to examine. This was about three years after Laurie had received his Ph.D. from LSU. "I looked at those pictures, and I didn't like them at all," he said. "There was something funny about the bird. I suggested that they go to the biology department and look at the pictures in detail under a binocular microscope." Laurie was one of the harshest critics of the photographs. "We concluded—because I argued so hard—that they were faked. If you look at them carefully, you can't see a bill and you can't see an eye. You can't see any legs. So I said they were fake. Lowery didn't like that. He was convinced they were good."

I also wanted to hear Laurie's take on the David Kulivan sighting. In some ways, Laurie is the resident skeptic of the LSU crowd, and I was curious how he received news of the sighting of not one but two ivory-billed woodpeckers. "I took Kulivan out on the back steps where I could smoke, and I quizzed him for over half an hour," he said. "Nobody can quiz people like I can." He laughed. "He came through with flying colors. You couldn't doubt him, you really couldn't."

Laurie asked Kulivan how far away the birds had been, and he pointed to some trees just thirty or forty feet away. "You're that close, how could you mistake them for anything else?" Laurie said. "Everybody agreed, and all his professors said he's a square-shooting guy, straight arrow all the way." Then he smirked. "On the other hand, to play the devil's advocate, it could also be the case that since it was April Fool's Day, he thought he'd come up with this little story just for fun, and he got trapped in it and couldn't get out. But it's either a hoax or he really did see it. I don't see anything in between."

Speaking about hoaxes got us onto the topic of how the ivory-bill has crossed over into the realm of Sasquatch and Elvis Presley sightings. Laurie suggested surveying people who believe ivory-bills still exist and finding out how many of them also believe in Bigfoot or the Loch Ness monster. "You might find that there's a great correlation there," he said, laughing.

As I was getting ready to leave, Laurie offered to tell me a Bigfoot story from the days when he was the curator of birds and mammals at the California Academy of Sciences. Of course, in California people were not chasing ivory-billed woodpeckers; they were after Bigfoot. From time to time someone would report a wild tale of a sighting to the academy, but people rarely provided any evidence. Then one day a man brought in a movie he had shot of a supposed Bigfoot striding away from him in the forest. "It looked like a real animal and was definitely not a bear," said Laurie. "It was clearly a primate — either a Bigfoot or someone dressed in a costume. But you don't know."

"So what did you say to the guy?"

"'Well, it sure looks like one,' I told him. What else could I say?" he said, laughing hard until he started coughing uncontrollably.

Like Laurie Binford, Bob Hamilton tends to be skeptical of many sightings — including his own. That's why in the early 1970s, when he was driving across the recently opened raised section of Interstate 10 that passes across the vast Atchafalaya and spotted a flying bird that matched the description of an ivory-bill, he didn't allow himself to count it. "I'm very conservative," he said. "I always question a sighting until I can double-check it, and there's no way I could follow up on that one. I thought it was probably an ivory-bill, but I didn't fully accept it in my own mind." Then, just two years later, when Bob was a regional editor of *American Birds,* he received a report from the director of the Louisville Zoo, who said he had just seen an ivory-bill fly across the interstate at exactly the same place.

I had dropped by Bob's house in an upscale Baton Rouge neighborhood shortly before resuming my search through the swamps. He was retired now but had been an LSU graduate student when some of the ivory-bill searches had taken place. The most interesting thing he told me about was the time he spent working in the Tensas River area in the 1980s, when the national wildlife refuge was being created. He spent a lot of time in the field there, and the thought that some ivory-bills might still be around was never far from his mind. At that time there were still some hunting camps and shacks in the woods and lots of old-timers who had been there before the big trees were logged. All the camps and other structures were slated for removal. "We met this guy who had worked with Tanner — you know, a local guide," said Bob. "He had hunted there every winter." I asked Bob if the man was Jesse Laird, whose son I had interviewed, but Bob didn't know. He confessed he was terrible with names.

Bob continued: "So I just asked him, 'When's the last time you saw an ivory-bill?' And he told me, 'Well, you know, I hadn't really seen one since the 1940s, but then last winter I saw one.' I asked him where he had seen it, and he said in the same place, near Bear Lake." This was part of the area where Jim Tanner had worked, which made the report particularly interesting.

"I thought at the time, *Well, the guy knows what he's talking about,*" said Bob. "I pretty well believed him."

Bob returned to the area with several other people, and some of them camped for a week. He left after three days of trudging through tangles of nettles; the juice soaked through his clothes and made his skin raw and itchy. It seemed so hopeless. The habitat was completely marginal. Bob pointed out how difficult it would be to find an unattached ivory-bill again even if the sighting was completely legitimate, as he believed it was. And what would be the use of finding it anyway? he wondered.

"I had a feeling that even if one was there, it wasn't breeding," said Bob. "Maybe he was just wandering. The habitat had changed, and he was just eking out an existence. I suspect one could live quite a while. So even if we'd found one, it wouldn't have been such a hopeful thing."

He and the others made a pact to go back there sometime and look again, but they never did. To my knowledge, that was the last credible sighting from the remnants of the Singer Tract.

Before I left, I asked Bob what he knew about the pictures George Lowery took to the AOU meeting. "I didn't have any trouble with the pictures myself," he said. "I didn't think they were fake. They were just lousy pictures." He explained that to many of the people who looked at them, the bird seemed stilted, because it wasn't sitting on the tree the way they were expecting it to. "I think the bird didn't look quite right because it was an ivory-billed woodpecker and not a pileated woodpecker, and none of us had ever seen an ivory-bill," he said. Bob was angry at how the pictures were received by Lowery's colleagues. "It was tragic," he said. "He got kind of laughed at with those pictures. And Lowery was a proud man. I'm sure it was devastating to him that people wouldn't believe him."

My last night at the motel in Baton Rouge, I decided to try to get in touch with David Kulivan and get his side of the story. I did a Web search and found one person with that name in the entire state, but when I called, it turned out to be his parents' number. His mother told me that he now lived in Virginia, so I did another search and found his number there. I thought, *This is good — maybe I can set up an interview and visit him on the drive back to New York.* I dialed his number and he answered on the second ring. But when I said who I was and what I was doing, I noticed an instant chill. He said he wasn't interested in talking about the sighting. I explained that he may well be the last person in the twentieth century to have seen an ivory-bill and it was vitally important that his recollections be preserved. He replied, "I've decided — and I've been advised — not to talk about this anymore." I was stunned. I didn't know what to think after that.

My friend David Luneau, who had met Kulivan during the Pearl River search, was philosophical about it when I told him later. "Maybe he just got tired of being hounded," he said. He also said he thought Kulivan was now working for the National Rifle Association as a lobbyist. Maybe someone in that position wouldn't want to be connected with something as intimately associated with environmental causes as the ivory-billed woodpecker. Did he really see those birds? We may never know the answer.

9

THE LAND OF DEAD GIANTS

*T*HE NEXT MORNING before dawn, I checked out of the motel and headed west toward the great Atchafalaya Swamp. It was good to be on the road again, good to be free of the city and to be without obligations. I had done all the LSU interviews plus some telephone interviews with people in other places. For the next couple of days, the Atchafalaya would be mine. Of course, I had no idea where I was headed. But that was part of the charm. I would just drive around until I found something interesting, then take off overland — or over marsh, swamp, and bayou. I had a compass, a GPS, and a couple of auto club road maps. What else could I possibly need?

I had promised Bobby that I wouldn't explore Fielding Lewis's secret hot spot until we could go back there together. And that was okay. We really needed to get a canoe or pirogue and some good topographical maps before going back in there. And it looked like the kind of place where you would want to have a friend along, in case you ran into trouble. We had made tentative plans to go back in late February or early March and perhaps take Fielding with us.

As the sun came up, I was driving on Interstate 10 between

Baton Rouge and Lafayette. The raised stretch of roadway where the highway crosses the vast Atchafalaya Swamp is a well-known part of ivory-bill lore. There Bob Hamilton and a handful of other people had believable sightings of large black-and-white woodpeckers that did not look at all like pileateds. Every ivory-bill seeker at some point will drive along this lofty highway, gazing from canopy level at the seemingly endless expanse of swamp forest. Your hopes are high. Your excitement is palpable. But usually nothing happens. I mean, what are the odds that you could just cruise past at seventy miles an hour and get an identifiable glimpse of an ivory-bill? Probably not as good as your chances of hitting the jackpot in a multimillion-dollar lottery. I'm sure there are birders who have spent their entire lives in this area and have driven this highway a thousand times without once seeing anything that gave them pause. But I still wanted to see for myself.

The Atchafalaya Basin is huge, containing some 850,000 acres of forest, swamp, lakes, and bayous between two levees. It is 115 miles long and 18 to 19 miles wide. I went back and forth across the Atchafalaya on the interstate a couple of times, looking for access points, but there were very few. Once I parked at a place where people launch small boats and went exploring for a couple of hours, dressed in my chest waders. It was tough going, as it always is in the swamp, and I didn't have any kind of boat to get past the deep-water areas. I also checked an area that was being logged. I suppose I was trespassing, but no one was around; the machinery stood silent. Nothing I saw was anything like virgin forest. The entire basin had been pretty much clear-cut by the middle of the twentieth century. But the woods had grown quickly here, and they now spread for miles. I saw plenty of dead and dying trees and woodpecker workings. It did not seem impossible that ivory-bills could exist today in a place like this — as long as they had been able to survive in a few nooks that had escaped cutting.

I decided to move my search south of the interstate and drove along the dirt road at the top of one of the levees. This was in the heart of the Cajun bayou country, and I hoped to run into some local people and ask about woodpeckers. This proved to be more difficult than I expected. I saw a toothless old woman sitting on a small bridge over the channel, trying to catch catfish. I guess she didn't notice me as I walked up behind her, holding some ivory-billed and pileated woodpecker illustrations in my hand. She gasped and just about fell off the bridge when I said hello. And then I could barely understand a word she said. I'm not sure whether it was because her missing teeth slurred her speech or because her Cajun accent was too thick, but I finally had to thank her and walk back to my car.

A short time later, I saw Tom Sawyer and Huck Finn (or their twin brothers) playing in the woods below the levee, and I climbed down to talk with them. This time I left the illustrations in the car. The boys were dressed in flannel shirts and worn jeans, caked in mud from playing in the swamp. But they knew their stuff. One of them gave me excellent descriptions of the pileated and red-bellied woodpeckers he often saw in the woods nearby. The other just nodded but never spoke. It was clear they had never seen an ivory-bill.

Then I thought I'd take a shot in the dark. I had found the phone number of Greg Guirard, a Cajun author and nature photographer who had written several books about the Atchafalaya. I was sure if anyone could help me tighten the focus of my search, it was he. Greg even had a scene in his novel, *The Land of Dead Giants*, in which the young protagonist puts his forehead against a tree trunk to feel the reverberations from a pileated woodpecker pounding away with its bill high above him. So I called him up and asked if I could stop by and talk with him about the Atchafalaya. He didn't seem at all surprised by this and invited me to come to his house right away. He gave me detailed directions about how far along the levee to drive and where to turn off on a dirt road into the woods.

His house is set in beautiful woodlands not far from the levee. When his family moved there in the late 1930s, it was a hunting camp and inaccessible by road. Greg was two years old at the time. He and his brother, who was a year older, grew up there. For the first few years they had no electricity, telephone, or other modern conveniences, and they had to travel four miles by boat to get to a little village and the road. Although Greg has all those conveniences today, his home still feels isolated, and you have to take a long, dusty drive along the levee to get there.

Greg was outside, sanding the top of a large cypress-wood table, when I pulled up. He sometimes salvages huge old cypress logs that were lost at the height of the lumber industry in the Atchafalaya and have lain underwater ever since. The wood is perfectly preserved, and he uses it to make furniture.

We shook hands and went inside, where Greg started brewing coffee. He is in his mid-sixties, but although he has a gray beard, his hair is still dark brown, and he seems youthful. I would have guessed he was forty-eight, at the most. His house is a modest structure but very pleasant, with lots of light streaming in through the windows in the afternoon. I noticed he had some interesting medallions dangling in a few places, which turned out to be the small, squarish bony plates from the hide on the back of an alligator, which give it its bumpy appearance. Some were stark white, others brown from being soaked in coffee.

In some ways Greg is obsessed with the cypress trees that used to tower above the swamp up and down the entire Atchafalaya Basin. He has written books about them. He has taken countless photographs of bleak swamplands filled with massive old stumps where sylvan behemoths once rose high above the water. One of the first questions he asked me was whether I had ever come across any of the big trees in my travels around the South — which was funny, because I was going to ask him more or less the same thing. I was searching for uncut tracts of virgin timber, hoping to find a tiny, out-of-the-way place where ivory-bills might still exist. He knew of no such places and was sorry to hear that I didn't either. Since boyhood he had been fascinated by these trees, and he felt almost cheated that they had been clear-cut before he was born. "I've been wanting to see some of those big trees all of my life," he said.

The logging had begun in earnest right after the Civil War, Greg told me. "A lot of land and lumber companies in the North were practically given the land down here," he said. "I've heard the prices ranged from twenty-five cents an acre down to eight cents an acre. It was swampland, but it was covered with those big cypress trees. Some were like enormous columns of wood, ten feet in diameter, rising ninety feet in the air."

The amount of lumber that came out of the Atchafalaya was staggering. In 1915 alone, a billion board feet of cypress were harvested in the basin, and this went on year after year.

When Greg was young, he talked to every old logger he could find and asked them about the old days there. Many times they would say, "You should have seen it when the big trees were here." And he would get frustrated and ask them, "Why did you cut them down if you liked them so much?" The answer was complicated. Most of the loggers were isolated, with no connection to any other group. Times were hard, the money was good, and there were thousands and thousands of trees. How could it ever end?

The loggers seemed to have no idea that dozens, if not hundreds, of other crews were out there cutting away. Many came from other states — Mississippi, Arkansas, Texas — to take part in the harvest. And the logging continued right up till the end of the 1920s. "They were surprised when there were no more trees to cut," said Greg. "So that was that."

Greg also laments the loss of much of the Cajun bayou culture of the Atchafalaya. He is old enough to remember when hundreds of people still lived in the swamps and bayous, miles from any road. They got around mostly in pirogues, poling them along through the shallow water. Families lived by catching catfish and picking moss. (Harvesting Spanish moss, which grows on trees in the swamp, used to be a lucrative business. The moss was cleaned, dried out, and used to stuff chairs, mattresses, and automobile cushions until synthetic foam was developed.)

"The village of Bayou Chene had a school, a Catholic church, a Methodist church, and a couple of bars," Greg said. And it was miles out in the swamp, reachable only by boat. "About six hundred people lived in the area, and kids were brought to school in a school boat."

According to Greg, politicians used to visit the town near election day, trying to pick up votes. "My grandfather would go out there," he said. "He was elected to five terms as sheriff. He had all the votes there, because everybody knew him. But he was a good man, unlike most politicians." Greg also remembers taking boat rides to Bayou Chene with his uncle, a physician with the health department. "He'd give kids shots and check them out," he said.

Not much remains of the village today—at least, not much that you can see. The Army Corps of Engineers built the two huge levees along the Atchafalaya in the 1930s. Before this, the basin was an even wider swamp, enclosed by the naturally formed levees of the Mississippi River and Bayou Teche. After the artificial levees went up, more and more of the Mississippi's water was diverted into the basin. "The place started to flood every springtime," Greg said. "Water would get into people's houses. That didn't happen before. By 1950 the little town was gone—the people had all left. So much sediment built up there. Some areas have eighteen feet of sediment over the old ground level. Bayou Chene was built on an oak ridge, but in spite of that, the sediment has covered it all. There's a village of houses under the sand there now. An old graveyard has a few tombstones showing in one place that people keep dug out, but that's the only thing left."

After visiting with Greg for a couple of hours, I decided to get back to my search. As it turned out, Greg knew the birds of the Atchafalaya well, but he had never seen an ivory-bill, despite spending countless hours in the swamp. He spoke with some friends—including one old Cajun in his mid-nineties who had been hunting, fishing, and trapping in the basin for the better part of a century and still went out in the swamp almost every day in a pirogue he built himself—but no one could help me. No one remembered seeing a bird like that. I left feeling blue and a little discouraged. But Greg had told me that Fausse Point, another ten or fifteen miles south along the levee, looked great and had some of the biggest cypresses he had ever seen, though they were not as large as the fabled giants he had seen in early logging pictures.

When I had driven the dirt road along the levee almost all the way to Fausse Point, I suddenly got to a place where the top of the levee was all torn up, as though it had been disked by a giant tractor. The ground was raised about three feet higher than the rest of the road and was chopped up in huge pieces, and it was like this for about the length of a football field. I had no idea what was going on. I saw construction machinery, but no one was there. By this time I was determined to go on. I put my car in low four-wheel drive and climbed slowly onto the devastated roadway. It was a long, bumpy ride to the other side as I got slammed this way and that with every movement of my car. At one point I started to get stuck and wondered if I should try to back out, but it was way too late for that. I continued on and finally got through.

Fausse Point was great. I walked the trails. I walked off the trails. I even donned my chest waders and tried to work my way along the edge of the water to get to some more interesting places, but I ended up bobbing up and down in the deeper water just offshore. I had cinched a belt tightly at the top of my waders to help keep water out, but I still got pretty wet. I didn't see or hear anything that made me think ivory-bill.

I continued south and a short time later caught a brief glimpse of a black-and-white woodpecker. I'm sure it was just a pileated, but I didn't get a good enough look to confirm it. To break the boredom, I once again pulled on my chest waders — which was hard to do, since they were so wet inside — and started bushwhacking cross-country, not knowing what I might find. I had a compass and knew if I took a heading the exact opposite of where I was traveling, I would eventually get back to the levee. It worked, sort of. A couple of hours later I popped out about a half-mile north of my car. Again I had not seen any likely-looking birds, and it was starting to get dark.

The map I had didn't show any of the dirt roads in the basin, so I ended up driving around endlessly on them, using my compass to give me an idea of the general direction I was heading. It was frustrating. Sometimes I would come to a dead end or the road would disappear across an agricultural area, and I'd have to double back. I wanted to go in the general direction of Franklin. I was hoping to connect with Fielding's friend Wilbur Cole sometime the next day. I was so tired and hungry and lonely, I probably would even have welcomed following Bobby on one of his shortcuts.

I finally got on a slightly better road and then — a miracle — I spotted a restaurant or club of some kind — a shack, really. I pulled into the dusty parking lot and shut off my engine. I could hear zydeco music playing loudly inside, with people hollering and a fiddle and an accordion droning in the background. I paused for a minute and let out a sigh. The place looked mildly scary, with beat-up pickup trucks with gun racks in their back windows looming in the parking lot. But I was starving. I walked in and sat at a bare wooden table at the edge of the empty dance floor. Seven or eight musicians, all middle-aged or older, plied their trade earnestly on a small raised section of floor at the front of the room. They were all skinny men with suspenders and potbellies. Most wore eyeglasses. A couple of them sat on chairs while they played; the rest stood up. The one thing they had in common was their complete obliviousness of the audience, such as it was. They clearly were playing for their own enjoyment and couldn't care less what anyone thought. But they were all good. It was an excellent band. One piece they played for a long time sounded just like that old limbo song from the early sixties, only it was sung, like all of their tunes, in Cajun French.

The dark-haired barmaid came over and asked what I would like. She had a rough homemade tattoo showing on her upper arm, but I couldn't see what it was in the dim light.

"I'd like some food," I said. "What do you have?"

"We got fresh alligator," she said.

I looked at her, expecting her to tell me a long list of other things or maybe give me a menu. She just stared at me, waiting for an answer.

"I guess I'll have that," I said. "Oh . . . and a beer." She brought me the beer right away, but the alligator was not as fast. I guess someone had to go out in the bayou to catch it. A couple of musical sets (and beers) later, I was still waiting. But when it finally came, it was great — smothered in a spicy étouffée sauce with crawfish and shrimp. I know you want me to tell you what alligator tastes like. I could cheat and say it was just like chicken, the way people always do with everything: iguana, rattlesnake, you name it. But with its bright white color, its texture, and its unusual consistency, it was nothing like chicken. As for its flavor, I don't know — all I tasted was the sauce.

I knew I would never find my way to a motel that night, so when I left the gator shack, I drove on a dirt road through a farm field and parked behind a windrow, then went to sleep in the back seat of my car, the limbo song still playing incessantly in my brain. In what seemed like five minutes, the sun was shining and it was time to get up. I took a compass heading, lined up on due west, and started working my way out of there, through the maze of endless dirt roads. Eventually I got to Route 90, which was the main road to Franklin, but there didn't seem to be any way to get on it, so I continued probing southward, taking every east–west road over to it, hoping there was an on ramp. Eventually I found one. I stopped a short time later at a truck stop and cleaned up as well as I could. I was looking like a hobo, so the shave and the change of clothes helped.

I decided to try calling Fielding's friend Wilbur again. When he answered, he seemed almost chipper. I asked him about the big woodpeckers he had seen in the swamp. "Yeah, I used to see them all the time," he said. "Black-and-white ones with big white bills."

I could feel my heart racing, and I felt dizzy. "Do you remember anything else about them?" I asked.

"Well, it was their way of hollering," he said. "I never heard a bird that sounded like that before."

He told me he lived in a small house behind a big house and gave me the most complicated set of directions imaginable. I saw something that vaguely matched his description, but it seemed more like a converted garage or a shack. I wasn't sure. I almost went ahead and cut through the yard to check out the little house, but something held me back. I started thinking, *I'd hate to get nailed for trespassing and have some police chief with a fifty-two-inch gunbelt run my ass out of town or shoot me in the foot and leave me for dead.*

I finally found the right place. Wilbur was friendly and invited me into his house. He was obviously very sick. I could hear his chest rattle as he breathed, and he had difficulty talking. The heat was turned up all the way, and it was sweltering. I tried to draw him out about his woodpecker sightings, but it was hard. He was so frail. By the end, I began to doubt that he had ever seen any ivory-bills. Not that I thought he was lying; he seemed perfectly truthful. It was just that he knew so little about birds. He had never heard of a pileated woodpecker or even a downy woodpecker. He had no idea there were woodpeckers of any kind in his neighborhood. The birds he had seen in the bayou may have been ivory-bills; I don't know. They were the only woodpeckers he had ever taken a second look at in his entire life. If they were ivory-bills, how ironic would that be?

Early the next morning I headed east, on my way through New Orleans and other places en route to the Pearl River. I pulled into Slidell a few hours later and started looking for a sporting goods shop. Ever since the big ivory-bill searches a couple of years before, the state had required birders to buy a hunting license before going into the Pearl River Wildlife Management Area. Only it's a special kind of hunting license — one that doesn't allow you to kill anything.

Finding a place to buy one was much harder than I thought it would be. I drove up and down the main street, looking for a likely store. I walked into a gun shop where various pistols were lined up in display cases and racks of rifles, shotguns, and assault weapons hung on the walls. The shop didn't sell licenses. I went to a drugstore, and the people there sent me off in another direction to a place I never found. I finally pulled into a marine hardware store, where they actually sold licenses. The clerk looked perplexed, though, when I described the kind of nonconsumptive, nonresident hunting license I was after. "Now why the hell would you want to buy a hunting license if you can't shoot anything?" he asked.

A short time later I was trudging through the woods, and it looked like excellent habitat. It had been decades since the trees had been cut in here, and they were maturing nicely. I recalled reading that Jim Tanner had visited here for a day or so in the 1930s, but the trees were much smaller, and he was unimpressed. But that was more than sixty-five years ago, and a lot of growth had taken place since then. I saw woodpeckers everywhere. This had been the place to be for the first two or three winters after David Kulivan's sighting — a real mecca for ivory-bill seekers. Everyone had come here. Now here I was in January 2004, and I was alone. And the conditions for hiking were much better than they had been during the search years, when all the low areas were full of water. This was much drier.

I spent the day exploring the woods, listening, looking, my camcorder in hand, switched on and ready. I stayed until it was almost too dark to see, listening to barred owls calling and following pileated and red-bellied woodpeckers as they worked the trees above me. But I saw nothing and I heard nothing that gave me hope. I wondered if the great flurry of activity and excitement surrounding the Kulivan sighting would turn out to be the last gasp of interest in this bird. I wondered if the ivory-bill might now slip gently into oblivion. I hoped not. I knew I wasn't ready to give up yet. I had lots of leads to follow and lots more people to interview.

For now, the search was over. I headed home as fast as I could travel. Both my four-year-old daughter, Gwendolyn, and my wife, Rachel, had come down with pneumonia, and our eldest daughter, Railey, had returned home from college to take care of them. I was overwhelmed with worry and guilt as I turned northward toward the heart of winter.

A trio of ivory-bill decoys that Bobby Harrison carved out of tupelo wood. *(Courtesy of Bobby Harrison)*

Below: Bobby climbs down after mounting one of the decoys on a tree at Bayou de View. He sets them up in the swamp with a camcorder trained on them, hoping to attract an ivory-bill and capture it on videotape. *(Courtesy of Tim Gallagher)*

Bobby Harrison (left) and the author stand together at Bayou de View a year after their ivory-bill sighting. (*Courtesy of Rachel J. Dickinson*)

Bobby still spends every free moment cruising through the bayou, clad in camouflage, searching for the elusive ivory-bill. (*Courtesy of Tim Gallagher*)

10

A BAYOU WITH A VIEW

*Y*OU NEVER KNOW when you get up in the morning what earth-shaking event might take place and change your life forever. For me, a chain of such events began when I checked my e-mail one day in February 2004. Just a few days earlier, a kayaker named Gene Sparling — the same man Larry Mallard had told me about a few weeks earlier — had spotted an unusual woodpecker foraging on a huge cypress tree in a long, narrow bayou in eastern Arkansas. When he saw the bird's unique color pattern — brilliant white on the lower half of its back, with two white lines extending up the back to its crested head — he knew immediately that he had never seen this kind of bird before. Inconspicuous in his kayak, he pulled into a secluded spot and sat watching it for almost a full minute. The woodpecker was so close he could see the minute details of the feathers and even some greenish staining on the lower part of its back, perhaps from going in and out of a roost hole or nest.

When he got home a few days later, Gene posted a long description of his trip on a canoe club listserver, and he included a couple of sentences about the woodpecker, buried toward the end of the piece. His e-mail report was forwarded to me, and I immediately called him up. I grilled him for about an hour. His sighting sounded better than a lot of the thirty-year-old reports I had been investigating, and it was less than a week old.

Gene has pileated woodpeckers nesting on his farm in Hot Springs, in the western part of Arkansas, so he is thoroughly familiar with that species. It seemed unlikely that a pileated was what he had seen. What struck me most about his description was that he said the bird seemed almost cartoonlike because of its quick, jerky movements and general nervousness. Its neck looked thinner than a pileated's, and its crest seemed to come to a point in the back.

I telephoned Bobby and told him about the sighting. Then I asked if he would mind calling Gene and talking to him. I was interested in getting his impression, to see if it was the same as mine.

After a long talk with Gene, Bobby told him, "It sounds to me like you've seen an ivory-billed woodpecker."

"You think so?" said Gene. "I don't have enough confidence to make that call, but I'm glad to hear you say that."

Before they got off the phone, Bobby was already planning a trip to the sighting area, at Bayou de View in the Cache River National Wildlife Refuge, and Gene was going to go with him. I mentioned this to my wife about an hour later, and she told me, "You should go along with him. You'll never forgive yourself if he sees an ivory-bill and you're not there."

I didn't need much encouragement. I did a quick search on the Internet to find a good airline ticket price and then called up Bobby. "Say, you think you could pick me up in Memphis on the way down?"

"No problem," he said. "I go right through there."

And that was it: the start of our adventure. A week later I was on my way south again, for the second time in a month.

Gene Sparling told us to meet him on a small country road near Clarendon, Arkansas. He wanted to look at a place where we could haul out at the end of our several-day-long float down the bayou. He had arranged with a local man called Frank to drop us off at a bridge crossing several miles north of where Gene had seen the strange woodpecker and to pick us up at the haul-out point.

We spotted Gene's red Toyota pickup, unmistakable with the canoe and kayak strapped to the top, a few minutes after turning off the main road. Gene greeted us enthusiastically, and we stood on the side of the road discussing the bird he had seen and our plans for the next few days.

Gene is an affable man with a deep, resonant voice and a slow delivery that reminds me a little of Eeyore's. Grizzled and bearded, with receding red hair and crow's feet etched deeply into his weathered face, he looks older than his forty-eight years. When we finished talking, Gene told us to follow him into Clarendon to pick up Frank.

As we drove along behind him, I said to Bobby, "You know, he either saw an ivory-bill or he's lying. And I really don't think he's a liar."

Bobby nodded. "I don't either," he said. "His story is completely believable."

Gene got confused on the way to Frank's house, and we went driving around and around in a residential area where everything looked the same. He finally found the correct house. Gene leaves his car at Frank's house every time he goes kayaking in this area. On this trip, Bobby parked his old van in front of Frank's house and left him with the keys.

Frank is a large, jovial man of about sixty-five who wears cowboy boots and a leather belt with a huge silver buckle. He teased Gene mercilessly as he drove us to our drop-off point, claiming that Gene must have a she-bear stashed somewhere in the bayou that he was always visiting. "No one would come out here just to look at a damn bird," he said. "I know you got a she-bear."

It was bad when Bobby and I first started canoeing along Bayou de View — real bad. Without any preparation, we clambered down below the overpass, loaded up the canoe — which Gene had borrowed from his parents — and pushed off into the latte-brown river flowing into the swamp. I sat in front and Bobby in the stern, with all our equipment piled high between us. I had had some fairly recent experience canoeing in the Adirondacks with my kids, and I had floated to falcon nests in Canada and other far northern places in the past, but I was rusty. Bobby hadn't touched a canoe since he was twelve, and it showed. It was a real grind hauling ourselves through that morass, at times practically clawing our way through the bayou, scrambling up and over logs and cypress knees and blasting through little chutes where the water pushed together to form a swift-moving stream. This is where you're in danger of flipping over. You bump into a submerged log or root, then overreact to compensate, and there you go — your canoe has turned over and all your gear and supplies are bobbing downstream as you lie submerged, with brown swamp water rushing into your mouth. *Blech!*

On that first day, it seemed that whenever we found ourselves rushing into a treacherous area, Bobby and I couldn't coordinate our movements to avoid the hazards. I would point the canoe toward the one open passage I could see ahead, but Bobby would inevitably steer in the other direction, and we would wind up blasting sideways into the teeth of disaster. It was the wildest roller coaster ride I've ever been on. Somehow we managed not to swamp the canoe, but a couple of times I had to jump overboard and horse the canoe in a different direction. Luckily, I was wearing chest waders. Unluckily, the water was sometimes deeper than the top of my waders and came flooding inside.

Bayou de View is a magical place where wildlife abounds. As we canoed through the swamp, wood ducks and flocks of mallards burst from the water around us. Herds of white-tailed deer, snorting a loud warning, splashed off across the shallow water at the edge of the woods. We saw beavers swimming past and otters playing. The loud calls of barred owls and great horned owls echoed through the dim recesses of the swamp, even at midday. But most impressive were the woodpeckers. Everywhere we turned, we saw pileated, red-bellied, red-headed, and downy woodpeckers, plus a few yellow-bellied sapsuckers. It excited us to remember that Jim Tanner had written that the woods in the Singer Tract had the most woodpeckers he had ever seen. This bayou had the same feel. Although on the first day we didn't see any of the huge trees that Gene had described, we passed some massive stumps, remnants of the logging done in the 1800s. And it seemed that there were trees in every state of decomposition, ranging from those that had just a few dying limbs to those that had tumbled to the swamp floor and were rotting away to nothing. It was perfect for woodpeckers, with lots of food and dead trunks and limbs in which to forage and dig roost and nest holes.

The three of us found a nice place to camp on some high ground near an area of open water. As I was pitching the tent, though, it began to dawn on me that I would not spend a pleasant night here. I had left home so quickly that I had forgotten to bring my good tent, down sleeping bag, and camp pad. They were packed in a bag back home.

I had said to Bobby when we met in Memphis that we should stop at a sporting goods store so I could buy the equipment I would need before we hit the swamp.

"Don't worry," he told me. "I've got an extra tent and sleeping bag in my van."

"You sure?" I asked. "It'd be no problem to stop and buy some more equipment."

"No, no," he told me. "I've got everything."

I wish I had gone with my instincts. As it turned out, the tent wasn't quite waterproof or bugproof and the sleeping bag had a broken zipper. And it was much colder than I had thought it would be. After sleeping fitfully for a couple of hours, I woke with a start at the nearby splash of a beaver pounding its tail flat on the water right next to us, and I never got back to sleep. No matter what I did with that sleeping bag, the cold air just flooded in, and it was too difficult to get more clothes from my bags in the middle of the night. They were packed securely in the canoe, and I couldn't even find my flashlight. The darkness of that swamp in the middle of the night was like nothing I had ever experienced. I couldn't even see my finger an inch from my eye. So I hunkered in the fetal position and shivered all night.

Still, it was great getting up the next morning. Bobby made his classic swamp breakfast, Dinty Moore stew in special waterproof packages for boiling. He put three or four of them at a time into a bubbling cauldron of brown swamp water completely unfit for human consumption, reasoning that the water couldn't get through the pouches to the food. Of course, we would never know if it did, because the stew was about the same color as the water. Gene said that the last time he was here, he had run short of drinking water and had pulled out his special survival water purification straw, but it had clogged up after a few quick sips. He didn't say what the water tasted like — it was probably a bit like Dinty Moore stew.

On the second day of our trip, we passed an area where a long-abandoned railroad trestle, built shortly after the Civil War, cut through the trees. The rails and even the rail bed were long gone, and only stout wooden posts rose up from the swamp water. We were starting to feel as if we were really out in the wilderness, far from civilization. We had been grinding along all morning, and it was tough. Bobby and I tried our best to keep up with Gene, but his kayak was much lighter and more maneuverable than our canoe. He could slip easily through places that presented impossible barriers to us: cypress knees, log jams, tangles of brush and debris. We often had to back up a long way and try a different route, fighting the current back upstream and weaving around obstacles.

It was an amazing experience spending time with Gene. He is a remarkable outdoorsman and has spent his life doing things like this — hiking, backpacking, horse packing, or kayaking for days or weeks at a time, in areas as close to wilderness as he can find. He used to lead kayak tours in Baja California, paddling out among the gray whales. He now owns a big farm in the mountains near Hot Springs and leads horseback-riding tours.

Gene was at his best threading his way stealthily through the bayou in his kayak. He would always range a hundred feet or more in front of us, pulling into little hiding places and sitting silently — watching, waiting for something to happen. His patience was boundless, and he had such a low profile in the kayak, he didn't look human. If anything, animals seemed curious when they saw him. We would come along behind him in our canoe and watch wood ducks, beavers, and otters flush from just a few yards in front of him. I had a feeling he would much rather have been out there alone, but he wanted someone to confirm his ivory-bill sighting so much that he put up with us.

Just as we were thinking what a wild place Bayou de View was, we started to hear the loud roar of highway traffic less than a mile downstream. As we approached the bridge at Highway 17, the din from semis was almost unbearable. Bobby told me that whenever he looked down on canoeists while he was driving past on a highway, he always envied them, wishing he could be down there instead of driving. And now here he was, one of the lucky canoe people. The only problem was that it was now a good hour past noon, and he hadn't eaten so much as a Snickers bar since breakfast. "Man, we gotta stop soon," he said. "I'm starving to death."

Looking around, I couldn't see any dry spots. The woods up and down the bayou in this area were inundated. Gene said he remembered some places downstream, a little past the highway, where we could stop for lunch. I said that was fine with me. Bobby didn't seem too happy, but we continued on.

We paddled the length of the "lake" south of 17 (it was more like what we would call a pond in New York) and turned right into a narrow channel leading through the trees. Gene had gone well ahead of us and was going to wait for us when he found a good place to stop for lunch. If it seemed that we had gotten lost, he would come looking for us.

As we paddled along, we talked and joked about floating through the trackless swamp. Then Bobby started to grouse that we were being way too noisy to see any ivory-bills.

"We don't need to worry about that," I said. "The road's so loud, they'll never hear us coming. And who knows, maybe Gene will chase one back to us."

And then it happened. Less than eighty feet away, a large black-and-white bird that had been flying toward us from a side channel of the bayou to the right came out into the sunshine and flew across the open stretch of water directly in front of us. It started to bank, giving us a superb view of its back and both wings for a moment as it pulled up, as if it were going to land on a tree trunk. "Look at all the white on its wings!" I yelled. Hearing my voice, it veered away from the tree and continued to fly to the left. We both cried out simultaneously, "Ivory-bill!"

Bobby reached for his camcorder while I tried to keep track of the bird. I kept pointing as it flew. I'm sure it landed on a tree trunk about fifty feet away, because I lost it for about three seconds, then I had it again, moving in a straight line through the woods, going up the bayou for another fifty or sixty feet, then landing again. It must have hitched around the trunk each time, because I couldn't see it. When we were almost to shore, I caught another glimpse of it flying at the same altitude in the middle of the woods. I lost it after about ten feet.

We clambered ashore, dragged the canoe onto the mud, and took off after the ivory-bill, our camcorders running. We staggered through boot-sucking mud and mire, over fallen trees, and through tangled brush and briars. It was impossible to move quietly. We didn't see the bird.

About fifteen minutes later we walked back to the canoe, just as Gene was paddling to shore, looking for us. I glanced at my watch. It was 1:30 on February 27, 2004. I said to Bobby that we should sit down separately right away and jot down our field notes, before we had a chance to talk about what we had seen and influence each other. At least we would have some kind of documentary evidence, even if we couldn't get a photograph. (Later, when I was back in Ithaca, Bobby faxed me his field notes and a sketch he had drawn right after seeing the bird; it was virtually identical to my sketch.)

My first impression of the bird was that it was definitely a woodpecker and looked larger than a crow. I know that it had white on the trailing edge of the wing, because that's what I honed in on and was looking for when I mentally evaluated it. The white was much whiter than I thought it would be, and the black much blacker — coal black, beautiful. I didn't notice any red on the bird, and I did not have a distinct impression of the bill, because I had focused at first on the wing pattern and then on keeping track of the bird. No knowledgeable person could have misidentified it. It was definitely not a pileated woodpecker. It looked completely different to me. And we had been seeing dozens of pileateds and pointing them out right and left, commenting on their field marks and other characteristics, constantly asking ourselves whether we could possibly mistake them for an ivory-bill. No way. The bird we saw was a different animal.

I'm glad that both Bobby and I saw the ivory-bill together. He has always been the most skeptical person about ivory-bill sightings I know. Although he did not believe that these birds were extinct, he rarely gave much credence to the reports that came in from time to time.

About half an hour after the sighting, he called Norma on his cell phone. She suffered from diabetes and asthma, and the medicines she took for both conditions often worked against each other and made her sicker. He was always concerned about her and usually called her whenever he got to an area with decent cell-phone reception. This time, he engaged in small talk for about ten minutes, asking how she was doing, how her latest tests at the hospital had gone. Then he stopped abruptly and let out a deep sigh. "I saw an ivory-bill," he said, and then he broke down and sobbed. "I saw an ivory-bill." Gene and I looked away, and it was all we could do to keep from crying ourselves. I saved my tears for a few days later, as I was driving home from Rochester airport in the dark.

Gene was ready to leave the bayou right away and start telling people about the sighting. He thought that people at the local office of the Nature Conservancy should know, and the officials at the Cache River and White River National Wildlife Refuges. "If we tell these people about the bird, they'll be able to save this whole bayou," he said.

"We can't do it," I told him. "You have no idea what could happen here. I mean, how would you like it if a couple of thousand birders showed up next week to look for the bird? We have to do this right, Gene. And besides, we've got nothing right now — no proof that the bird really exists."

"What do you mean?" he said. "You both saw it — you said it couldn't have been anything else."

"Yeah, but who the hell are we?" I said.

"You're the experts, right? You're from Cornell. That's why I brought you here."

"Look, Gene, I'm a bird magazine editor, and Bobby teaches art and photography. We're not scientists, and even if we were, we would still need solid proof."

Gene was fuming. "We have three eyewitnesses who saw this bird. Three! What more do we need?"

"We need a picture or a video. Believe me, even if the director of the Lab of Ornithology had been in the canoe with us, he would say the same thing. We've got nothing. But we still have a few more days to spend out here. Let's set up camp somewhere close and start searching. This is the second sighting of the bird in this area in two weeks. We really ought to be able to nail it on film."

We agreed to keep things cool for a couple of days. We could always revisit this conversation in a few days if we couldn't find the bird. We floated downstream about a quarter of a mile and pulled out on a nice piece of higher ground on the east side of the bayou. A massive cypress tree, well over a thousand years old, towered high above us nearby, surrounded by tupelos, and second-growth oaks and other bottomland hardwoods grew above the waterline. It seemed to be an excellent place for an ivory-bill. Who could say? Maybe we would wake up the next morning and find a nest right outside of camp. We put up our tents and dubbed the place Camp Ephilus II, in honor of the camp Arthur Allen set up within sight of an active ivory-bill nest in the Singer Tract in 1935.

At dusk we fought our way back upstream to the place we had seen the bird. Another great old cypress, perhaps seven feet in diameter, stood not far from where the ivory-bill had been. We could see at least one excellent woodpecker hole. Could it possibly be an ivory-billed woodpecker's roost hole? Or maybe it was a nest. Anything seemed possible and perhaps even probable to us that day. We sat silently tucked away at the side of the bayou, waiting for a bird to fly into the hole or make a *kent* call or a double rap. In the quiet of the swamp, with its thick, damp air, we watched and waited for over an hour. Nothing showed up. When it was too dark to see, we headed back to camp, shining our tiny flashlight beams into the abyss of darkness ahead. Gene had hung little strips of white toilet paper on branches to mark the way, and we followed them in the darkness like Hansel and Gretel.

The next morning we floated downstream to check some other areas. Gene kept talking about some interesting habitat in the Dagmar Wildlife Management Area, to the south. We searched desperately for a roost hole or evidence that an ivory-bill had been feeding in the swamp. These birds are masters at peeling bark from a tree when it is still fresh and tight, to get at the huge beetle larvae underneath. Under the trees where they had been working, there would be pieces of bark, or strips of it would be hanging from branches or the trunk. We had seen some of this kind of work in the White River refuge. (When I saw that, I told my wife on the phone, "You know, for the first time today, I felt like we might really find an ivory-bill.") Of course, some bark sloughs off a dead tree naturally, and some can be peeled off by animals such as bears or by hunters hitching up a tree with a portable deer stand. But some of what we saw was definitely the work of woodpeckers. Ivory-bills? I can't say. I'm sure that pileated woodpeckers sometimes do this kind of thing too, but according to Jim Tanner and others, bark peeling is far more prevalent with ivory-bills than with other species.

At one point that morning, some wood ducks exploded from the water in front of us and flew off through the woods. Bobby cried out, "Look!"

"They're just wood ducks," I said.

"No. Not those," he said. "Over there, to the right."

He was pointing far to the rear and the right of us. Whatever he had seen was gone, but he felt certain it was our bird again, giving us one more tantalizing fly-by. That was all we got that day, and there was nothing the next or the next.

On our last day in the swamp, a powerful windstorm came up. Shocking in its violence and intensity, the wind roared through the forest canopy, bending and shaking the tops of the tall trees. Huge limbs creaked and moaned and frequently came crashing down near us, causing an explosion of water. At times it felt like being in the target zone of a mortar attack. For the entire day we rarely saw or heard any birds. We knew it was over — we would go home empty-handed. The question was, what could we say about this sighting? Would we even tell anyone?

Bobby wanted to keep the sighting completely secret, at least until we had found a nest or roost hole and taken a series of photographs of the bird. Then we would have positive proof before going public, so we could never be branded crackpots. But Bobby was mostly concerned that scientists would come in and close off his access to the bird. In his worst nightmares, he imagined that world-famous nature photographers would be brought in to take pictures, and he would end up staring at huge spreads in *National Geographic* and saying, "These should have been my pictures."

Being a photographer, I was sympathetic and also somewhat worried myself. But I was starting to see that our discovery was too big to handle by ourselves. We needed help and advice. I told him that we had to get the Lab of Ornithology involved. After a long silence, he agreed.

I hadn't slept for more than an hour each night for several days. I had tossed and turned for hours in my sleeping bag, wondering what I should do. Again and again I pictured myself telling John Fitzpatrick, the lab's director, about the bird. I tried to imagine his response. Fitz is a serious scientist. When he was younger, he discovered several species of South American birds that were previously unknown to science, and he is universally respected. A former president of the AOU, he has been the director of the Lab of Ornithology since the mid-1990s. How would he receive this news? Would he throw me out of his office? Would he tell me to go get psychiatric help? Would he tell me to start looking for a new job? I had no idea. But I did know that he was very interested in the ivory-billed woodpecker and had led a search in the Pearl River area after David Kulivan's sighting. Whatever the case, I knew I had to tell him, and soon.

This was a tough decision for me. Although I had many times imagined myself finding this bird — that's what keeps all ivory-bill chasers going — I thought I would have some hard documentary evidence in hand before I made an announcement. I didn't want to do it this way. But I knew Gene was going to push the issue. He was determined to tell the world, and he didn't want to wait.

That last night, Gene wanted to build a huge bonfire at Camp Ephilus II. He said it looked like it was time to have the big talk that we had put off. I agreed. But we never got around to building the fire. As soon as we pulled into camp and hauled out our gear, we started in. Within minutes, we were shouting at each other.

"There's no damn way we can announce this now, Gene," I said. "We've got absolutely nothing. We need proof."

Gene seethed with anger. "These people have a right to know," he said. "The Nature Conservancy has done great work here. This bird's being here could really help save land up and down this drainage."

"Only if people believe it," I said. "Otherwise, it'll just draw in a bunch of birders and Bigfoot chasers and do nothing good for this place *or* the bird. And look, I'd have to put my career and the well-being of my kids on the line over this. A lot of good people have been ruined because they claimed they saw an ivory-bill."

Gene was adamant. It was as if this discovery had given him a newfound purpose in life. He believed he could help save this place he loved so much, and maybe a lot more land throughout the Mississippi Delta.

"Ever hear of John Dennis?" I said. "Here was a guy who went to Cuba in 1948 and shot the last picture ever taken of an ivory-bill nest. You'd think that if anyone knew what an ivory-bill looked and sounded like, it would be him, right? And you'd think that people would believe him. Well, when he said he found ivory-bills in east Texas in the 1960s, they laughed at him. Said he was either mistaken or crazy, or maybe just making the whole thing up."

"But you're from Cornell," said Gene. "And there were two of you. They'll believe you."

"You think so?" I said. "What about George Lowery? He was a respected scientist, the head of the Museum of Natural Science at Louisiana State. He showed two snapshots of an ivory-billed woodpecker at the AOU meeting in 1971 and said that a dog trainer had given them to him and didn't want his name to be known, or the place where he saw the birds. You think they believed Lowery?"

Gene frowned.

"Hell, no," I said. "You know, Gene, all I'm asking for is a few days. Let me tell the director of the lab about this and see what he thinks we should do. If he's not interested, you can do what you want, and I'll back you up. But if you go off now and tell people that someone from Cornell came and confirmed your ivory-bill sighting, I'll deny it. I'll say it looked like good habitat and I had some interesting glimpses of birds, but that's as far as I'll go. Too much is riding on this."

Gene finally agreed to hold off telling anyone about the sighting. I promised him that I would tell John Fitzpatrick about it first thing Monday morning and then let him know what Fitz said.

The next morning we broke camp and headed back to the bridge at Highway 17. We had called Frank, the man who had dropped us off on the first day, and asked him to pick us up there instead of at our original rendezvous point, several miles to the south. He must have thought we had just wimped out, and we didn't say anything to change his mind.

While we were away, Frank had had to move the van, which now had a large bubble on the side wall of the left rear tire in addition to all its other problems, into his back yard.

"You drove that thing here from Huntsville?" he asked Bobby. He let out a whistle. "You a gamblin' man. Scared the hell out of me just driving it around to the back of my house."

Bobby got defensive. "What are you talking about? It's a great car."

"Yeah?" I said. "Would you let your daughter drive it?"

"Not even across the street," he admitted, laughing.

After loading up the canoe and kayak and all our gear, we pulled out of the little dirt parking lot at the base of the bridge and drove east on Highway 17. Frank said that he would take us on a quick tour so we could get an idea of what the rest of the area was like. My heart sank as soon as we drove away from the bayou. All around us for miles it was Dogpatch — vast fields full of crops, small farming towns with names like Cotton Plant, black tenant farmers resting on the front porches of their shacks. How could I expect anyone to believe that ivory-bills existed in a place like this? There were no endless tracts of wilderness here — just a long, narrow strip of bayou, only a mile wide at best through most of its length. And yet this might be the only thing standing between the ivory-billed woodpecker and its final, absolute, undeniable extinction. I still couldn't help picturing my friend Ken Rosenberg, the director of the lab's conservation science program, laying his eyes on this place and shaking his head, though. "Come on, Tim. Ivory-bills here?"

Bobby dropped me off at the Memphis airport a couple of hours later. Before he left, he asked me if I was going to tell Nancy Tanner about the sighting. "Only if I have proof," I said.

11

THE THIRD DEGREE

I GOT INTO ROCHESTER AIRPORT about midnight, and I still had a good two-hour drive home in the dark. I was dog-tired, but even so, I couldn't fall asleep when I got into bed. I was still imagining what it would be like when I made my big announcement to Fitz — which I would be doing in just a few hours.

At 8:30 sharp I was standing outside his office, waiting for a convenient moment to talk with him. I looked terrible — ashen, thoroughly exhausted, with messed-up hair and bags under my eyes. He told me later that when he saw me hovering there, he was afraid I was going to tell him I had an incurable illness. If ivory-bill fever is an illness, he wasn't far from right.

As if I were plunging into an ice-cold lake, I thought it would be best to jump right into my story. "I don't know how to say this, Fitz," I said. "I feel like I've crossed over into the crackpot zone, but ... I just got back from the South last night, and I'm absolutely certain that I saw an ivory-billed woodpecker."

He was sitting at his computer when I said that. Peering over his glasses, he stared at me intently, sizing me up, trying to figure out if I was kidding. After a few seconds, he stood up quickly and closed his office door. He said he had a meeting in a few minutes but he wanted me to tell him the major details of my sighting right away. I gave him a thumbnail sketch of the preceding week and a half. I said someone had forwarded to me an e-mail written by a kayaker who had seen an unusual woodpecker while exploring a section of old-growth woods in a bayou in eastern Arkansas. I had telephoned him and been so impressed with his description and his seeming integrity that I had taken vacation time and flown there at my own expense, intending to spend a week canoeing with a friend through the area where he had seen the bird — blah, blah, blah. "And on the second day . . ."

By the end of my story, Fitz was visibly stunned. "Are you positive about what you saw?"

I told him, "In some ways I almost wish I could have come in here and said, 'I'm almost certain' or maybe 'I'm pretty sure I saw an ivory-bill.' But I couldn't. It would have been a lie. I'm absolutely positive that this bird was an ivory-billed woodpecker. I can't think of anything else that it could have been. It could not possibly have been an unusually marked pileated woodpecker or something like that. It was different in other ways. It flew differently. The black was blacker and the white was whiter than on a pileated. This was definitely a different animal."

Fitz pressed me for more details. "How big was it? Describe the pattern of the white on its wings. What did it fly like? Did you see its bill?"

I fielded question after question. "It looked larger than a crow . . . The white definitely went all the way down to the trailing edge of its secondaries . . . It flew straight and fast — it definitely did not have a bounding flight . . . No, I didn't notice the bill. I was focused so intently on the trailing edge of the bird's wing that its head and bill were in my peripheral vision. I remember focusing on the trailing edge of the wing and confirming in my mind, *Yes, it's white all the way to the very end*. Then I checked it one more time to be sure. Then we both yelled, 'Ivory-bill!'"

At that moment, Fitz and I noticed the sound of several people talking and shuffling around in the room adjacent to his office. He suddenly realized he was more than half an hour late for his meeting with several Lab of Ornithology researchers who had just returned from a three-week stay in Cuba, where they had worked on a biological inventory of the famed Zapata Swamp and other important wildlife habitats. Fitz said he would like to talk with me more about my sighting, and he invited me to sit in on the meeting. "But don't mention any of this yet," he said. "There's nothing I'd like to do more than go in there and tell them, but I need to think about this."

I glanced around the room as we walked in. In attendance were Greg Budney, the curator of the sound collection at the lab's Macaulay Library; Ken Rosenberg, the director of conservation science; Eduardo Inigo-Elias, the director of the international conservation program; and Andy Farnsworth, a graduate student. Tim Barksdale, a filmmaker from Montana, had gone on the expedition with them to shoot high-definition television footage of Cuban birds, but he was not at the meeting.

They seemed surprised to see me — no doubt partly because of how bad I looked. Andy went right into his story, talking animatedly about all the great birds the group had seen in Cuba. The others added their comments and opinions as he spoke.

Back in the mid-1980s, Lester Short and several colleagues had reported a handful of ivory-bill sightings in a small forested area in Cuba — a place where, like the United States, the birds had been thought to be extinct for decades. And in many ways, the Cuban habitat was in much worse shape than it was in this country. The rediscovery of the ivory-bill there had generated intense scientific interest and media coverage, but all of the sightings consisted of brief glimpses totaling about a minute or two, and the researchers were never able to get even one photograph or sound recording of the birds. Subsequent searches in Cuba were relatively fruitless — researchers had perhaps a couple of tantalizing glimpses here and there, but nothing substantial. Some ornithologists now even openly doubt that Short and the others had really seen ivory-bills. They say things like "If you want to see an ivory-bill bad enough, a crow flying past with sunlight flashing on its wings can look pretty good."

But Cuba has been a hot destination for ivory-bill chasers ever since. And all the travel restrictions that the U.S. government has put on Americans who want to go there have only made it a more desirable place to explore. Everyone who had been on this most recent expedition to Cuba had dreamed of seeing an ivory-bill.

During the meeting, my mind kept drifting away — about 1,135 miles, to be exact — to a lonely bayou in eastern Arkansas. How ironic it seemed that Fitz and I were sitting there with these guys, listening to their story, when we knew about an ivory-billed woodpecker that I had seen less than a week earlier in a swamp only a twenty-hour drive from Ithaca. It occurred to me that we could all climb into a van and by the next morning be searching in a place where we would probably be far more likely to see an ivory-bill than we would anywhere in Cuba.

My thoughts came back into focus when Ken Rosenberg started talking about ivory-bills. The ornithologists now knew specific areas where birds had been seen in the past, and they had even heard one tantalizing report from a man who said he had found an ivory-bill nest with a couple of young birds during the past year. But if this was so, why hadn't he snapped a picture or made a videotape of it? Ken didn't know. Maybe the man didn't own a camera. But apparently he had given them reliable reports of other rare species earlier, so they certainly wanted to check it out. They would have to wait for next year, though — and that was only if they were able to get permits to visit Cuba again. This opportunity could easily slip away.

Andy and the others told us some funny stories about their adventures. One day as they were walking back to camp, Andy noticed a long line of leaf-cutter ants, each carrying a tiny piece of brightly colored nylon fabric that looked vaguely familiar. When he got to camp, he saw thousands of ants swarming over his tent, tearing it apart and carrying it off, piece by piece.

Someone told another story of how some of the team and their local guides had been picked up by Cuban police and taken away for interrogation, while the rest of the team stood beside a lonely road near Guantanamo for several hours, wondering what to do. Tim Barksdale was carrying his high-definition television camera (worth more than $100,000), which he thought might be seized, and his insurance policy didn't protect him from confiscation by foreign governments. In the end, though, the detainees were set free to continue their work.

Fitz was busy for the rest of the day, but he kept dropping by my office, sometimes closing the door and talking for ten or fifteen minutes. One time he stuck his head in the doorway and asked, "Are you sure you haven't come to your senses and realized this was all a dream?"

"No, I'm sure it happened," I said. "It definitely happened."

"Good," he replied, and gave me a thumbs-up.

Earlier that day, when I told him about the ivory-bill sighting, he had said that it was so important to keep this secret, he wasn't even going to tell his wife, Molly. But he later confided that he had ended up telling her about it a few minutes after the Cuba meeting. He felt he needed to discuss it with someone, and he knew he could trust Molly to keep it quiet. He asked me who else knew. "Besides me, just Bobby Harrison, Gene Sparling, and our spouses," I said. He asked me if I would mind not telling anyone else about the sighting unless I discussed it with him first, and I agreed. I also said that I thought Gene was eager to tell more people about the ivory-bill sighting. I suggested that he call Gene and get him on board with the project.

I spent the rest of the day in a stunned silence, though I could already feel a great weight lifting from my shoulders. I felt almost euphoric. Just before I left for the day, Fitz asked if he could interview me on tape the next morning, for historical purposes, and I said that would be fine. That night I slept well for the first time in a week. It was now Fitz's turn to lie awake. In some ways, no one had more to lose than he did. He was a respected scientist. I hoped for both our sakes that we would soon get conclusive evidence, such as a photograph or videotape, to prove the existence of this elusive bird.

The next morning, Fitz went downstairs to the Macaulay Library to round up a tape recorder and microphone. When he got back, we went to his office and sat down to talk. It felt as if I were on the witness stand, being cross-examined by a prosecutor. I sat on a chair as Fitz paced back and forth, pitching questions at me. He asked me to explain in minute detail everything that had happened.

"You said it looked darker than a pileated woodpecker. What about a crow? Maybe the light hit the bird just right as it flew past and the reflection made part of the wings look white."

"No," I said. "To me a crow's plumage looks shiny, almost like armor. This was not like that at all. It had a softer sheen. But it was blacker than a pileated, almost purple-black. I'll never think of a pileated as being black again — it's dull black, almost brownish black."

"What about a vulture? I'm sure there are lots of them there."

"No, I'm positive it wasn't a vulture. It was nothing like that."

"What about a hooded merganser?"

"I didn't see any hooded mergansers."

"Why not? There should be some there this time of year. They have white on their wings."

"Yeah, but not enough. And besides, I know hooded mergansers. To me, they're a little buzz-bomb duck, just a cut above a bufflehead. There's no way it could have been a hooded merganser."

"What about a wood duck?" he asked.

"Look, Fitz, there's absolutely no way it was a duck!" I said. "I'm positive it was a large black-and-white woodpecker."

"Why a woodpecker?" he asked. "What was it that made you think woodpecker?"

"I don't know . . . It was my general impression . . . the bird's gizz," I said. (*Gizz* is a term that originated in World War II

Britain, when plane spotters would try to determine whether a distant airplane was friend or foe by getting a "general impression of its size and shape"; hence *gizz*, though I don't know how it came to be spelled with two *z*'s instead of two *s*'s. Birders worldwide have since taken up this term.)

"I don't believe it when people talk about gizz," Fitz said. "You have to be able to describe what made the bird seem like a woodpecker."

"Well, for one thing, it landed on the side of a tree. Nothing that size but a woodpecker would have done that."

"But you never actually saw it perched on the trunk of a tree, did you?" he asked.

"No. But I'm sure it landed at least three times, because it would stop for several seconds at a time before flying again. It must have hitched around the other side of the trunk from me, as shy woodpeckers always do."

"How do you know it didn't land on a branch each time?"

"At that height, those tupelos and cypresses really don't have any branches."

He pulled out a framed painting by David Sibley that showed several views of ivory-billed woodpeckers, including one in flight. "Did the wings look like that?" he asked.

"Well, yes," I said. "The extent of the white looks right, but there's something . . . The way it's holding its wings is wrong. The wings of the bird in this painting are held too far down . . . the wingstroke is too deep. The bird I saw was making very shallow wingbeats, almost as if it was just moving its primaries. It had a very stiff-winged look."

Fitz finally turned off the tape recorder and looked at me. He said that he believed my story and that he considered me to be at the level of a professional field ornithologist. He also said that locating and studying the ivory-bills in eastern Arkansas would now be the number-one research and conservation priority at the lab.

12

BACK TO THE BAYOU

*T*HE PROBLEM WAS what to do next. Fitz had enormous responsibilities and commitments in the immediate future. Though he wanted nothing more than to get down to Bayou de View as soon as possible, he couldn't go yet. But whom should he send? We sat together in his office pondering this. The members of the Sapsuckers, the Lab of Ornithology's big-day birding team, were an obvious choice. Each May they competed against the top birders in America (and some from overseas) in New Jersey's famed World Series of Birding, the object of which is to find the most species of birds from midnight to midnight on the day of the event. Fitz is the cocaptain of the Cornell team, with Ken Rosenberg. Other team members include Kevin McGowan, Jeff Wells, and Steve Kelling.

The bar has been raised considerably in this event since the early 1990s, when I was captain of the Sapsuckers. At that time the top scores barely passed 200 species. (The best we ever did when I was captain was 184 species — and that was 10 more than the team had ever found before.) Now the winners sometimes pass the 220 mark. And the ranking of the Sapsuckers has also improved immensely. They are almost always in the top two —

they tied for first in 2001, won a clear first place in 2002, and came in a close second in 2003 and 2004. So the Sapsuckers are great birders. The problem was deciding which of them should go. Fitz was concerned that the secret would leak too soon.

What about Ken Rosenberg? He's a fantastic birder. But he might tell his brother, Gary, who is a tour leader and well connected in the birding world. What about Kevin McGowan? Well, his seventeen-year-old son, Jay, is an avid birder, and he would probably have to tell Jay. Can we trust someone that young to keep a secret?

And it went on and on. After eliminating all the Sapsuckers for reasons like this, Fitz brought up Andy Farnsworth, who is certainly a fabulous birder. I remember how great it was ten or twelve years ago when Andy was a Cornell undergraduate. He and his friend Ned Brinkley, who was working on a Ph.D. in comparative literature, were a couple of the most fanatical birders this area has ever seen — and in Ithaca, that's saying a lot. They seemed to be everywhere, searching every likely clump of evergreens for northern owls and scanning up and down Cayuga Lake for vagrant water birds or gyrfalcons, and the rare-bird sightings tumbled in. It reached the point where some people started to wonder if some of the sightings were made up, but when someone went to check them out, they almost invariably proved to be accurate.

More recently, Andy's skills had gotten even better. He is now an international guide for a top tour company and leads people on birding trips throughout South America. And what made him even more attractive as an ivory-bill searcher was the fact that he had already seen and heard other *Campephilus* woodpeckers, such as the pale-billed, powerful, and Magellanic woodpeckers in Latin America. Although these birds are quite different from the ivory-bill, they do make the double-rap signal that is characteristic of the genus.

Andy is also a master of digiscoping, which was another recommendation. This is a relatively new phenomenon among birders. You get a pocket-sized digital camera, hold it up to the eyepiece of a spotting scope or binoculars, and take a telephoto shot through it. I've seen some amazing results using this technique — some good enough to publish in a book or magazine. Andy hoped to be able to get a quick digital image of the ivory-bill if it landed near him. Of course, that was a big if.

Some birders say that Andy is like a young Ted Parker, which is the highest compliment a birder could ever receive. A phenomenal ear birder, Ted had an encyclopedic knowledge of bird vocalizations and could identify more than four thousand species by sound alone. He personally recorded more than ten thousand of the bird songs and calls in the Lab of Ornithology's Macaulay Library. He became the world's leading authority on neotropical bird distribution and identification and has been called by many the greatest field biologist of the twentieth century. Ted died tragically at the age of forty in a 1993 airplane crash during an aerial survey he was conducting in Ecuador for Conservation International.

Fitz decided that Andy would be the perfect person to send to Arkansas to help find the ivory-bill. As we sat together in his office, he called Andy at home in Manhattan, switching on his speakerphone so I could take part in the call.

"Conceptually, could you fly somewhere in the eastern United States tomorrow and camp out for a week?" asked Fitz.

"Conceptually, yes," said Andy, without missing a beat. "Why? What's going on?"

"We have a ground zero," said Fitz.

"Really? That's awesome!" said Andy, who seemed to know instantly what Fitz was talking about. Apparently Fitz had had a conversation with him at a party several weeks earlier in which he had discussed what he would do if they ever had another ivory-bill "ground zero" like the Pearl River. "Just tell me where you want me to go," said Andy.

Fitz told him that he couldn't give him any details, but that he should book a ticket to Memphis for two days later. He said that I would meet him at the airport and drive him to the site of the search. That's it. For all Andy knew, I might have taken him blind-folded on an eight-hour trip — which would be enough time to get anywhere in the Deep South.

Before he got off the phone, Fitz asked Andy if he had done much canoeing.

"Yes," he said. "I've had lots of experience in whitewater ca-noeing."

"I don't think we'll see much whitewater," I said, laughing.

So for the third time in a month I was heading south. This time I flew from Ithaca's tiny airport — yet another mistake. I flew on one of the small commuter planes, which are particularly sensi-tive to turbulence. It was the worst flight I had ever been on. Dur-ing the first leg, to Pittsburgh, we were buffeted constantly as we flew through dark, thunderous clouds. Once it felt as if the plane had hit a brick wall and fallen twenty feet straight down. Every-one's drinks flew into the air, covering the bottom of the overhead luggage carriers with Coke, ginger ale, and coffee, which dripped down on us for the rest of the trip. I was sitting beside a loud-mouthed businessman from New York City, who babbled cease-lessly about all the wonderful things he had done in his life. But worse was the guy behind me, who was terrified we were going to crash any second.

"What's happening? Why is the plane losing altitude?" he asked frantically as the plane dropped uncomfortably close to the woodlands, pastures, and farms below.

"No big deal," said the New Yorker. "We must be heading into Pittsburgh."

"When are we supposed to get there?" the other man asked.

"About nine-thirty," I said. I glanced at my watch. We still had a good forty-five minutes to go before we were due to touch down, so it was way too early to be descending to land. This just fright-ened the man more. Even the New Yorker was concerned that the pilot had not come on the intercom to soothe us and explain what was going on.

I laughed. "Maybe he's too scared to take his hands off the controls to talk on the microphone," I said. No one smiled.

The Pittsburgh airport finally came into view, and we made a rough landing, slamming down on the tarmac and bouncing a couple of times. Once we were on the ground, the pilot did get on the intercom to apologize for the rough ride. He said no one had told him there was any turbulence up ahead.

Andy was flying out of New York City and had booked a flight that was scheduled to stop in Atlanta before continuing to Memphis. The only problem was, Atlanta was experiencing fierce storms and his flight had been canceled. He rebooked on a different airline that traveled by another route. He would arrive several hours later than originally planned, and it would cost three times the original price.

On his old itinerary, Andy was supposed to get to Memphis a couple of hours before me and just wait. As it turned out, I arrived first. I was taking the shuttle to the car rental company when he called me on my cell phone. He had just landed and was on his way to the baggage claim. I said I would pick him up out front as soon as I got the car. I had a pleasant surprise at the rental company. They were all out of full-size cars, so I got a free upgrade to a Chrysler Pacifica, which looked like a giant PT Cruiser but had the feel of a sport utility vehicle. I figured it would be great off-road, but I didn't tell that to the agent.

I picked up Andy a few minutes later in front of the terminal, and we were on our way. I hardly knew where to begin with my story. I decided to wait until we were out of town to get started, so I wouldn't miss a turnoff and have to figure out how to get back on the right road. I asked him if he had any idea what this was about. He said he assumed we had a lead on an ivory-billed woodpecker. I nodded and then started telling him the details. He was completely enthralled, hanging on every word as I told him about what Gene Sparling had seen. I gave him the long version of the story, letting it build slowly in a powerful crescendo. I'm sure he assumed we were going to check out Gene's sighting and had no idea that it had already been confirmed. He became more and more excited as I told him that I had been here just a few days earlier with a friend and had paddled through the bayou in the sighting area with Gene. But his jaw dropped when I told him about the close fly-by.

"No!" he exclaimed.

"Yep," I said. "It flew right past in front of us at close range. I honed in on its back and confirmed that the white went all the way down to the end of its secondaries. Then I checked once more and reconfirmed it. Then we both yelled, 'Ivory-bill!'"

"That's awesome!" he said, using one of his favorite words.

Andy is thirty-one, but he looks much younger. A trim man with short dark-brown hair, he looks like a young Bobby Kennedy. His powers of concentration are . . . well, awesome. As soon as we got to the bridge at Highway 17 and parked, he stood away from me and just listened, his hand cupped to his ear. He spent a lot of time like that during the next few days — and he usually heard more birds than anyone else.

We hooked up with Bobby soon after we parked. Except for a short trip home, he had been out in the bayou almost constantly since we had seen the ivory-bill. He was determined to get the first picture or video of the bird. He had brought two camcorders (one of which he had just purchased) and set them up at strategic places in the swamp, hoping for another fly-by. He left them running constantly, changing the videotape and batteries every four hours. One camcorder was aimed right at the spot where we had seen the bird. The other was pointed at a freshly excavated woodpecker hole about a quarter of a mile north of the bridge.

Gene Sparling was supposed to meet us early the next morning and bring his parents' canoe for Andy and me to use. The plan was for Bobby to ferry Andy and all of his gear to Camp Ephilus II so he could set up his tent. Then he would come back for me. Andy was planning to spend several hours in camp just listening, hoping to pick up a *kent* call or a double rap, while Bobby and I went exploring.

Bobby had a new canoe, a used one he had bought from a

neighbor for a hundred bucks. It was much smaller than the one we had used last time and seemed very tippy. This was offset somewhat by Bobby's newfound skill as a canoeist. I could hardly believe he was the same person I had cruised down the bayou with just a few days earlier. This was a new Bobby — strong, dynamic, a real outdoorsman. And he was starting to look trim, almost athletic, after paddling for so many miles in the past couple of weeks.

"It's great," he said. "I'm eating twice as many Baby Ruths and Snickers bars, and I'm losing weight. And I stopped taking my blood-pressure medicine." He took a big swig of Mountain Dew from a plastic bottle as we spoke. I remembered that the first day we had paddled through the bayou, he had told me he was at the age when, especially given his sedentary life, he could easily keel over and die of a heart attack from exertion, like one of those men you hear about who drop dead shoveling snow from their driveway.

The weather was still cool, so the snakes hadn't come out yet. And this time I had the tent, sleeping bag, and pad that I had used the last time I had camped in Greenland, so I knew I would have some warm, comfortable nights ahead. And I had taken Bobby's advice — I had brought along a good supply of Dinty Moore dinners to boil.

After pitching our tents and unloading our camping gear, Bobby and I stepped into the canoe and shoved off, letting the current catch us as we pulled into the main channel of the bayou. Tall trees rose up all around us, including an ancient cypress that was probably already five hundred years old when Columbus sailed to America. I looked back toward camp just before it passed out of view. Andy stood at the far edge of the water, bent slightly forward, with his hand cupped to his ear: a portrait of concentration.

As we paddled down the bayou, every hundred yards or so we would spot something interesting — a part of a tree trunk or limb with the bark stripped off; a freshly excavated woodpecker hole —

and head into the heart of the swamp to check it out. It was always a challenge. There is no such thing as a straight line in the swamp forest. You head in the general direction you want to go and then have to turn left or right and wind around trees and huge cypress knees that thrust up from the muddy water. In places the water is so shallow that your canoe bottoms out. Then you have to step out into the mud and haul the canoe behind you. At times you sink up to your knees and start to wonder if you'll be able to pull yourself out. In your really paranoid moments, you start remembering every B movie you've ever seen involving quicksand and men in safari clothes sinking slowly from sight.

After a couple of hours of silently threading our way through the swamp — well, as silently as we could, given that we were often grunting and straining to pull the canoe through mud — we decided to stop in a nice-looking area with enormous trees and just wait and listen. The raucous laughter of pileated woodpeckers rang out through the woods. And red-bellied woodpeckers were all around us, drumming on trees and making their distinctive *churr* call.

Bobby pulled out a tuna snack package and started opening the can and draining the liquid. I watched as he carefully ladled out the tuna with a tiny wooden spoon, mixed it with mayonnaise and pickle relish, and smeared the concoction onto crackers. He popped a couple into his mouth and washed them down with Mountain Dew.

"Got another one of those handy?" I asked. He reached into his black zippered satchel and tossed one to me. As I opened the package and started making my lunch, we talked.

"You know, I really wish we could have done this without telling anyone else," said Bobby. "Like we always planned. Get pictures of the bird first before bringing in other people. Now there's half a dozen people who know about the bird and have come looking around. And it's only going to get worse."

"I know what you're saying, Bobby," I told him. "But I don't see what else we could have done. Gene was the one who found the bird. We never would have seen it without his help. And if the Nature Conservancy really can buy up all this land and save it, that would be so great."

It turned out that Gene had told several people about the bird shortly after our sighting. When Fitz called Scott Simon, the director of the Arkansas chapter of the Nature Conservancy, about getting permission for our researchers to enter TNC land along Bayou de View, Scott already knew the whole story. So the research effort had instantly evolved into a partnership between the Lab of Ornithology, the Arkansas TNC, and a handful of independent participants. Just seven days after Bobby and I saw the ivory-bill, Scott hosted a conference call involving all of the principal players, and we have had one every week since. The search team immediately expanded.

David Luneau was one of the first to show up. Bobby ran into him just three or four days after our sighting. But I was glad he was on board. Although we had spoken on the phone a few times earlier, I had met him for the first time just a month and a half earlier, in Little Rock. I had taken an instant liking to him, as though we were old friends. He seemed good-natured and easygoing, with an infectious sense of optimism. From the start, as a member of the Zeiss ivory-bill search team at the Pearl River, David was the one who was most confident that the ivory-bill still lived.

Another Arkansas birder who soon joined the search was Mel White, a book author and freelance magazine writer who has a regular column in *Living Bird*. Mel and I are old friends, and we have traveled together in Africa and a couple of other places over the years. The night before I drove to White River to meet Bobby for our first search there, I had stayed at Mel's house in Little Rock. Over glasses of single-malt Scotch, we debated whether the ivory-bill was extinct. He was convinced that if it was still around, some birder would have seen it by now. "I really hope you prove me wrong," he said. "But I don't see how they could have gone unnoticed for so long."

Scott Simon has also been a great asset to the team. He has a single-minded focus — an ability to fix on a goal and quickly develop a step-by-step plan to accomplish it. Within days he was figuring out which pieces of land should be preserved and in which order. He and Fitz were also approaching donors, both to help fund the research effort and, more important, to acquire vital pieces of bottomland forest habitat that were subject to logging and clearing for agriculture. Scott also has excellent people skills and has managed, single-handedly at times, to keep our fragile coalition together when the inevitable personality clashes take place.

That night in camp, Bobby sat on a log near his tent, holding a small cookstove on his lap. He turned on the fuel jet and kept striking matches and holding them over the burner, trying to get it to light.

"I wish you wouldn't hold that on your lap while you're doing that," I said. "I've seen too many of those stoves flare up when you're trying to light them. You could end up like a human torch, running through the woods in flames."

Bobby laughed. "I've been doing it like this for years, and nothing's happened yet."

"It doesn't mean it couldn't happen this time or the next time," I said. "But I guess I could always kick you into the bayou to put the flames out."

When he finally got the stove lit, he set it on the ground and walked to the bayou to fill up a stewpot with sludge-brown water. He set it on the stove and turned up the flames to full power, so the stove looked like a blowtorch with sooty black plumes coming up the sides of the pot. I watched him tear the cardboard from a couple of the plastic stew packs and set them beside the stove.

"Anyone want any Dinty Moore?" he asked.

"I'll take one of the roast-beef-with-mashed-potatoes meals," I said.

"The stew's better," he said.

"I know, but I feel like roast beef tonight."

"You want two?"

"No, one will be fine," I said.

"How about you, Andy?" he asked. "How many you want?"

Andy got a slightly disdainful look on his face. "I don't want any, thanks," he said. "I've got my own food."

All we had seen him eat so far was granola and trail mix and tiny boxes of raisins — the kind that conscientious parents send to day care for their kids' snacks — and this was really starting to get to Bobby. He had been offering Andy beef jerky, candy bars, and bottles of Mountain Dew all day, and Andy had turned up his nose at everything except for one of the small tuna lunch packs.

"You really ought to eat some of this stew, Andy," said Bobby. "A man can't live on the kind of stuff you've been eating."

Andy shrugged and smiled, then opened up another small box of raisins and started eating them. Bobby shook his head. The water in the stewpot was boiling over now, sizzling as it ran down the sides and hit the flames. He picked up the three dinner packs and slipped them sideways into the bubbling water.

We drifted off to sleep that night with the loud hoots of great horned owls echoing through the bayou and a soft wind blowing through the treetops. It was great to be back in the swamp.

The next morning David Luneau pulled up his canoe beside Camp Ephilus II as we were heating up coffee.

"Hey, David, it's great to see you," I said, walking over to shake his hand. "I was hoping you'd come here and prove I didn't have some kind of hallucination."

He laughed. "Yeah, I bet you'd like someone else to see that bird right about now," he said.

"I feel like I'm really hanging out alone on a limb with the Sasquatch chasers and Elvis sighters."

"You definitely are," he said.

Although it had been only nine days since our sighting, David had already spent countless hours paddling up and down the bayou, exploring every likely-looking nook he saw. Every time he had a few hours to spare from teaching at the University of Arkansas, he would blast down to Bayou de View — about a seventy-minute drive from Little Rock if you travel very, very fast. He would go to work every morning with a canoe strapped to the top of his van and a full suit of camouflage clothing on the passenger seat. As soon as he finished his morning class, he would race to his van and leave. Sometimes he could spend only an hour or so at the bayou before hauling out his canoe and rushing back to teach another class. He hadn't told anyone at the university what he was doing, and he was constantly ditching faculty meetings. "Someday I may have to explain why I'm never there and why I duck all new responsibilities," he told me later. "My work life will be greatly simplified once the announcement about the bird is made, but I do understand the need to keep it quiet."

Bobby was in the same boat. Although his dean and the president of Oakwood College already knew about the rediscovery of the ivory-bill, they may not have realized what an earth-shaking event it was. From the start, when the participants in the search were asked what their personal goals were, Bobby insisted that his college should receive the recognition it deserved for its part in the discovery. "They let me take time off and gave me a lot of the funding I needed to search for this bird," he said. (Of course, he had also completely depleted his savings account to keep going.) Bobby wanted more than anything for Oakwood College to stand beside Cornell and the Nature Conservancy when the announcement was made.

Andy decided to join David and search to the south of camp. Bobby and I headed north up the bayou to the other side of Highway 17. We both liked that area, especially in some of the drier parts, where nice stands of hardwoods grew. He showed me the tupelo with the fresh woodpecker hole about fifty feet up — the hole on which he had one of his camcorders trained. The camcorder was bolted to the trunk of a nearby tree and pointed directly at the hole. He reasoned that this might be the bird's roost hole. It certainly looked like it could be. It had the perfect oblong shape and was the right size. And this tree lay in the same direction the ivory-bill had been flying when we lost sight of it.

I had gotten in touch with Gene by cell phone earlier, and he was running late. He expected to get to Bayou de View by late morning. Bobby and I decided to go back to the bridge to wait for him. Gene arrived in his red pickup truck a short time later.

"Hey, Gene, long time no see," I said.

He laughed. "Good to see you again," he said. He asked me if I would mind driving him north to where Highway 38 crossed Bayou de View, so he could float south again through some of that great hardwood habitat and end up at Camp Ephilus II by evening. We left a few minutes later, and Bobby went exploring alone.

In the six days since I had seen him, Gene had gone through some personal changes and also spent a considerable amount of money. He had a brand-new digital camcorder with extra oversized batteries so he could keep it running constantly as he drifted down the bayou. Maybe he would have another sighting like the one that had started this stampede, and this time he would be ready and get the definitive video of the long-lost bird. He had also bought yards and yards of camouflage material — the shredded-looking kind that turkey hunters drape in front of them to break up their outline.

"Boy, you're really getting into this, Gene," I said. "So how are you managing to keep your business going when you're spending so much time out here?"

"I made up my mind," he said. "I'm canceling the rest of my life to do this."

I helped him take his kayak off the top of his truck and carry it to the water's edge. He carefully packed it with all the gear he would need for the next few days. Then came the hard part — attaching the camouflage. He draped it on top of the kayak and held it in place with large rubber bands that he slipped over the hull in front and back. After putting on his splash skirt and getting inside the kayak, he pulled the camouflage over his head. I'm not sure what he looked like—maybe a cross between an alligator and a log—but he definitely didn't look human. I wondered what people would think if they saw him float past under the bridge at Highway 17. Maybe this kind of thing is the source of some of the swamp monster legends.

"Hey, if this'll buy me a couple of extra seconds when I'm coming up on an ivory-bill, it'll be worth it," he said. With that, he pushed off and paddled swiftly downstream.

"See you tonight," I said.

I got back to the small parking area beside the bridge just as David was paddling to shore with Andy. We unloaded the canoe from Gene's car and promptly headed south toward the place where Bobby and I had seen the ivory-bill.

"Okay," I said. "We were coming up right here, and we were ... wait a second ... just a little closer ... Now, right here—when we saw the bird flying up from that bayou to the right. It crossed the channel in front of us right there, just above the level of that bend in that tree. It banked with its back to us as if it were going to land on that tree there. Then it heard us shouting, I guess, and veered off and continued to the left. Bobby was scrambling to get his camcorder out, and I was pointing at the bird, trying to keep it in sight. I lost sight of it there for a few seconds, when it must have landed on a tree. Then I saw it again at the same level, flying to the north another fifty feet, then landing for a couple of seconds. Then I saw it one more time for about ten feet before I lost sight of it. We pulled ashore right there and went scrambling after it."

"That's awesome!" said Andy.

"But we never found it," I said. "It's only been about nine days since then."

Andy and I explored a lot of areas immediately adjacent to where the sighting had taken place and found several trees with fresh woodpecker workings. Whether any of the damage was done by an ivory-bill was difficult to say, but some of it looked

promising — newly peeled branches with long strips of bark floating in the water below. Andy's technique was to pause from time
to time in a place that seemed good and just sit, sometimes for
half an hour or more. He would cup his hand to his ear and lean
forward, listening intently, often with his eyes closed. Then we
would move on. We rarely spoke. I could feel myself getting into
the slow-motion rhythm of the swamp — hearing, breathing,
sensing my surroundings as much as seeing them.

Gene showed up sometime in the late afternoon, well before
dark, to set up his tent. We were all at camp when he paddled to
shore and got out of his kayak. As he stood up, his splash skirt
hung down like some weird, ugly prom dress.

"Hey, Gene, nice skirt," said Bobby.

We all laughed. "You've been in the swamp way too long,
Bobby," I said.

Bobby decided to paddle north of the bridge to watch the woodpecker hole. He needed to pick up his camcorder, but he also
wanted to wait there until dark to see if an ivory-bill showed up.
He had picked up his other camcorder earlier and moved it to
a place about halfway back to camp from the woodpecker hole.
This one was pointed at some freshly peeled bark on a tupelo. He
hoped that whatever was working on the tree would show up
again and be captured on videotape. The only problem was that
this was at least fifty or sixty feet off the main channel in dense
swamp forest, and he would have to find it in the dark.

About an hour and a half after nightfall, there was still no sign
of Bobby. It was a dark, moonless night, and the only illumination
he had was a cheap flashlight he had bought at a dollar store. The
batteries actually cost more than the flashlight. If the light went
out, he would never be able to find his way back. Gene started getting worried. He paced back and forth at the edge of the water
and then stood peering out into the darkness.

"You know, Bobby's been gone an awfully long time," he said.
"You think we ought to go look for him?"

"I don't know," I said. "Maybe we should give him a little more time. It won't do anyone any good if we all get lost out there." But half an hour later, I was fretting too. "It's not like Bobby to be late for a meal," I said. I turned on my flashlight — which I had also bought at the dollar store — and shined it in the direction he would be coming from. A minute later, Gene was standing next to me with his light, and then Andy joined us and shone his light.

"Let's give him fifteen more minutes and then go looking for him," I said. After a little while I spotted a tiny light twinkling in the distance through the pitch-black swamp. "There he is," I said.

Gene turned to me and said under his breath, "Don't tell Bobby I was worried about him, okay?"

Bobby finally pulled ashore and stepped out of his canoe. I grabbed the gunwale and hauled the canoe most of the way out of the water. He was soaking wet and cold. "What happened to you?" I asked. "I had a feeling when you missed supper that something had to be seriously wrong."

He laughed. "You know, everything was going good," he said. "I stayed at the roost hole till it was dark, then took down the camcorder. Then I came back and found the other one and took it down. But when I was coming out of there, I was holding the flashlight in my hand while I was paddling, and it slipped out and fell in the water."

Bobby had watched the flashlight sink halfway to the bottom and just hang there, suspended with the light still on, pointing upward. He kept reaching for it, but it was like bobbing for apples; every time he touched it, he nudged it farther away, and the current was moving it quickly downstream. He knew if he leaned too far, the canoe might turn over and flip the camcorders and everything else into the water, leaving him shivering in the dark on a cold winter night in the swamp. If the water short-circuited the flashlight before he could get it, he would never be able to find his way to camp. He finally jumped over the side and went wading after it. "When I pulled it out, it was all full of water," he said, laughing. "I could hear it slosh around inside when I shook it."

After he climbed back into the canoe, he realized that he had another problem. He had gotten turned around chasing the flashlight and had lost all sense of direction. He couldn't remember which way the channel was. He paddled around this way and that, looking for clues about where he was. The temperature hovered in the high thirties, and he was wet and cold and shivering — definitely at risk for hypothermia. Then he remembered that he had been heading toward Venus when he went deeper into the swamp to get his camcorder. To get back out, he would have to go toward Sirius. It worked. He eventually found the channel and followed Gene's toilet-paper markers until he saw our flashlights twinkling like stars up ahead.

That night Bobby splurged and ate three packages of Dinty Moore, washed down with a sixteen-ounce bottle of Mountain Dew.

Before I left Ithaca, Fitz had specifically instructed Andy and me to search by car along the perimeter of the bayou, looking for alternate access points and checking habitat. A couple of days after Bobby got lost, we decided to take some time off from canoeing and head out in my shiny new rental car. We had a Delorme guide to Arkansas, and Andy took copious notes everywhere we went. He seemed genuinely fascinated by the area. And the bird life was great, with plenty of interesting hawks and waterfowl. Everywhere we went, Andy snapped digital pictures through his binoculars.

The car did turn out to be a great off-road vehicle. We drove for miles on dirt roads, sometimes coming across flooded areas and having to back up and go speeding forward so we had enough momentum to avoid getting stuck in mud. We went up and down the bayou near the sighting area, then worked our way to the south near Interstate 40 and checked the wildlife management area, which had several lakes and a lot of hardwoods. It seemed like the kind of habitat Jim Tanner had described at the Singer Tract, at least in terms of the species composition of the trees in the forest, though they were much younger and smaller than the ones he had seen. We then drove north to the Black Swamp, almost getting mired in a treacherous muddy patch on the dirt road.

We finished our local scouting early, and we were eager to keep going and check other areas. I had been talking up the White River to Andy almost constantly. "That's the mother lode," I told him. "It has to be. It has more than 160,000 acres of bottomland forest. There's nothing like it left anywhere. That bird had to come from somewhere, and I'm betting it was there."

It didn't take much talking for us to convince each other that we had to go to White River. We headed south, trying to keep as close as possible to the swamp to see how good the forest was between Bayou de View and the area I was most interested in at White River. It was almost fifty miles from where Bobby and I had seen the bird to where Mary Scott and Bob Russell had had their encounters a year earlier, but the two areas were connected by a strip of swamp forest that was almost continuous. I knew Andy and I would have to take a whirlwind tour, but I was eager to explore the place again, and the weather was much better than the last time.

We went right to the refuge headquarters to see Richard Hines. He had told me earlier that the dirt road leading to the spot we wanted to go to had been washed out. I needed to find out whether it was passable yet.

"You won't be able to get your car across, but you can walk across it," he said. "You'll have to park your car at the levee, though, because we've got the gate locked." He told us that a flood surge was making its way down the Mississippi — "The pulse had reached Cairo, Illinois, by this morning" — and when it got to the refuge, the water would back up at the White River and flood the forest, making it impassible for who knew how long. I had noticed the last time I was there that many trees — even the oaks and other species that grew on higher ground — had tidemarks several feet up their trunks. This made me all the more eager to get out there as soon as possible.

Richard said he had to drive there anyway and would be glad

to open the gate and take us to where the road was washed out. When we left, though, we would have to walk the mile or two back to the gate to get to our car.

I ended up taking a backpack full of heavy camera equipment. It wasn't that I thought I would have an opportunity to photograph an ivory-bill — I just didn't want to leave my gear where it would be easy to steal. But this was not my biggest mistake — that was my choice of footwear. I was wearing a great pair of hiking boots that I had walked in for miles through rugged terrain in the Rocky Mountains and the Arctic. I almost left them on, but then I thought, *These are the only things I have to wear tomorrow when I fly back home. If I have to wade through muck and water where the road is washed out, well, these boots will not be fit for airline travel.* I had a knee-high pair of black wellies in the car that I could use to get through the mud. Okay, they were one or two sizes too big, and they slipped around on my feet as I walked. But we weren't walking that far, right?

Wrong. Andy was so excited when we got to the woods on the other side of the washout that he just took off. Although he is shorter than I am, he is amazingly fast on his feet. He still stopped from time to time to listen, but not for anywhere near as long as before, because we had such a small amount of time left to search that day. I had almost brought my hiking boots along, slung across my shoulder, so I could put them on after I got through the mud. I wish I had done that. Before I had gone half a mile, I knew I was getting blisters, even though it didn't hurt much at that point. A few years earlier, when I had been working on a whale research project, which involved camping five miles offshore on the pack ice, interviewing scientists, and photographing Inuit hunters as they attacked bowhead whales, I had frozen the bottoms of my feet. I didn't even realize it until I went back to a research station onshore and took a hot shower. I had no feeling in my soles. When I was barefoot, it felt like I was standing on a half-inch-thick piece of carpet padding. And it hadn't improved much since then. I could step on a sharp rock or other object and not feel it until it had done some deep damage to my foot. So I never walked around without shoes anymore, even indoors.

Of course, I would never think of telling a young guy like Andy that I was too much of a tenderfoot to go on — "I'll just wait here, sonny, and rest my feet until you get back." If anything, I walked faster and completely ignored my feet while the bottoms became completely blistered, the blisters popped, and my soles bled.

The forest was wonderful. Even the second-growth trees in much of this tract were big. I could just imagine what they would be like in another fifty or one hundred years. It already seemed like great habitat for an ivory-bill. It was full of woodpeckers, all eking out a healthy living. We didn't see or hear anything that looked like an ivory-bill, but Andy was clearly impressed with the place and eager to return later and do some more searching.

By the time we got back to the car, we had walked eight miles. My feet had been damaged to the point that I was no longer protected by the peripheral numbness. They hurt like hell. And I didn't want to look at them until I was in a motel and could soak them in a bathtub.

On the way back to Brinkley, I insisted that we stop at the St. Charles store for a catfish dinner. Unfortunately, it was not fish night, so I ordered a huge cheeseburger. Andy was fascinated with the place and all the men dressed in full-body camouflage, talking about hunting and fishing and farming. He kept looking around and saying, "This is awesome!" Before we left, he bought a camo baseball cap with "St. Charles, Arkansas" embroidered on the front.

The next day Andy and I returned to Memphis airport, he on his way to New York City, me on my way to Ithaca. More than two weeks had passed since Bobby and I had seen the ivory-bill, and no other searchers had spotted it yet. As I limped through the terminal with my feet bleeding into my socks, I thought to myself, *This is not going to be easy.*

13

WHERE SAPSUCKERS DARE

$\mathscr{I}$T WAS MID-MARCH, I was back in Ithaca, and the bird hadn't been seen for two and a half weeks. The clock was ticking. It seemed pretty clear that discreetly sending two or three people to Arkansas to find where the ivory-bill lives and document it with a camera was not going to work. We just didn't have enough information about this particular bird or birds — or, for that matter, about the entire species — to be able to figure out what was going on. Jim Tanner's research in the late 1930s was the only in-depth study of the ivory-billed woodpecker ever undertaken, and we had no way of knowing how much of what he had learned about the birds' natural history was directly applicable to the bird or birds at Bayou de View. The old Singer Tract contained thousands of acres of prime habitat for these birds, but Bayou de View is far from optimal and in many ways does not even resemble the habitat that Tanner said ivory-bills require. He estimated that ivory-billed woodpecker territories average about six square miles in size — enough space to accommodate thirty-six pileated woodpecker territories. But how does this translate in a linear setting like Bayou de View, which is less than a mile wide in some places? Would one pair's territory stretch for twelve miles along the bayou? Or could it be even longer? We had no way of knowing.

I tried to imagine how a bird of this size, a bird this specialized, could eke out a living at Bayou de View. Perhaps it had a regular foraging circuit, visiting various dead and dying beetle-infested trees that were miles apart. It might take days to complete such a circuit. If this was the case, what were the chances that a handful of searchers could catch a glimpse of the bird, much less take a picture or record its calls? It seemed a discouraging prospect.

We really needed to find the bird's roost hole to get decent photographs as it went in or out of the cavity. In my more hopeful moments, I imagined that there might be two birds and that one might even be incubating eggs in its nest cavity. The bird Gene Sparling had described had red on its head, so it was certainly a male. Bobby and I did not see any red on our bird. It's possible that the bird *did* have red on its crest and we just failed to see it, but red shows up well in decent light. And in the days that followed our sighting, we saw many pileated woodpeckers and always noticed the red on them. If our bird indeed lacked red, then it was certainly a female, which would indicate that the bayou might have at least one pair of ivory-bills. But no matter how I rolled this around in my mind, the nagging thought was always there: what if this was a lone bird — one solitary remnant of a dying race that somehow managed to hang on into the twenty-first century?

John Fitzpatrick wouldn't buy that. "The odds against your stumbling upon the last ivory-billed woodpecker are astronomical," he said. "It's much more likely that this bird is part of a population, however small. This bird had parents. Where are they? Where did it come from?"

Fitz had a topographic map of the Bayou de View drainage in the conference room beside his office. When I got back from Arkansas, he showed it to me and explained his theory. "Look at this," he said, pointing at the map. "Bayou de View is a finger, and here's the palm." He traced the bayou south to where it spread out into Dagmar Wildlife Management Area. "This must be where the bird came from."

I agreed that Dagmar had nice habitat. I had looked around it with Andy the week before. It had a large tupelo swamp plus many acres of bottomland hardwoods, although it was all second growth, and most of the trees were not large. Something that kept looming at the back of my mind, though, was that the real palm of the hand might be the White River National Wildlife Refuge, which dwarfed anything in the Bayou de View drainage. But for now, Bayou de View would have to be the focus of the search. After all, two ivory-bill sightings had taken place there in the space of a month. The question was, who should we send now?

The answer had to be the Sapsuckers — all of them are top birders and all are enthusiastic about finding rare birds. Despite Fitz's earlier worries that the secret would get out prematurely, the time had arrived to take advantage of their enormous skills as birders. Fitz sent an e-mail around, inviting the team members to have lunch with us in the Kingfisher Room, a large conference room on the Lab of Ornithology's second floor, overlooking Sapsucker Woods Pond.

The Sapsuckers are an interesting crew. Two of them, Ken Rosenberg and Kevin McGowan, have been on the team almost since it was formed. Fitz joined the team in the mid-1990s, soon after he became the lab's director. Steve Kelling and Jeff Wells have been Sapsuckers for about ten years.

Ken is a remarkable birder, particularly for someone with poor eyesight. He is a master of birding optics, which is why he usually writes the binocular and spotting scope reviews for *Living Bird*. For him, these products are absolutely essential tools, since he would be useless in the field without them. When I watch him carefully scan a mudflat, poring over the subtle markings on every shorebird, I am reminded of a microbiologist studying bacteria through a microscope. Ken is also a fabulous ear birder. I'll never forget one World Series of Birding when we were both on the team. Ken was driving the car at 70 miles per hour with his window cracked slightly when he suddenly slammed on the brakes and came skidding to a halt. He said he had heard a snatch of the song of a Blackburnian warbler. We all jumped out of the car and confirmed the bird, then added it to our big-day total.

In many ways, Kevin is the resident skeptic. He wants to see empirical evidence for everything. This may be because he was the curator of Cornell's bird collection for a long time and is used to dealing with evidence that you can see and touch, such as bird specimens. He is careful and precise, and if he says he saw something, there is no doubt that he did. Like Ken, he has less than perfect vision. He is obsessed with visual clarity to such an extent that he insists on using only real glass lenses in his eyeglasses, not plastic, despite the extra weight. He currently works on on-line projects such as eBird and AllAboutBirds for the Lab of Ornithology, and along with Ken he is a technical editor for *Living Bird*.

Steve Kelling is the techno-guru of the lab. He heads the information technologies group, which floats high above the rest of the lab in the third-floor mezzanine. Sometimes when he talks to me about his work or about certain supercomputing applications, I suddenly realize that I have no idea what he's talking about, as if he is speaking in a foreign language. So I always try to steer the conversation back to birds. Steve is also a superb birder. Three years ago, when he spotted a stray long-billed murrelet (an Asian species) at nearby Cayuga Lake, people from all over the country came to see it.

I first started noticing Jeff Wells around the lab several years ago, when he was still a Cornell graduate student. He seemed very serious at the time, almost scary in his intensity. Either he has mellowed since his hair turned gray or I just didn't know him well enough back then. He has a great sense of humor, and his subtle comments always make me laugh. Jeff is a career conservationist and until recently worked for the National Audubon Society, although he was based at the Lab of Ornithology. His powers of observation are phenomenal, especially as he stands at the edge of the woods listening to the song or call of a distant bird.

Kevin, Fitz, Steve, and Ken all went to the Pearl River in early 2002, along with Kurt Fristrup, to deploy or pick up the twelve ARUs the lab installed there, so they had already had a taste of searching in a swamp for ivory-bills. Like everyone else, they came up empty that time. And the only interesting sound recorded on the ARUs turned out not to be the double rap of an ivory-bill, as many had hoped, but a couple of distant gunshots.

Although these guys are good friends of mine, I was filled with dread when we sat down together in the conference room. Fitz and I were sure that they had some inkling of what was going on. We were completely wrong. They confessed later that they were convinced Fitz had brought them together to announce he was leaving the Sapsuckers and I would replace him. The World Series of Birding was coming up soon, and Fitz had seemed completely disengaged from it. Like me, he had become obsessed with the Arkansas ivory-bill, and he couldn't focus on the upcoming competition.

Fitz said I had something to tell them, and he let it go at that. Everyone looked at me as they started eating their sandwiches. I took a deep breath, exhaled, and then jumped right in, going through the whole story again for what seemed like the hundredth time — the backwoods kayaker in Arkansas and his remarkably credible sighting; my trip with Bobby down the bayou; our fly-by sighting. A few sentences into the story, no one was eating anymore. By the time I finished, the men were sitting in stunned silence. Ken finally stood up. "Can I shake your hand?" he asked. Then everyone smiled broadly. They each shook my hand and congratulated me on the sighting. The room was electric with excitement. The question was not if but when they could go to the bayou. The prospect of seeing an ivory-bill was so far beyond anyone's wildest dream, they wanted to leave for Arkansas immediately.

The original plan had been to split up the group so a couple would go right away, a couple the next week, to spread out the coverage. But the season was progressing fast in Arkansas, and the trees were starting to leaf out, which would greatly reduce visibility. Fitz decided to send the whole team as soon as possible for a one-week blitz. Kevin was so enthusiastic that he volunteered to stay for two weeks and take along his son, Jay, who was also an excellent birder.

It still amazes me how quickly the Sapsuckers got ready and headed south. The meeting took place on Tuesday. By Saturday they were on the ground at Bayou de View with all their gear. I had to postpone my plans to go with them, because my youngest daughter had come down with pneumonia for the second time in six weeks, and my wife and I were worried about her.

After taking their various flights to Memphis, the group (except for Fitz) converged at a motel in Brinkley, Arkansas, not far from the bayou. Eric Spaulding, of the lab's Bioacoustics Research Program, also arrived; he had come to install the first of the ARUs in Bayou de View. Although they did not have any canoes yet, they were all too antsy to sit around in the motel, so they drove to the Highway 17 bridge and began checking out the area. Kevin and Jay headed north on foot, trying to skirt the edge of the bayou on dry land. Jeff and Ken tried the same thing to the south, while Steve and Eric stood on the bridge, hoping for a lucky flyover. It didn't happen. And trying to slog along the periphery of the swamp proved impossible.

Fitz arrived later that afternoon, and everyone traveled south to Clarendon for a meeting with the Arkansas chapter of the Nature Conservancy to discuss plans and logistics. Jeff had worked out a preliminary scheme for surveying the bayou, which involved establishing a grid of survey blocks measuring two hundred meters by two hundred meters around the sighting area, assigning two-person teams to a designated area in the grid for twelve hours a day, and having each team carry out counts of all bird species present, starting a new count every half-hour. Jeff reasoned that this would force people to move slowly and, as he wrote in an e-mail, "maintain focus on deep listening and paying attention to everything.

"After covering the projected home range around the sighting location, I suggest we move the same methodology to survey areas immediately north and south," wrote Jeff. "This would effectively and systematically saturate a twenty-four-kilometer stretch of the corridor."

This all sounded great, but the swamp has a way of scuttling the best-laid plans of scientists and other seekers of lost species. It is a place of infinite hardship to those who don't know it well, with vast expanses of flooded forest that all look the same; partially submerged roots, branches, and cypress knees waiting to flip you from your canoe; confusing meanders in the bayou that constantly send you to dead ends; huge areas where the water is too low to float a canoe and too deep to walk through easily; boot-sucking muck and mire; and huge trees that block satellite reception, making it difficult or impossible to take GPS readings. And I haven't even begun to talk about poisonous snakes. How would the Sapsuckers cope with these challenges? They would soon find out. That night the Nature Conservancy lent them some canoes and a Jeep to haul them. The next day they hit the swamp.

The group rendezvoused at the bridge early, put the canoes in the water, and clambered aboard. Some were better canoeists than others, but they were all eager to penetrate the depths of the swamp. A flotilla of Sapsuckers headed south, led by Gene and Bobby. A short time later, they stopped and sat in awe at the place where the ivory-bill had flown across the bayou less than a month earlier.

Jeff, Steve, Ken, Kevin, and Jay established a transect soon after, spreading out and stationing themselves at points a couple of hundred yards apart across the bayou — setting up a kind of human mist net the bird would have to go through if it flew up or down that section of Bayou de View (a mist net is a gossamer-fine, almost invisible net that researchers use to trap birds when they band them). Meanwhile, Fitz and Eric were installing ARUs both north and south of the sighting area. Bobby and Gene had gone off exploring. The Sapsuckers sat and waited. And waited. And waited.

As planned, every thirty minutes they started a new count of the bird species they saw or heard, but they rarely moved. They had quickly discovered that Jeff's grid system was impossible to implement, at least in the way he had planned. Going from place to place on foot was horrendous and sometimes involved trying to move through hip-deep mud, hoisting themselves along by brute force, grasping at any solid anchor — a tree trunk, a stout limb — to haul their bodies forward. And it was too noisy. Sitting still and silently seemed to be the best plan. Each person was dropped off by canoe at a stump or a log and left to sit and watch and listen.

An hour passed. Then another hour. And another. And another. And these were not quick hours. It's amazing how slowly time can pass when you're deep in the swamp. It's a fluid kind of place; all of your visual references are gone. Most of the time you can't even tell the position of the sun in the sky, so your sole clue to the passage of time is your watch. The only way to cope is to give in to it. Camping out in the swamp with Gene and Bobby had made it easier for me than it would have been if I had spent every night in a motel. I got into the rhythm of the place. There's something about hearing the slap of a beaver's tail, the snort of a deer, or the call of a great horned owl or a barred owl from the tree above your tent. The swamp no longer seems alien; you feel like part of it.

For the Sapsuckers the waiting was interminable, and they saw nothing noteworthy. By the time they returned to the bridge and hauled out their canoes, the giddy exhilaration, the heady optimism, and the confidence that finding the ivory-bill would be a slam-dunk were long gone.

On Tuesday, Jay heard what sounded like three different double raps as he sat on a log — first in the distance; then, a few minutes later, much closer; and finally very near. But he never saw a bird. Was it an ivory-bill, some other bird, or just the wind making branches strike together in the treetops? He didn't know. Jay also caught a glimpse of a large dark bird flying away, and it appeared to have white on its wings. But was the white in the right places for an ivory-bill? He couldn't say. Steve saw a bird fly into a tree near where he was sitting, and it apparently disappeared into a hollow. As he suspected, it later turned out to be a wood duck.

Eric Spaulding flew home on Wednesday, but Andy Farnsworth had arrived the night before to step into the breach. The Sapsuckers got their second wind. Through sheer strength of will, they dug in their heels and forced themselves to keep going enthusiastically. I had experienced this kind of thing before, during the World Series of Birding. There is always a point in the late afternoon when you're physically and emotionally exhausted, depressed, and demoralized. I call it the big-day blues. And then you rally and push on strongly all the way to the end of the day, at midnight. Of course, the Sapsuckers were facing a whole new level of hardship. This was not just a twenty-four-hour birding marathon but day after day of the toughest physical and mental exertion imaginable, with few payoffs.

Steve Kelling became the most determined swamp rat, slogging farther and farther on foot into areas inaccessible by canoe. Fitz had been scheduled to fly back but changed his ticket so he could stay in the swamp with his teammates. He joined the human mist net, and together they began a long swamp sit. They were still there ten hours later, but no one was complaining.

Late in the day, Fitz made an interesting discovery. While gazing at the topmost section of an enormous old cypress, he noticed that many of the branches had been stripped of bark, revealing beetle tracks grooved in the exposed wood. Was this the work of an ivory-bill? No one could say without actually seeing the bird debarking the tree, but it was the most interesting piece of physical evidence they had found. And it was close to where Gene had made his original sighting. (Although Gene had never been able to pinpoint the exact tree where he saw the bird, he had always described it as being in this area.) Since that day, this cypress has been known as the Fitz Tree.

The next day the plans changed again. Everything was fluid. No one had any fixed notions of how to proceed with the search. It was seat-of-the-pants science. People spread north, setting up several parallel two-person lines. Ken and Jeff went the farthest upstream and stationed themselves in some areas that Bobby and I had thought were promising on our initial float down the bayou.

By Friday morning the Sapsucker saga was nearly over. Fitz had already left for home, and Ken was on his way to Memphis to catch a plane. Later in the day, Andy, Steve, and Jeff would also depart, leaving only Kevin and Jay representing the New York contingent. But not for long: during dinner, Kevin got a call from Bill Evans, another Ithaca bird researcher, saying that he was flying from Ithaca to Houston on other business but planned to drive to Bayou de View to help with the search for a few days. Fitz had called him up and invited him to join the effort. He would arrive sometime late Saturday night.

Bill Evans is one of those borderline geniuses you tend to run across in birding. He is tall, in his mid-forties, with thick gray hair and a boyish face. I have known him for several years and have always been fascinated by his research, which he initiated and has largely funded himself for about a decade and a half. It started one spring night when he was an undergraduate at the University of Minnesota. Back then, he always camped out during spring and fall migrations so he could watch all the newly arrived birds that flew through the area. He wanted to be in the field at dawn so he could experience the migration firsthand as it was happening, not just on weekend birding trips. On this night he was camping on a bluff beside the St. Croix River and had just finished a shift delivering pizza. It was a balmy evening, and he lay awake for hours, listening to the sounds of the night — especially the calls of migrating birds flying high overhead. Sometimes he would pick out one that sounded familiar. A black-billed cuckoo? It sure sounded like one. And then he heard another and another. Although black-billed cuckoos are not rare, they are secretive and hard to find by day. And yet now he was hearing dozens of them. He started counting them and in less than an hour had tallied more than one hundred.

Bill had an epiphany that night as he pondered what could be accomplished from a conservation standpoint if the various flight calls of birds could be identified and catalogued. Perhaps an automated bird-census system could be developed — one that could count the numbers of birds of each species flying over at night during migration. "At that moment I saw the rest of my life unfold before me," he told me a few years ago. "I envisioned recording these nocturnal flight calls and using them to document bird populations for conservation. I literally saw all the key components on that one night. It just overwhelmed me."

Of course, figuring out the concept was just the initial step. The flight calls would have to be identified; many of them differ significantly from the daytime songs and calls of the particular species. And many of them are just single notes, less than a second in duration. For more than a decade, Bill traveled extensively, setting up sound-recording equipment where he knew certain species would be passing over so he could identify and tape their flight calls. He amassed a huge collection of calls, and the lab's Bioacoustics Research Program developed a pattern-recognition software program that automatically identifies many of them. Andy Farnsworth has since picked up the torch and as a Cornell Ph.D. student is studying the nocturnal flight calls of migrating birds, looking at the function of the calls and flight-calling behavior.

I too headed to Arkansas late that week, after my daughter recovered. But I didn't go right to Bayou de View. I decided instead to visit White River again with Bobby. A couple of days earlier, he had called me to complain about the Sapsuckers. He seemed to resent it that his swamp had been invaded by these aliens — these damn Yankees. "You should see these guys," he said. "They say they want to keep this thing secret, then they come down here carrying thousands of dollars' worth of optics, wearing Cornell Lab of Ornithology hats, and pointing at every bird they see and calling out its name. They fit in down here about as well as a landing party from Mars."

And things sounded just as bad from the Sapsucker side. I think a lot of it was a clash of cultures. Northerners seem to feel a visceral repugnance for a southern accent. Southerners can't stand stuck-up Yankees. And I was caught in the middle. I live in the Northeast, I work for Cornell, and I'm a former Sapsucker. But at the same time, I sincerely like Bobby.

By this time, visiting Arkansas felt like going home, especially when Bobby and I went to the community store in St. Charles for an early morning breakfast. There's no latte or cappuccino within a hundred miles of that place, but the coffee was fresh and the bacon and eggs set me straight for hours. And I felt good. My feet had largely healed from my long walk in the too-large rubber boots the last time I explored White River, the floodwaters had receded, the washed-out road had been repaired, and the sun was shining. What could be better?

Bobby was having mechanical troubles with his van, so he borrowed his wife's Jimmy, which handled much better than the old Safari. We parked, hauled the canoes and all our gear to the edge of the bayou, and pushed off as soon as everything was ready. It was good to be out in the swamp again. Bobby had borrowed a canoe for me from his neighbor, so we no longer had to squeeze all our equipment into one canoe—which was good, because Bobby's canoe was small. Unfortunately, mine was even smaller, and tippier. We were so eager to get away from the dirt road, into the real backwoods area, that we raced down the bayou, paddling as fast and hard as we could. Amazingly, Bobby started pulling away, leaving me in his wake. As I mentioned, he had gotten a lot better at canoeing between our first trip down Bayou de View and the second time I saw him there, but this was ridiculous. He looked like someone from the canoe Olympics, pulling so hard on his paddle that the hull seemed to plane on top of the water like a speedboat. And I was paddling with all my might.

I finally caught up with him when we reached a long stretch of shallow, murky, plant-laden water that was almost impassable. My little canoe sat somewhat higher in the water and had less weight than his, so it moved through this morass with slightly less difficulty than his. But it was a tough slog. If I hadn't wanted so badly to see what it was like on the other side of this rough stretch, I would have given up right away. But with each foot or two we advanced forward, we were farther and farther past the point of no return. When we finally broke through to the other side, back into open water, we were exhausted. We pulled over to some dry land for a quick lunch of tuna and crackers, followed by Snickers bars. As usual, Bobby washed his food down with a sixteen-ounce Mountain Dew. After all the paddling he had been doing lately, he could eat and drink whatever he liked with impunity.

As we sat there, we spotted a big cottonmouth lurking just offshore. It seemed to raise its head slightly and glower at us. It was not the last we would see. This late March morning the snakes came out in full force. They were everywhere — swimming in the water, lurking in the cypress knees, hanging in the low branches near the water — so we spent as much time watching out for them as we did looking for woodpeckers. We took a long hike into the woods, hoping to stumble across an ivory-bill. Instead we stumbled across more snakes. In a small stand of old-growth hardwoods, I asked Bobby to stand in front of a big oak while I took a picture to show the size comparison between a portly man and an even portlier tree. He almost stepped on a six-foot-long snake draped across the roots. He jumped into the air for a second in horror. It was only a rat snake. *Phew.*

We took off cross-country. At one point we could hear a large woodpecker working slowly on a tree, making low, deep thuds with its bill. As we made our way toward it, a large dark shape flew off through the treetops in the direction of the sun. But these

are the kinds of sightings that are worthless, barely worth men-
tioning. We heard no *kent* calls or distinct double raps on our slog
across the higher ground. But the habitat was beautiful, with
larger trees than we had seen anywhere, though the big trees certainly were not wall-to-wall. They tended to stand somewhat isolated from other trees their size, with many smaller trees around
them. We saw nothing at all that resembled the huge cathedral
stands in the giant redwoods.

Bobby and I spent all that day and the next exploring the Sugarberry Natural Area, the only significant tract of old-growth
hardwoods in the White River refuge. Scrubgrass Bayou meanders around Sugarberry, forming a sausage-shaped piece of land
almost a mile wide and about two and a half miles long. Connected to the surrounding woodlands by only a tiny strip of land
at its southwest corner, Sugarberry is practically an island. Apparently the loggers didn't get around to cutting it when the surrounding timber was felled. We walked through some promising-
looking areas, taking GPS readings at trees with woodpecker
workings or cavities. This was some of the best habitat we had
seen in all of our travels through the South.

On Saturday afternoon we canoed back to the Jimmy and loaded
up our canoes and gear. I couldn't get a cell-phone signal the entire time we were at the White River, so I hadn't been able to
check in with the Sapsuckers and see how they were doing. By
the time we had driven a few miles back down the levee, I was
able to make a call. I tried the motel where everyone was staying.
The person at the front desk told me that most of the people had
checked out the day before. Kevin and his son were the only ones
still there. No one answered when I was put through to their
room, so I left a message. Then I tried calling Kevin's cell-phone
number, but I had no luck there either.

Bobby and I checked in at the motel in Brinkley so we could
wash off the accumulated swamp sludge and change our clothes.
It was close to dinnertime, and we were both starving. We tried
calling Kevin one more time without success and then decided to

go to his room and see if anyone was around. The door opened slightly and Jay peered out at us. He seemed shell-shocked after his eight-day vigil in the swamp. Kevin didn't look any better. He seemed tense, edgy, like someone who had been lost in the wilderness for weeks. I suggested that we go to the local Mexican restaurant and load up on burritos and dark beer. I think we all needed a good relaxing meal prepared by someone else. I know I had had enough packaged beef stew, jerky, and tuna with crackers to last a lifetime.

Lauren Morgens had just arrived from New York to help with the search effort, so we invited her to go with us. Lauren, a slender woman with long dark hair and brown eyes, is in her early twenties and loves a good adventure. A veteran tall-ship crew member, she has sailed around Cape Horn, through the treacherous seas off the tip of South America. She was eager to start exploring the swamp the next morning. It was good to talk with someone so young and enthusiastic — someone not yet exhausted from days of slogging through the trackless swamp.

Bill Evans was due to arrive soon, but by the time we had finished eating our food, drinking our beers, and talking excitedly about ivory-billed woodpeckers, he was still a couple of hours away. Bobby and I decided to turn in early. We felt a little wimpy about sleeping in a motel. To make up for it, we planned to be back out on the bayou before dawn. We would have to check out of our room by 4 A.M.

We pushed off our canoes well before the first rays of sun began lightening the eastern sky, and we drifted southward, letting the current do most of the work. Floating down a bayou in the dark is a remarkable experience. If you have an overactive imagination, you might sense all kinds of strange monsters taking shape in the darkness, moving furtively just outside the bounds of your vision. The transition into morning was stunning, with the light glistening through the branches, dazzling our eyes. The swamp was beautiful. Even the coffee-brown water looked good.

· · ·

This was my last day on the bayou for this trip. I had to go back to Ithaca for a week or so to catch up on my work with *Living Bird*. Late that evening I would be flying into Rochester again and then making the long drive home.

Kevin McGowan's stay at Bayou de View would also soon be coming to an end, but before he left, he had one more thing he wanted to try — flying in a helicopter over the bayou, searching for more trees with woodpecker workings. Gene had already found another huge cypress with stripped bark on its topmost branches, like the Fitz Tree. They might be able to spot more of them from an aerial vantage point. They could also scout for areas of good habitat that we could check thoroughly on the ground later. Perhaps they might even catch a glimpse of an ivory-bill flying though the swamp.

Kevin had made arrangements to go out early on Wednesday morning. He would ride in the front passenger seat beside the pilot; Bill Evans and Gene would ride in back. But before they left, they stopped at a restaurant in Brinkley for breakfast. Gene in particular had a large appetite and filled up on extra helpings of fried potatoes. A short time later, as they walked to the helicopter, he said, "This'll be great, even if I get sick." Famous last words.

Before they had been airborne for ten minutes it started. First Gene turned noticeably green and leaned his head against the window. He held one hand hard against his mouth and started reaching for a bag with the other. And then he exploded, vomiting again and again and again.

"It was amazing," said Bill. "You wouldn't think someone could throw up that much." But Bill spoke with admiration about how Gene never stopped searching the treetops during the flight. "Most people would be worthless if they got that sick," he said.

Gene kept pointing at peeled branches as the helicopter reeled sideways high over the treetops, trying to give the passengers a better view. "Look at that cypress tree down there," Gene would say. "It's got [*glorph* . . . gasp . . . *arrrgh*] bark stripping on those top [*ooph*] limbs." This went on for most of the two-hour flight.

Long after every trace of food Gene had eaten for the past few days was gone, he still convulsed and groaned. And the overpowering stench of vomit in the helicopter made everyone nauseated.

As soon as the helicopter landed, Gene felt better — everyone felt better. And the overflight had been productive. They found three more trees with visible bark stripping on the higher branches — one near the Fitz Tree and two farther south, in the Dagmar Wildlife Management Area. The next day, while canoeing near one of the newly found bark-stripped trees, Lauren and Kevin heard a distinct double rap. Both of them had heard other *Campephilus* woodpeckers make this signal — Lauren in Costa Rica, Kevin in Peru — and it sounded perfect. But though they waited there a long time, they didn't hear it again.

That double rap was the most promising clue Kevin experienced in his entire two-week stay in Bayou de View. On Saturday afternoon, he and Jay caught a plane in Memphis and returned home. So the last Sapsucker had departed. It was April 3, 2004 — thirty-six days after Bobby and I had seen the ivory-bill — and we still had no evidence that this elusive bird inhabited Bayou de View. Had the ghost bird vanished yet again?

14

TRYING TO PROVE THE EXISTENCE OF A GHOST

*E*VEN BEFORE KEVIN AND JAY left Bayou de View, the next wave of searchers from the Cornell Lab of Ornithology were headed south: Ron Rohrbaugh, David Bonter, Tina Phillips, and Mindy LaBranche of the citizen science program; Elliott Swarthout and Melanie Driscoll of bird population studies; Sara Barker Swarthout of conservation science; Martha Fischer, David Brown, Mike Andersen, and Jim Goetz of the Macaulay Library; and Jeff Gerbracht of the IT group. Eric Spaulding had returned to install more ARUs. Searching for the ivory-bill was quickly becoming a lab-wide project.

John Fitzpatrick's older brother Jim was driving down from Minnesota to join the search and was bringing his own canoe. And the cinematographer Tim Barksdale would soon be driving from his home in Montana, hoping to capture the ivory-bill's image with a high-definition television camera. Excitement was building by the day.

The new arrivals were an interesting mix of people. Ron Rohrbaugh, the director of Citizen Science, had grown up in a small town in rural Pennsylvania and spent his entire life in the woods, hunting, fishing, and birding. He got along well with the Arkansas crowd — both the searchers and the local people he met in the woods. As a bow-hunter, he was used to dressing in camouflage and moving through the woods silently, nearly invisibly — vital assets to an ivory-bill seeker. Ron is in his late thirties and has brown hair that parts naturally in the center and a thick beard. He is friendly and outgoing, and people trust him instantly.

On one of his first days in the field, Ron explored the dirt roads that ran through the agricultural areas bordering the bayou, looking for new access points to the swamp. He approached everyone he encountered and struck up a conversation. When he spotted a man driving a tractor in an area he was particularly interested in, he smiled and said, "Say, bud, do you know who I should see to get permission to park over there next to the bayou?" The man stared at him in amazement. "How did you know my name is Bud?" he asked. It turned out that Bud owned the property and was happy to give permission for this young psychic to park in his field.

Elliott Swarthout works on the lab's House Finch Disease project, tracking the spread of an infectious eye disease that has been devastating house finch populations across the East during the last few years and is now spreading westward. Like Ron, he is a longtime bow-hunter. The two of them brought a multitude of useful field skills to the group, plus one great advantage — these guys do more than just tolerate sitting motionless in the woods for hours at a time; they actually enjoy it. Elliott came with his wife, Sara, the project leader of the lab's ongoing Birds in Forested Landscapes project. A tall, thin strawberry blonde with freckles, Sara is an intense cyclist who rides miles every day in all kinds of weather. She and Elliott spent their six-month anniversary together in the swamp.

All of the searchers in this group were good canoeists and all-around outdoor types — the kind of people who spend most of their vacations camping in the wilderness. They added an extra element to the search: they all love the swamp and enjoy being there.

The first interesting sighting by the new arrivals took place on Saturday, April 3 — the same day Kevin and Jay flew home. Martha Fischer and Jeff Gerbracht were canoeing in Dagmar Wildlife Management Area, about three miles south of the primary search area, when they briefly played a recording of an ivory-billed woodpecker from the 1935 Cornell expedition. A few seconds later, a large dark bird flew past about a hundred yards from them. Martha thought it looked like a woodpecker, but she couldn't tell whether there was any white on its wings. Jeff thought it looked significantly larger than a pileated, and he said that he *did* see white on the bird's wings as it flew away from them. Because of the discrepancy in their reports, the sighting was inconclusive. The one that occurred two days later was not.

Monday, April 5, 2004: Despite the bright sunshine, it was chilly on the bayou that morning. Jim Fitzpatrick had ferried David Brown with his huge high-definition television camera, dropping him off at Stab Lake in Dagmar. David planned to stay there all day, hoping to shoot a high-quality video of anything that flew past his hiding place. Jim continued south in his canoe, passing through tiny Pawpaw Lake a short time later. He was trying to float slowly and quietly with the current, hoping to explore some areas he hadn't checked thoroughly yet. But each of the channels he tried to go down petered out; the water was too shallow to float his canoe. The water level on the entire bayou had dropped significantly in the previous few days, making it difficult to canoe to places that had been easy to reach earlier. He finally decided to return to Pawpaw Lake to take a break and eat his sandwich. It was about 10:15, and he had worked up an appetite from all his paddling.

Jim is in his fifties, with a bushy mustache and a gruff voice. A Vietnam War veteran, he has a high capacity for enduring hardship and adversity. He is also a powerhouse of a canoeist. I had met him several years earlier at an annual meeting of the Raptor

Research Foundation, a group he has served as treasurer for a long time. He is a lifelong duck hunter, and according to Fitz, Jim is better at identifying waterfowl than he is.

Jim stopped near a large fallen tree on the east shore and backed his canoe into some cypress knees. He was fumbling around in his daypack when he happened to take a look north up the lake. At that instant a large bird appeared, coming right at him, flying above the trees. "I just thought to myself, that's a really big pileated," he said. A few seconds later the bird turned slightly westward and started flying down the opposite shore, still about thirty feet above the treetops, giving Jim an excellent view of its profile. He watched it veer slightly farther west to get around a huge cypress.

"When it cleared the tree, I finally realized that the wing pattern was all wrong for a pileated," he said. "I was seeing white on the downbeat as well as on the upbeat — and not that little star shape like a pileated; it was a full-blown patch of white." And the bird didn't fly like a pileated woodpecker. "There was no undulation in its flight," he said. "It was flapping briskly and strongly, like a loon. The flight seemed exquisitely efficient. He didn't waste a lot of body movement. He just cooked right along. That's when I realized, holy shit! That's not a pileated!"

Jim knows the pileated woodpecker well. "I've been a bird bander for thirty-some years," he explained. "I've held them in my hand; I've banded them. I know their relative size and their wing shape. That bird was just not a pileated.

"At that point I finally lost it," Jim continued. "*Shit! What do I do now?* I was there by myself. I started paddling hard, and then I stopped." For a few seconds he was bewildered. *Should I stay here? Should I go? Should I stay here? Should I go?* He tried calling Ron on his cell phone but got his voice mail. He finally stopped and tried to breathe slowly. After taking a GPS reading, he scribbled down some notes about what he had seen, recording the time and his position, and drew a sketch of the bird.

Jim said he was 98.5 percent sure that the bird was an ivory-bill. His attitude was, *I just saw a bird I've never seen before. If it wasn't an ivory-bill, please tell me what it was; I'd like to know.*

Tuesday, April 6, 2004: Ron and David were hiding on the edge of Pawpaw Lake, about two thirds of the way down its eastern shore. They had the big camcorder aimed at the treetops on the opposite side of the lake, so that if the bird tried a fly-by like the one Jim had seen the day before, they would nail it on videotape.

It had been a pleasant morning with a phenomenal amount of woodpecker activity. The woods resounded with their calls and their drumming — red-bellieds, pileateds, downies, and more. It was just past noon and nothing had happened yet. Suddenly they spotted a large black-and-white bird slipping through the woods on the opposite side of the lake, maybe seven or eight feet high. David tried to swing his camcorder around, but it was already too late: the bird had landed on a big dead tree and quickly hitched around to the other side. According to Ron, the bird's color pattern was similar to that of a red-headed woodpecker — the upper part of its back was black, the lower part white — but it was huge, larger than a crow. "I remember the black-and-white color pattern flashing as it flew," he said.

The two men froze. They were familiar with the old snag the bird had ducked behind, which had several large woodpecker holes. Could this actually be the bird's roost tree? They decided to sit and wait with the camcorder aimed directly at the big snag. When Elliott and Mindy paddled up three hours later, they were still waiting. At this point they finally approached the tree, but they found nothing. The bird had apparently slipped away unseen.

Bobby and I were on Bayou de View the morning after Ron and David's sighting and planned to spend that day and part of the next there before returning to White River. It was tough making our way through the low water. We frequently had to climb out of our canoes and drag them through the sludge, and we often sank deep in our waders. The bottom of my coat was caked with mud from the times I sank up to my hips. And snakes were everywhere.

Cottonmouths are famous for climbing into people's boats and canoes, so we had to watch carefully for snakes lurking on low branches or floating up to us on the water. I remember looking ahead in the shallow water and seeing a snake move, which chilled me for a second. It turned out to be a harmless water snake. A few minutes later Bobby dug his paddle deep into the sludge we were pushing through, and a huge triangular head reared up — it was just a submerged tree branch he had hooked on his paddle. Half an hour later I saw another floating branch and paddled calmly past it; this one turned out to be an enormous cottonmouth. And so it went.

When we got to Pawpaw Lake, Tim Barksdale was set up with his video heavy artillery. His canoe was tucked in the same place Jim Fitzpatrick had sat just a few days earlier. His high-definition television camera stood on a bulky tripod in front of him, ready to sweep the tops of the trees if another large black-and-white bird tried to sneak past.

I like to think of Tim as a banker gone feral. Several years ago he worked as an executive at a bank in Missouri, sitting in an office each day dressed in a three-piece suit. And he had been successful. But then he threw it all away to become an itinerant cinematographer, traveling to faraway places from the high Arctic to the tropics to photograph wildlife. He looks tough. In his mid-fifties and balding, he has long gray hair pulled back in a ponytail and a huge bushy beard. He is now an associate of the Lab of Ornithology, and his video collection is housed at the Macaulay Library. Fitz had invited him to Arkansas to document the bird, and he was determined to spend as many months as necessary there to make it happen.

We pulled our canoes up beside his and sat talking quietly about the recent sightings. I told him we planned to go to the White River in a day or so to continue our explorations there. We were especially interested in some areas that have large numbers of beaver-killed trees, which Richard Hines had told us about. Richard said that beavers were a major problem there and no matter how many were trapped, it didn't seem to put a dent in their population. Bobby and I had both perked up when we heard that. The beavers were girdling all these trees and killing them, providing habitat for wood-boring beetles and their larvae — an ideal food for ivory-bills. What if the beavers were responsible for the survival of a small population of ivory-bills there? It seemed feasible. We wanted to examine some of these trees, determine how long they had been dead, and see if they had any signs of bark stripping. We had already seen bark stripping in other parts of the White River refuge. It was all very intriguing. Tim was interested and said that he and Jim Goetz, who was assisting him, might also soon visit White River.

As we sat side by side in our canoes, the wind kept trying to catch us and make us drift away from Tim's canoe, which was jammed securely into the cypress knees. Bobby grasped the gunwale of Tim's canoe and put his foot into my canoe to keep all three together. Suddenly a floating snake reared up and opened its mouth right under his leg. "Cottonmouth!" Bobby almost fell backwards out of his canoe as he pulled his leg out of the way. The snake must have been hiding in the cypress knees the entire time we were there.

A day and a half later, we drove into the lower section of the White River refuge again, but this time we bypassed the Sugarberry Natural Area to look for some of the beaver-killed trees Richard had mentioned. When we finally parked, we didn't unload the canoes or even put waders on. The area was mostly dry and brushy. We took off on foot, making our way through thick underbrush and thorns in places. After a couple of hours of hiking, we caught a glimpse of an interesting bird. We didn't get a good enough look to have any idea whether it was an ivory-bill, but we definitely wanted to see it again. A deep slough lay between us and where the bird had flown. Luckily, just a hundred yards away a fallen tree spanned the water, creating a convenient bridge. We made our way carefully across it, winding around all the dead branches sticking up this way and that from its horizontal trunk. When we got to the other side, we jumped down and headed off in different directions to look for the bird.

A short time later I made my way back to the fallen tree, just in time to hear the deep pounding of a large woodpecker back across the slough. The bird was not drumming as a signal; it seemed to be working very slowly and deliberately to get at the grubs in the wood. I pulled myself up onto the log and started racing across it, going faster than I should have. Halfway across, a branch I stepped on broke cleanly, and I went down hard on my left knee. The broken-off stub of the branch was sticking up like a sharp knife, and it cut deeply into the side of my knee. Blood gushed out instantly and spread in a quickly widening circle, already as big as a baseball, on my pant leg. I pulled my jeans down and held my hand hard against the wound for several minutes. Eventually the bleeding slowed to an oozing trickle and then stopped. I must have been a sight, sitting on a big log across the slough, covered in blood, with my pants pulled down around my ankles.

I didn't know where Bobby was. I figured I would clean myself up as well as I could and try to get back to the car. I had some extra-large Band-Aids in my backpack, plus a couple of pocket-sized Kleenex packages and a canteen full of water. I sat there for maybe half an hour, carefully cleaning the blood away from the wound with tissues and drying it so the Band-Aids would stick. Then I taped it all up, wrapped a bandage around it, and pulled up my jeans — all while sitting on top of a horizontal tree trunk with branches sticking out every which way. I finished off by swallowing a few ibuprofen tablets and then stood up, as good as new. Well, almost. I had to hop on one foot, clinging gingerly to the limbs the rest of the way across, and then ease myself to the ground. I picked up a limb for a walking stick, took a compass reading, and headed back through the brush in the general direction of the car.

Later that afternoon I popped out onto the dirt road about a hundred yards north of our car. I was beat, and my knee was throbbing. Bobby was still looking around in the woods somewhere. I limped to the car and sat down in the shade. Bobby showed up a short time later.

"What happened to you?" he asked, looking at my blood-soaked jeans.

"You wouldn't believe it," I said.

Under any other conditions, I'm sure I would have gone to a doctor and gotten stitches and a tetanus shot. But the amount of trouble that would have entailed would have put an instant end to the trip. Just getting back to a reasonable-sized town and finding a doctor would have taken hours. And I still wanted to look for ivory-bills. I took some more ibuprofen, and we went to check a few more places. That night in camp I boiled some water in a pan — bottled drinking water, not swamp water — and cleaned the wound more thoroughly and dressed it again.

Because it was hard for me to walk quickly and cover long distances with my injured leg, we decided to canoe to Sugarberry the next morning to look around some more. We would have to check the beaver-killed trees some other time. The weather had turned bad in the night. It was drizzling as we paddled down Scrubgrass Bayou and finally put in on the other shore about a mile and a half farther on. We took off hiking toward an interesting stand of trees we had visited earlier, hoping the rain would ease soon. It didn't; it just rained harder. We finally stopped under a big tree to get some shelter, but it was useless. We stood there getting wetter and wetter, the rain dribbling down our backs, soaking us to the skin.

After more than an hour, we had both had it. We hiked back to the canoes as fast as we could and paddled back to camp. Bobby was a maniac, racing along twice as fast as I could go. I was a little off balance with my left leg stuck out straight as a board in front of me in the canoe. Eventually I reached the place where he had hauled his canoe from the water. He had already taken most of his gear up the bank to the car. He came down and helped me with my canoe. We were soaked and freezing as we drove to Brinkley. My teeth chattered all the way there.

The bad weather we had been in didn't reach all the way north to Bayou de View. It had drizzled some there that morning but cleared by noon. We decided to spring for a motel so I could give my injured leg a long soak in a tub and we could get a good night's sleep and a decent meal cooked by someone else. A short time later, we ran into Ron. There had been another sighting that day on Bayou de View.

Saturday, April 10, 2004: Mindy LaBranche considered herself the least likely of the searchers to see an ivory-bill. One of the main reasons was her skepticism. Down deep, no matter how much she tried to keep an open mind, she just couldn't bring herself to believe that this species still existed. Sure, she was willing to come and spend time in the swamp and work on an interesting project, but really—an ivory-billed woodpecker? You might as well be looking for a passenger pigeon.

When it comes to woodpeckers, Mindy is no slouch. She has far more experience than any of us with rare woodpeckers. She spent eight years at North Carolina State University, earning both a master's degree and a Ph.D. studying the endangered red-cockaded woodpecker. Now in her forties, she heads the Urban Bird Studies Program at the Lab of Ornithology. She has long, curly gray hair, usually worn in a ponytail, and wears wire-rimmed glasses. A no-nonsense person, she is mature enough not to be caught up in some kind of group hysteria, so what happened that day is particularly interesting.

Mindy was stationed about midway down Pawpaw Lake on the eastern shore—about the same place where Jim, Ron, and David had been when they had had their sightings. It had been drizzling lightly most of the morning, so she put her camcorder into its case to protect it. Shortly past noon the rain stopped, but it was still dreary and overcast. She was gazing toward the south when she spotted a large black-and-white bird flying from west to east above the forest canopy at the southern edge of the lake. *It's a big pileated woodpecker,* she thought to herself. She lifted her binoculars to her eyes for a closer look. The bird seemed different somehow, though that knowledge dawned on her slowly.

"I kept seeing the top of the wing and the white trailing edge of the wing," she said. And she thought, *I don't remember seeing white on the top of a pileated woodpecker's wings. And this isn't flying like a pileated. The wings aren't the right shape, and the stroke is too strong. And it's too big.* "But I still didn't know what it was," she said. "I kept seeing white. When it came up, I could see white under the wing on the trailing edge. And when it came down, I'd see white on the trailing edge of the top of the wing."

Mindy was suddenly aghast. As the bird vanished from sight, tears filled her eyes, blurring her vision. She slowly lowered her binoculars and sat there repeating over and over, "The trailing edge was white, the trailing edge was white, the trailing edge was white . . . This can't be a pileated."

I interviewed Mindy on camera that night back at the motel. All of the searchers had gathered there to drink a few beers and talk about the latest sightings. I started grilling her about what she had seen. I was annoyed that so many people were throwing out percentages about how sure they were that they had seen an ivory-bill. Ron and David were maybe 85 percent sure; Jim Fitzpatrick was 98.5 percent; now here was Mindy saying she was 99 percent sure of her sighting.

"What's all this crap I keep hearing about people being 90 percent sure, 95 percent sure that they saw an ivory-bill?" I said. "What is it about your sighting that gives you that one percent of doubt?"

Mindy shot right back: "Because the bird is freaking extinct! For years I've been convinced of that. And that's why I can't be a hundred percent sure."

As we spoke, I left the camcorder running, and it was still taping for a while after the interview was over. When I played it back later, it was interesting to watch the expressions on her face while conversations went on all around her. People were laughing and joking nearby, and she would occasionally laugh along with them, throwing out a comment or two. But every time she stopped talking, she would withdraw into herself. Her face at times looked almost horror-struck, almost like that of a person in shock — or perhaps like someone who has . . . well, seen a ghost.

Sunday, April 11, 2004: We all met at the parking area beside the Highway 17 bridge and unloaded our canoes. Tim Barksdale had brought his high-definition television camera. He and Jim Goetz wanted to interview Bobby and me on camera at the place where we had seen the ivory-bill. Several other members of the search team were also launching their canoes. Ron and Mindy were in one canoe, and Melanie Driscoll, who works with Elliott on the house finch disease study, shared another canoe with Mickey Scilingo, a birder from Ithaca. We paddled downstream together until we reached the spot on the bayou where Bobby and I had had our sighting. We turned our canoes out of the current and let the others go by, waving at them as they floated past.

Tim asked us to paddle back up the bayou, then turn around and float past him again . . . and again . . . and again. I guess this footage was something that could be used if anyone produced a film or a television program about the rediscovery of the ivory-billed woodpecker. Tim had us show him the exact spot where the woodpecker had flown across the bayou and describe the sighting in intricate detail. Then he interviewed us extensively as we sat in our canoes, out of the current.

Bobby and I both longed to be searching for the bird. This would be my last day on the bayou for a while. I had some business to attend to back home, and my left knee had ballooned up from the gash, which was now infected. I envied the other searchers, who at that very moment were fanning out to the south, continuing their vigil.

Melanie had been dropped off on some high ground at the power-line cut just south of Stab Lake a short time after leaving us. People had been watching this area closely for a week or more, because any bird moving up or down the bayou would have to cross this open area, providing an excellent view. Melanie started her first point count at ten o'clock, jotting down each bird she saw or heard from her vantage point. Just as she was about to begin her ten-thirty count, she saw a large black-and-white bird fly out of the trees just north of the power line. It was east of her and heading south. She immediately locked onto the bird with her 10x binoculars and tracked it the entire time it was in view, until it disappeared in the trees to the south.

She wrote down detailed field notes within minutes of her sighting. "My first impression was of a very large black-and-white bird with much of the body dark and most of the white being on the wings," she wrote. "I saw approximately three downstrokes of the wings. On each upstroke, I saw a flash of white on the trailing edge. On each downstroke, I saw a large white patch on the trailing edge of the near wing. I also saw a flash of red on the crest but did not see enough detail to detect shape or to see how much of the crest was red."

Melanie is in her early thirties, with long, straight brown hair and brown eyes. She tends to look you in the eye when she speaks, and you can't imagine that she would make up a story and try to present it as fact. She is also an excellent birder and an experienced field biologist with first-rate observation skills. She said the bird was larger than a pileated woodpecker and seemed to move in a more stately way. Its neck was extended and thinner than that of a pileated. When she put her binoculars on the bird, she was certain that the wing pattern was similar to that of a red-headed woodpecker, but this bird was far, far larger.

Melanie continued in her field notes: "I am shaking and feel like I could cry. Every pileated woodpecker I have watched, carefully looking for any hint of extra white, has felt like I was reaching, searching. This felt like the bird shouted its ID at me."

Several days later, back at the Lab of Ornithology, I was one of the people who asked her in detail about her sighting. She spoke with utter confidence and assurance. She was completely believable. "I feel one hundred percent certain that it was the bird," she said. "I estimate that I watched it for eight seconds or less. But my very first thought was, *Oh my God, that's the ivory-bill.* Then I got the binoculars up and saw it clearly, with no glare from the sun."

The list of people who had seen the bird had grown by five in the space of a week, but there was still no solid documentary evidence — no videotape, no photograph, no sound recording.

15

SWAMP RATS

$\mathcal{B}$OBBY HARRISON, David Luneau, and Gene Sparling were amazing all through this period. They were a constant presence in the swamp. The searchers from Cornell and other faraway places came and went, but the southern boys were always there. Bobby took off from work every day he could get away. He left town after his last class of the week and didn't return from the swamp until his first class the next week. And sometimes he arranged for substitutes to teach his classes so he could stay out longer.

David was the same way, but since he lived much closer to the action than Bobby did, he rarely missed a day after he heard about our sighting. He would teach a class and then drive to Bayou de View as fast as he could. He sometimes even returned to campus the same day to teach another class. To make this more feasible, he installed an electric trolling motor on his canoe so he could drift and paddle downstream as far as he wanted and still be able to power quickly back to his car.

The first time Bobby saw David's setup his eyes lit up, and he asked him all about where to get a motor like that and how much it would cost. When I joined him again at Bayou de View a couple of weeks later, Bobby's canoe sported a brand-new trolling motor with a huge DieHard car battery to power it. Unlike David, he used it to go both upstream and down — not because he was lazy, but because it was an amazingly unobtrusive way to move through the bayou. Every paddle stroke a canoeist makes is visible dozens of yards away to any wildlife — especially if the canoeist has a shiny metal paddle with a yellow plastic handle and blade, as some of the searchers did. Every time you raise your paddle, the sun reflects off the metal and the bright color flashes through the woods. Using this small, nearly silent electric motor, Bobby found it easy to approach wildlife. He could get within a few yards of otters playing in the swamp, and he could approach within fifty feet of pileated woodpeckers, which spook easily, without flushing them. But the trolling motor had a downside for Bobby: his weight and his blood pressure shot up again once he stopped paddling, so he had to go back on medication.

In addition to using a trolling motor, Bobby wrapped camouflage tape around his paddles and put foam-rubber pipe insulation along the gunwale so that when he did paddle, the noise would be muffled if he accidentally hit the canoe with his paddle on the downstroke. And his canoe was sludge green, to blend in with the swamp. The first canoe we had used was red. He had come a long way.

Bobby, David, and Gene were some of the first to embrace the idea of camouflaging themselves, hoping to gain a few seconds and get a few yards closer to the birds. David had always dressed in camo whenever he went into the swamp. Gene went a big step further, draping shredded camouflage material over his kayak and even pulling it up and over his head, as I have noted. As usual, though, Bobby won the prize. He dressed in camo clothes. He draped shredded camouflage material over himself and his canoe. And then he smeared gobs of multicolored camouflage greasepaint all over his face. He looked truly scary, like some whacked-out survivalist hiding deep in a bayou. He wrapped his camcorder and tripod tightly with camouflage tape, which gave it the look of a deadly automatic weapon. I'm sure he scared the hell out of a few hunters and fishermen who spotted him lurking at the edge of a channel, tucked in cover, as they floated past. Bobby didn't care. He just wanted to photograph a woodpecker.

I was constantly amazed by the innovativeness of these guys. David installed automatically triggered still cameras, setting up eight of them at woodpecker workings up and down the bayou. Bobby did the same thing with camcorders, always having a couple mounted on tree trunks, filming likely-looking pass-through spots, woodpecker holes, and bark-stripped branches. When he got back home, he would spend hours playing back the videos in real time on his television.

Some of Bobby's ideas bordered on the crackpot and made people laugh — like the time he bolted a camcorder to the top of a hardhat and canoed down the bayou with it strapped on his head, automatically filming everything he looked at. But he had to scrap that idea after a couple of days. His neck got so sore he could barely move his head for a week.

Bobby always kept a camcorder running. He mounted an expensive Gitzo tripod in the front of his canoe with a camcorder screwed on top of it, set at wide angle. He would film the panorama in front of him for hours as he paddled along the bayou. He figured that if an ivory-bill flew past the bow of his canoe, as the one we had seen had done, he would capture its image on video. He reused the videotapes over and over.

David also had a camcorder running constantly, but he kept his lying in front of him in the canoe so he could grab it quickly and point it at a bird. He practiced this quick-draw action frequently with pileated woodpeckers that flew past. I kept expecting Bobby to lose his camcorder and tripod if his canoe tipped over, but it was actually David who dropped one overboard.

Sunday, April 25, 2004: Two weeks had passed since Melanie Driscoll's sighting, and no one had seen anything resembling an ivory-bill. This was frustrating after the flurry of sightings earlier in the month. Considering how much time David Luneau had spent in Bayou de View, it must have been especially galling for him that he had not seen the bird yet. But the weather had been terrible — it had rained almost steadily for a week.

Now that the weather was clearing, David was eager to get back to the swamp. His brother-in-law Robert Henderson had agreed to go with him, so David pulled up at Robert's house before 5 A.M., and they were on the water at Bayou de View by 6:20. They sat facing each other in the canoe as they cruised down the bayou — David in back, Robert in front — so they would have a 360-degree view of the surrounding swamp forest. In the terse field notes David wrote that day, he commented on the scaled trees he examined, the excellent habitat he explored, and the automatic still cameras he checked, like a fur trapper going down his trap line.

It happened just after 3:30 in the afternoon, as the two of them approached camera number T2 (David had given each of them a letter-and-number designation). He had just raised his trolling motor out of the water, locked it in the up position, and picked up his paddle. At that instant, a large black-and-white woodpecker burst from the other side of a tupelo, just a couple of feet above the water, and flew straight away from them. With the paddle in his hands, David didn't have time to grab the camcorder, but he swung the canoe to the left, trying to keep the bird in view.

"What was that?" he asked.

"I don't know," said Robert. "I sure wish I could see it again."

David looked down at the camcorder in front of him. It had been pointing in exactly the direction the bird had flown, and it was running. The entry he jotted down in his field notes for 3:40 P.M. reads, "Saw B&W Wp [woodpecker] fly away. Never got anything but a rear-end look. Right at camera T2. Caught it on video briefly." You would never know from that matter-of-fact note that he had just nailed the first videotape of our feathered phantom.

David told me later that he would never have mentioned the sighting if not for the videotape. "I just didn't get a good enough look," he said. "Whenever I see a large woodpecker flying, I look at the wing pattern to see whether the white trails or leads the black, which usually takes just a split second. This was particularly frustrating, because I only saw the bird from the rear. When it finally did turn, it was too far away to see the black-white relationship with my naked eye."

When the two of them got back to Robert's house, David hooked up his camcorder to the television and played back the video on the larger screen. The film was far from perfect. The camcorder had automatically focused on Robert, who was in the foreground on the right side of the screen. The background was in soft focus. But even so, you could definitely see a large black-and-white bird flying straight away from the camcorder — a bird with an inordinately large amount of white on its wings. David turned the camcorder off immediately. He knew that a video image would degrade slightly every time it was played. This videotape was bad enough to begin with; he didn't want it to get any worse.

"When I got home, I made a digital copy on my computer, so I could watch it repeatedly without worrying about harming the tape," he said. Then he had a thought: what if he had unknowingly captured the woodpecker's image slightly earlier on the videotape? The bayou had curved around just before he flushed the bird. Maybe there was another image from a different angle. He backed up the tape to a point several minutes earlier and copied it onto his computer. "As I watched the area where I thought the bird would be, I noticed a black-and-white object on a tree," he said. "After watching this part of the tape many times, I began to have more confidence that the flying bird was really our quarry."

David showed the videotape to Bobby soon after he made it, so I called Bobby to get his opinion. He laughed. "It makes a bad Bigfoot movie look good," he said. "But you know, I do think it's the bird. I especially like that black-and-white shape on the tree. The size is perfect. And I've been to that tree and looked at that spot on its trunk. There's nothing like that on it."

A week later, none of us at the Lab of Ornithology had seen

the tape yet. David was being coy. He didn't want to send this over the Internet; the danger was too great that it would somehow be leaked. But he didn't even want to mail a copy. He invited us to come to Arkansas to view it. A short time later, Fitz visited David in Little Rock, and David agreed to download a copy of the video directly onto Fitz's laptop so he could take it back to Cornell.

Fitz brought the digitized video to Marc Dantzker, the motion-picture curator at the Macaulay Library, to see what he could do to enhance it. Marc is one of the most enthusiastic and energetic people I've ever met. In his mid-thirties, he seems to be on a constant coffee high. And he has a distinctive look, with a completely shaved head and a dark goatee. I was there when he first viewed the video, and his perpetually high excitement level shot through the roof. He immediately took the digital file of the video into "the cave," a small film studio in a back downstairs hallway of the library, and went to work.

I was surprised at how good the video looked when I first saw it, unenhanced and played in real time. My expectations had been low after hearing the comments of Bobby and a few other people. But when I saw it, my immediate impression was *That's the bird.* Marc's work on the movie only confirmed that for me. He stayed up most of the night in the studio, separating the entire video clip into individual frames, then sharpening it, increasing the contrast, enlarging, and cropping more tightly on the bird. Then he reassembled it into a viewable motion picture. Marc didn't add anything to the video — he just attempted to make it clearer. The results were astounding. In the blown-up film, I could see what appeared to be a large bird with a black-crested head and a white bill peering out from behind a tupelo. A second later, a wing flared, showing a large quantity of white, and the tail came out as the bird pushed off and flew away powerfully. Freezing the frames and slowly advancing them one by one, I saw the bird flying directly away. It had a large black body with a black tail and black primary flight feathers showing; the rest of the flight feathers shone brilliant white, top and bottom, all the way to their trailing edge. I was completely floored. Virtually all of the ivory-bill's major field marks were there, albeit fuzzy.

In the weeks that followed, it was interesting to see how people responded to the film. Everyone who was familiar with what an ivory-billed woodpecker looks like seemed utterly convinced that this was the real thing. To my mind, we crossed a crucial threshold when Kevin McGowan finally said that he thought the bird in the video was an ivory-bill. "I wanted to believe before," he told me. "But it's in my nature to be skeptical. I just couldn't help but have doubts, even though I trusted the abilities of some of the people who'd had sightings. It wasn't until I saw David Luneau's video that I really accepted the existence of this bird."

Is this video good enough for the six o'clock news? Probably not. The average person doesn't know enough about what an ivory-bill looks like to know what he or she is looking at. But for everyone involved in the search, this was just what we needed to keep our energy level high — especially as we entered the summer doldrums and the number of sightings plummeted.

Wednesday, May 5, 2004: It was about 3:30 in the afternoon as Bobby motored his canoe quietly up Bayou de View, about a mile south of Camp Ephilus II. A large bird suddenly flushed from the base of a tupelo up ahead. Bobby felt certain it was an ivory-bill, which made him wonder: what were these birds doing so close to the water? One thing he had noticed earlier offered a possible clue. He had seen a red-bellied woodpecker catch and eat a crawfish at the base of a tupelo. Could the ivory-bills be eating these small, lobsterlike crustaceans too? He had also noticed big spiders down low on most of these trees — another possible food source?

In late May, Bobby flew to Ithaca to spend a few days mining Cornell's Rare and Manuscript Collection for clues about ivory-billed woodpecker behavior. The collection contains the personal papers, photographs, and field notes of Arthur Allen and Jim Tanner — a real treasure trove for any ivory-bill seeker. There is something magical about holding the notebook and reading what someone wrote when he was actually sitting beside an active ivory-billed woodpecker nest. And if you read closely, you might find interesting unpublished observations or vital clues that will help you in your search — at least, that's what you hope for.

In some ways, ivory-bill seekers are like biblical scholars, who dig deep into the text, trying to parse the hidden meanings, which sometimes requires going back to the ancient scrolls written in Aramaic and doing their own translations. These field notebooks are our scrolls, and this time Bobby hit pay dirt, solving a mystery that I had been working on for several years.

Many people in my generation of ivory-bill seekers — certainly Bobby and I — were first inspired by John Dennis's rediscovery of the species in the Big Thicket of east Texas in 1966. To think that the whole thing might have been a mistake, or, worse, a fabrication, as some people claimed, was completely disillusioning. Based on everything I had read about John Dennis, I couldn't bring myself to believe it. He had spent at least a couple of years searching the swamp there, living in a rustic cabin with few amenities. He had had a number of sightings and on a foggy morning in May 1968 had even tape-recorded the *kent* calls of the bird. John William Hardy, the chairman of the Department of Natural Science at the University of Florida at Gainesville, analyzed Dennis's recording and wrote about it in a 1975 article in *American Birds*. Hardy maintained that the bird John Dennis recorded was either an ivory-billed woodpecker or a blue jay imitating one, and he believed it was the former.

My dream was to get a copy of the tape from John Dennis and have it analyzed by sound technicians at the Macaulay Library and the Bioacoustics Research Program. Surely with all the technological advances that have taken place in the past three decades, we would be able to determine once and for all the identity of the bird on the tape. It was a nice dream. The problem was, I had waited too long. When I finally got around to calling John

Dennis, he was on his deathbed, suffering from cancer of the sinuses. His face was partially paralyzed, and he had difficulty speaking, so his wife relayed my questions to him and then told me his answers. Eventually he got so excited thinking about the ivory-bill again, he took the phone from her and spoke directly to me. It was obviously difficult for him. I asked him about his ivory-bill recording and explained what I wanted to do with it. I'll never forget his words as he struggled to answer: "I gave . . . it . . . to . . . the Lab . . . of Ornithology."

I was stunned. I hadn't even thought about asking anyone in the Macaulay Library. When I did, though, I hit another dead end. No one knew anything about it, and not one person who had worked in the library in the 1960s was still there. Of course, everything had been in upheaval at the lab at that time, a couple of years before. Our new facility was under construction, and many of us worked in a temporary office building five miles from Sapsucker Woods. A lot of things were in storage. I had just about given up hope of ever finding the recording when Bobby came to Ithaca.

He stopped by my office on the way to the Rare and Manuscript Collection so we could drive there together. I knew all the reference librarians well and wanted to help him get started. He had a printout that listed all of the Tanner papers, letters, photographs, and field notes in the collection. "Look at this," he said, pointing to something on the sheet. I glanced at it for a second, and then did a double-take as I read it more closely: "John Dennis recording (1935?)." Bobby and I looked at each other and smiled. Obviously someone at the library had found a tape with Jim Tanner's papers when they were cataloging them. They must have thought it was from the 1935 Cornell expedition. Surely this had to be the missing John Dennis tape.

We jumped in my car and raced to the library, about four miles away, in the center of the Cornell campus. The tape was supposed to be in box number 3, which the reference specialist Laura Linke brought out for us on a cart. My hands were trembling as I pawed through the contents of the box, quickly pushing back each file folder. And I found . . . nothing. My sense of disappointment was crushing. But I made myself go through the box again — slowly, carefully. And then we saw it: a small manila envelope with something bulky inside. It was a spool from an old reel-to-reel tape recorder, with a few yards of audiotape on it. I explained to the librarians what the tape was and how important it might be. I asked if I could take it to the Lab of Ornithology for analysis, and miraculously, they said yes — they would let me keep it for a week.

Everything started to make sense when Bobby found a letter to Jim Tanner from John William Hardy, dated February 6, 1974. "Have you heard the Dennis tape?" he wrote. "It is clear and clearly not the Cornell recording distorted. And yet there can be little question of its maker — almost certainly an ivory-bill. I'll be happy to provide you with a copy for your own ears if you wish." So in private Hardy was convinced that the calls were really made by an ivory-bill, even more than he had conveyed in the *American Birds* article. The mystery of how the recording ended up with Jim Tanner's papers was solved, but the question remained: did Tanner ever listen to it? And if so, what did he think of it? So far I have been unable to find any correspondence from him referring to this tape.

Greg Budney, the audio curator at the Macaulay Library, and some sound technicians have now listened to the tape and compared the sound spectrographs to the 1935 Cornell recordings, and most agree that John Dennis did indeed record an ivory-billed woodpecker in the Big Thicket of east Texas on February 25, 1968. "I have no doubt that it's an ivory-billed woodpecker," said Budney. "And the tape is not the one that Allen and Kellogg made."

This duplicate recording from Hardy is a poor copy, however. Apparently something was wrong with the tape speed when it was recorded, so it wavers somewhat. Although Bob Grotke, the Macaulay Library's sound engineer, improved it as much as he could, he was still dissatisfied. But this encouraged people to look through the sound library more thoroughly, and someone located twenty hours' worth of tape submitted years earlier by Dennis. A sound technician reviewed the entire tape and close to its end found what is apparently the original cut of the Dennis tape. It's eerie. John Dennis's voice comes on, speaking hauntingly in a whisper right in the field, talking about an ivory-billed woodpecker that is at that moment calling from just 150 feet away.

So now we know that John Dennis was right. He most likely did have at least one ivory-bill out there in the swamps of east Texas in the late 1960s. Too bad we didn't determine the truth of his observation until after his death.

When I think of John Dennis, I sometimes have a strange feeling of déjà vu. So many aspects of his rediscovery of the bird — so many of the things he wrote about in his articles and letters — are similar to what we have been experiencing in Arkansas. He wrote that the birds he was seeing were not like the ones Jim Tanner studied in Louisiana. The Singer Tract had been closed to hunting for years. The birds there had little reason to fear people, so they could afford to be more visible, more vocal. The birds of the Big Thicket could not. They were shy, retiring, and easily spooked, just like the ivory-bill we had encountered at Bayou de View. True, no one has yet labeled us crackpots. But as I write this, only a handful of people know about the sightings and about our field-work in Arkansas. Who knows what will happen after the redis-covery of this species is announced to the world?

Tim Barksdale stayed all summer at Bayou de View, sitting on a platform he built ten feet up in some tupelos, dressed from head to toe in camouflage. Bobby, David, and Gene were almost always there too, cruising up and down the bayou, searching, hoping. I went there only once in the summer, and it was nothing like the place I had known in winter and early spring. This was a thick green jungle, humid and buggy, with poor visibility. I didn't even see many pileated woodpeckers. But despite what Jim Tanner had written about the uselessness of searching for these birds in summer, these guys hung tough. They knew there was absolutely no possibility of seeing an ivory-bill if they stayed at home; at least they had a chance if they were on the bayou.

Wednesday, June 9, 2004: As Bobby paddled up the bayou south of Camp Ephilus II, a large woodpecker dropped from the trunk of a cypress tree about fifty feet up and flew toward another cypress. "I immediately did a mental checklist of field marks: large woodpecker, white trailing edge on wings, white secondaries, black back," he wrote in his field notes. "It was the ivory-bill."

Of course, this sighting didn't sit well with some of the other searchers. Bobby had had a lot of sightings, and people were starting to doubt him. I had more faith in him, though. Bobby is one of the most honest people I have ever known, and I knew he wouldn't lie. And he really does have an excellent visual memory. On photography trips with him, I have been amazed by how well he can describe things he has seen for only an instant, as though he has a photograph of it in his mind that he can refer to. I think this is why he's so good at finding his way back when he goes off exploring in swamps.

But Bobby didn't care what anyone thought. It only made him more determined to get his own videotape. He continued to come up with new ideas and to experiment. His finest moment came when he designed an ivory-billed woodpecker decoy. This was another idea that people snickered at, but he went ahead with it anyway. He figured that at worst, it wouldn't work. But at least he was doing something. It seemed crazy just to keep floating up and down the bayou or sitting waiting for something to happen. He could still do that, but why not do something proactive at the same time?

His idea was to set up one or two of these decoys in likely places and aim camcorders at them. He had bought a couple of discontinued Hi8 camcorders at a clearance-sale price. The advantage of using them was that they could be set to record for up to four hours, whereas the newer digital models were good for only an hour. And he bought extra-capacity batteries, each with enough juice to last for ten hours.

Bobby carved his decoy out of tupelo — probably the most common tree in the swamp — and painted it broadly in the distinctive color pattern of the ivory-bill. Any bird passing within one hundred yards up or down the bayou would be able to see it. It didn't take long to pay off.

Saturday, September 4, 2004: Just before ten in the morning, Bobby set his decoy 15 feet up on the trunk of a tupelo about 250 feet west of where he had seen the ivory-bill on June 9. He attached a camcorder to a nearby tree, aimed it at the decoy, and started recording. The decoy was clearly visible from 400 feet north on the channel and 300 feet south. Bobby reasoned that if an ivory-bill was using the channel as a daily flyway, it would have to see the decoy. And he felt certain that if it did see it, it would respond in some way.

When he had finished setting up his equipment, he pushed off, heading north using his trolling motor. He went exploring up a secondary channel until he reached a dead end, then turned back, heading to a fork that would take him to the main channel of the bayou. "As I was making my way back, I could clearly see the decoy about 250 feet away, directly in front of me," Bobby wrote in his notes. A few seconds later, a large bird burst from the base of a tupelo just 80 feet in front of him, to the right of his canoe. "The trailing edges of its wings were white," he said. "It moved fast and upward into the canopy."

Bobby stayed in the area about twenty minutes looking for the bird, but he couldn't find it. That night he decided to get a motel room just so he could use a television screen to play back his videotape and see if he had captured the bird's image. The black-and-white decoy stood out well from the grayish background of the swamp as he watched the video. Only ten minutes into the tape, a large bird shot past the upper left corner of the screen. He could see a distinct flash of white.

Bobby was already planning to come to Cornell again in a few days to do some more ivory-bill research, so he kept news of the video quiet. He wanted to walk into the lab and hand it to Fitz himself.

Interestingly, the same day Bobby videotaped that bird, Joan Luneau, who is married to David's brother Guy, saw a bird she felt strongly was an ivory-bill fly across the break in the woods at the Highway 17 bridge. Neither of them knew of each other's sighting until days later. David said Joan is an excellent birder.

Marc Dantzker set to work on Bobby's tape the minute Bobby arrived. There wasn't as much to work with as there had been with David's tape — this was the briefest glimpse imaginable. But after it was enlarged and slowed down, most people who saw it were convinced that the bird in the video was an ivory-bill. In one of the last frames before it vanished from view, you could see a black body, black on the wings, with a large expanse of white. Then Fitz spotted something else interesting: the bird actually flew through the frame a second time, going from left to right across the bottom of the screen just thirty-three seconds later.

Bobby's video is far from being a high-quality, undeniable rendering of this bird. The best thing about it is that it shows conclusively that a decoy can lure in a passing ivory-bill. So we now had one more vital tool in the upcoming field season, set to begin in early December 2004.

In late November, another key player joined the search team: Martjan Lammertink of the Netherlands. Although he's only thirty-three, Martjan is already a renowned expert on large woodpeckers and a veteran of other searches for ivory-billed and imperial woodpeckers. My favorite story about him concerns a solo expedition to Cuba he launched as a nineteen-year-old in the early 1990s. He had long dreamed of going there to search for ivory-bills. When he got out of high school, he worked in a dairy for a year and a half, saving up all the money he earned. As soon as he had enough, he bought a ticket to Cuba and left. He hired local people to help him explore areas in Oriente Province, where ivory-bills had been seen at least up until the mid-1980s. He spent three months searching, hiking through rugged terrain for weeks and interviewing countless people, but he went home feeling doubtful that the species still exists in Cuba. "Almost certainly extinct," he wrote in a lengthy paper about the expedition. The habitat he visited had been largely ruined for the birds, and although he found quite a few older people who were familiar with the bird called *el carpintero real,* the royal carpenter, none of them had seen one in the past fifteen years. Martjan didn't find any of the characteristic ivory-bill foraging signs, such as stripped bark, even on beetle-infested trees.

A couple of years later he got the urge to travel again, this time to the Sierra Madre Occidental of northern Mexico, to search for the imperial woodpecker. I first heard about Martjan after this expedition, because I had long dreamed (and still dream) of searching for this species myself. The mountains in that part of Mexico are extremely dangerous because of all the large poppy- and marijuana-growing operations there, patrolled by AK-47–wielding guards who think nothing of shooting suspicious strangers who come snooping around. More than one biologist has been killed there. The ornithologist Noel Snyder warned me emphatically against going into some areas. He had studied the thick-billed parrot in those mountains and had some close calls. He was filled with admiration for Martjan, who spent months there and seemed to go everywhere, completely oblivious of the danger.

Martjan laughed when I spoke with him about that, and he told me a little about Borneo and other places in Indonesia where he had studied large woodpeckers. Some of the towns he had visited look perfectly normal, with paved roads, stop signs, and gas stations. But every so often, he told me, ethnic tensions would break out, and suddenly he would see rows of human heads hanging from traffic lights and lampposts. I guess Mexico is pretty tame compared with that.

The paper Martjan wrote about his foray into Mexico after imperial woodpeckers was just as pessimistic as his Cuban report.

The high-altitude old-growth pine forest habitat the birds require had been largely destroyed. And over the years the local people had shot many of these birds for food.

This year's Arkansas expedition was not Martjan's first foray into the United States searching for ivory-bills. He was on the Zeiss team during the 2002 Pearl River search. I remember asking him sometime after that if he thought there was any hope that the ivory-bill might still live in the United States. I expected him to give me a pessimistic assessment, but he surprised me. He said he had seen a lot of great habitat during his month in Louisiana — much better than anything he had seen in Cuba — and he was hopeful the birds might still exist here.

Martjan and his wife, Utami Setiorini, stopped in Ithaca for a couple of days in mid-November before continuing on to Arkansas. It's amazing to think of this tall, thin Dutchman with short light-brown hair and chiseled European features being able to blend in so well in countries where most of the people look so different from him. Utami, who is Indonesian, couldn't be more different from Martjan in appearance — she is short, dark, and petite. They seem a perfect couple. Utami was Martjian's field assistant when he was studying in Indonesia, so she too has a lot of experience in woodpecker research. They were both clearly excited about the chance to search for ivory-bills. While they were here, we showed them David Luneau's videotape. After viewing it, Martjan had no doubts. "It's an ivory-billed woodpecker," he said confidently. "Probably a female."

16

THE LAZARUS BIRD

$\mathcal{A}$s I BEGIN THE FINAL CHAPTER in this narrative of the ivory-billed woodpecker's twenty-first-century rediscovery, it is the last day of November 2004, and three fifteen-passenger vans chock-full of field equipment have just shoved off from the Lab of Ornithology's loading bay, en route to Arkansas. At the wheels are Ron Rohrbaugh, now the primary project manager; Elliott Swarthout, the field supervisor of the Bayou de View search team; and Peter Wrege, a behavioral ecologist at Cornell who is the field supervisor of the White River search team.

The last few weeks were a blur as people scrambled to prepare for the launch of the field season. Led by Ron and the project coordinator, Sara Barker Swarthout, the group developed research protocols, put together a training manual, arranged funding, hired project staff, bought canoes and other equipment, and oversaw all aspects of the search preparation.

Clearly, the scope of the effort has expanded enormously since last season. Bayou de View will be searched thoroughly, but we will also send searchers deep into White River National Wildlife Refuge. It is vital that we do more now than just gather additional evidence to prove the existence of a bird or two. We need to establish whether any ivory-billed woodpeckers are breeding in Arkansas, and if so, whether enough of them exist to form the basis of a viable population. Every government agency involved and every potential supporter will want to know that.

When I try to imagine the upcoming search, it seems daunting. White River refuge is like a vast ocean of trees, tens of thousands of acres in area, and we have to comb through it all, straining our ears to hear tiny tin-horn toots and peering deep into dense forest and swamp to catch a glimpse of these secretive birds. But we have already done overflights and taken a series of aerial photographs of the entire drainage. We have a good idea of which areas to concentrate on — places with numerous dead and dying trees that will attract foraging woodpeckers.

Of course Bobby Harrison will be there. And he has already started designing some inventions he hopes will lure a passing ivory-bill. He recently created a flat, bark-covered bird feeder that he intends to put on the trunk of a tree in good habitat. It will contain suet and perhaps even mealworms and should attract a variety of woodpeckers. Will an ivory-bill take the bait? I don't know, but it will be interesting to see. Bobby has also carved a few more decoys, which will be used in a later phase of the search. Initially, teams will just be scouting, without using decoys or playbacks of ivory-bill calls. If and when these are employed, they will be used sparingly, just to determine whether ivory-bills are present in a particular location. And they will be used only when camcorders and sound recorders have been set up and are running to record any response from a bird.

As the new field season begins and researchers fan out across Bayou de View and White River, I'm full of excitement and eager to get back to Arkansas. But I also feel heartsick in some ways. I often think of Mary Scott's words: "I hope you have the smartness to do the right thing . . . If you make the sighting known, you doom the bird. So far, we've shown as a species that we're incapable of doing the right thing."

Science has never yet done right by the ivory-billed wood-pecker. At a time when the species was clearly in trouble and needed to be studied and protected, ornithologists were still shooting ivory-bills to add specimens to their collections. And decades later, when many feared that the species might be extinct, mainstream ornithologists pooh-poohed the reports of anyone with the temerity to say that he or she had seen an ivory-billed woodpecker. Even respected ornithologists such as George Lowery and John Dennis were laughed at for believing that the bird still existed. This had a chilling effect on any effort to try to find and help these birds. Some researchers passed up chances to check on credible sightings; it just wasn't worth putting their careers at risk when just admitting that they believed the ivory-bill still might exist could subject them to ridicule from their colleagues.

To me, this is the opposite of what true science should be. Scientists should approach every question without bias, weighing the available data and rendering judgment with an open, dispassionate mind. This has been anything but the case with the ivory-billed woodpecker for almost a century. The belief that this bird is extinct has been held so strongly for so long that it has become a tenet adhered to by many ornithologists as rigidly and dogmatically as the tenets of the most fundamentalist religious sects. It's time to change that.

I want to think that we'll do the right thing this time. I need to think that. And I have seen encouraging signs. Both Scott Simon, the director of the Nature Conservancy's Arkansas chapter, and John Fitzpatrick, the director of the Cornell Lab of Ornithology, are passionately committed to restoring the unique bottomland swamp forests of the South — one of the most neglected and forgotten habitats in all of North America. The Nature Conservancy has been working toward this end in Arkansas for several years through its Big Woods initiative, but the rediscovery of the ivory-bill has accelerated the process by at least tenfold; thousands of acres of bottomland forest have been purchased outright or optioned since February 2004. And Fitz has been fund-raising for land acquisition with a zeal I have never seen before, even in someone with his level of enthusiasm and charisma. These people and others are planning a centuries-long process of regeneration to restore these woods to something resembling their primeval state.

Unfortunately, it is far too late to save a significant piece of existing old-growth bottomland swamp forest. Back when people were saving Yellowstone, Yosemite, and the giant redwoods, they didn't even think about the southern forests. Logging companies took countless millions of board feet of lumber from the Atchafalaya, year after year. And even as late as 1940, when we had the chance to save a remnant of primeval swamp forest at Louisiana's Singer Tract, we didn't do it. We let it go. Consequently, no one in our generation or the next or the next will have the chance to see the spectacle of a southern forest with trees nine feet in diameter towering more than a hundred feet high. They are gone — obliterated in the nineteenth and twentieth centuries.

What happened to the vast bottomland forests of the South during the past 150 years is one of the greatest environmental tragedies in the history of the United States, and few people know about it. These are still one of our most neglected and abused habitats. Nothing symbolizes what we have lost more than the ivory-billed woodpecker. Just to think that this bird has made it into the twenty-first century gives me chills. It's as though a funeral shroud has been pulled back, giving us a brief glimpse of a living bird, rising like Lazarus from the grave.

I think the best we can hope for now is that through our actions, our great-great-grandchildren may have something we never had: thousands of acres of old-growth southern swamp forest with massive trees rising more than one hundred feet above them. That's what I want. At least we know that the great forests of the South are capable of coming back, given enough time and protection. We may not know for decades whether the same can be said of the ivory-billed woodpecker. As wonderful and gratifying as it is to know that this species still exists, it may well be hanging on by the most tenuous of threads. We don't yet know what the presence of this bird or birds at Bayou de View represents. We're so lucky that it made its way up this narrow finger of swamp forest into an area that is small enough to search effectively. But ivory-bills are nomadic. The tide that brought the bird up this narrow finger could easily recede, and the species could vanish again. It wouldn't be the first time. I hope we don't give up on it again.

I believe the attention that this bird's rediscovery will bring to the southern swamp forest habitat will ultimately be a good thing, as more and more of it is preserved. And that can only be good for the ivory-billed woodpecker, provided that the species can hang on just a little while longer. Considering how much the bird has already gone through, I have faith that it will.

EPILOGUE

As I write, it is early March 2005, the ivory-bill search is in full swing, and I'm sitting at home in upstate New York, looking out my window at a frozen landscape. Snow has fallen steadily all morning, whipped by a howling wind, piling up deep drifts in my yard. I should be out shoveling, but I can't face it yet. It's been a tough winter — here and in the swamp.

There were days in December when the searchers couldn't go out because the bayou was frozen. I remember paddling back to the haul-out point one day at dusk this past January and having to break through thin ice for the last hundred feet or so. And at the White River search area, much of the land below the levee has been flooded this season, so our teams have often had to use john-boats or canoes in places where we were able to drive last year. But the searchers have hung tough.

With a core group of about seventeen full-time searchers, supplemented by part-timers who join the effort for a week or more at a time, we have been able to field around twenty-five searchers a day, split between Bayou de View and the White River search areas. It's hard work. Martjan early on came up with the idea of completing a careful, thorough search of Bayou de View and parts of the White River area for ivory-bill–like roost cavities, which have entrance holes that are larger and usually more oblong than those of other woodpeckers. These are all being catalogued, and searchers are being assigned to sit near each of them at least once for a couple of hours around dusk to see if a bird — if *the* bird — flies in to roost. This has been particularly difficult in the White River refuge, because people have often had to find their way out of the swamp in the dark without the benefit of a path or a channel. But the cavity search has proven to be a useful process, creating an inventory of possible roost or nest holes and also making people slow down and really concentrate. And the vigil did lead to one interesting observation in November.

John Fitzpatrick had invited Marshall Iliff, a top birder and a tour leader for a major international birding tour company, to join the search effort a couple of months earlier. Marshall's skills as an observer and his experience watching other *Campephilus* woodpeckers in Mexico and Central America made him an obvious asset to the team.

On November 9, Marshall spent several hours searching some areas north of Highway 17. The previous day had been fairly cool on the bayou, but on this day the weather was pleasantly warm, which seemed to increase the activity of the woodpeckers. The rolling, rapid-fire drumming of pileated woodpeckers resounded through the swamp for much of the day. Marshall also heard downy, hairy, and red-bellied woodpeckers and at least one yellow-bellied sapsucker.

In the late afternoon he paddled to a place where he could watch two excellent woodpecker cavities. This area was particularly interesting because of its diversity of tree species — oaks, red maples, sycamores, large cypresses, and more. On some trees, strips of bark had been peeled away in ivory-bill fashion.

As Marshall sat quietly, he suddenly heard a distinct, though distant, *BAM-bam*. He listened closely, hoping the sound would be repeated, then decided to try mimicking the sound by hitting a paddle against the side of his kayak. Amazingly, twenty seconds later he heard a distinct *BAM-bam*, apparently in response to his signal. Marshall rapped again with his paddle and immediately started taking out his tape recorder. He heard two more double raps before he got the recorder switched on and then another a few seconds later. He pounded again and got another response. The bird appeared to be moving. He heard the noise several times straight ahead of him; then, a minute later, it sounded like it was to his right, a fair distance away. Were two birds signaling back and forth? Or was one bird moving quickly from one place to another and then back? He didn't know. He never caught sight of the bird or heard any calls.

By the time Marshall set his recorder down to take some notes, he had been recording for perhaps thirteen minutes and was sure he had some great material. But then he noticed with horror that the switch on his shotgun microphone was in the off position. Most of these high-quality microphones are independently powered with an internal battery, and they amplify the sound before it reaches the recorder. It's easy to forget to turn them on (and, conversely, to turn them off when you're finished recording, thus depleting the battery). I've done it myself, and I sympathize with Marshall.

Although Marshall turned on the microphone and kept recording, it was too late. Whatever had been making the sound had stopped, and he didn't hear it again. According to Marshall, the sounds he heard at Bayou de View were very similar to the double raps he had heard pale-billed and crimson-crested woodpeckers make in Latin America, except that they were somewhat louder — which is probably to be expected, because an ivory-bill is significantly larger than either of those species. He said that they definitely did not sound like gunshots, which tend to hang in the air longer and are not as sharp and resonant as the double raps.

In a sound spectrograph — which is a computer-generated snapshot of a sound showing its pitch, loudness, and duration — the double rap of a *Campephilus* woodpecker has a distinctive look: two sharp peaks, the first one significantly taller than the second, with a small space in between. That interval between the peaks, which averages about 75 milliseconds in most species in this genus, together with the difference in intensity between the first and second rap, is what makes these double raps stand out from other knocking sounds in the woods. True, two trees or limbs might bang together occasionally on a windy day and create a double-rap sound, but the odds are extremely low that this would produce the perfect spectrographic signature of a *Campephilus* woodpecker. And a gunshot looks nothing at all like a double rap on a spectrograph.

Of course Marshall's observations that day generated great excitement among the search team. Early the following morning, he returned to the spot with David Luneau and Tim Barksdale. The three of them spent the day scouring the area, hoping to see or hear an ivory-bill. They didn't detect anything promising, and the following day rain kept them away.

And that was it — for months. All through the rest of November, December, and January, the searchers came up empty. Although a lot of people, including me, visited the spot where Marshall had sat on November 9, no one heard any double raps in the area. But one very good thing came out of his observations that day: the team installed an ARU on a tree at that location. If the ivory-bill — or whatever it was — repeated its performance, maybe this time it would be recorded and could be analyzed in minute detail by sound technicians.

We had our first ARU breakthrough on February 7. Beth Howard, one of the sound technicians working on the project at the Lab of Ornithology, was running through spectrographs from sounds recorded in December at Bayou de View when she spotted something that looked like a classic *Campephilus* double rap. It had been recorded at dusk on Christmas Eve in the same area where Marshall had heard the double raps, albeit more than six weeks later. Beth and Mike Powers started searching through the sounds recorded on other days around that time. They found a double rap that had been recorded on Christmas Day, also at dusk. Could this be an ivory-bill doing a last double rap before entering its roost hole?

Interestingly, none of the searchers had been in the bayou on those days. They were all taking a Christmas break.

The technicians compared these sounds with the double raps of another *Campephilus* species, the powerful woodpecker, and the spectrographic signatures were strikingly similar — the classic twin peaks, with the second peak significantly lower than the first and the perfect interval in between. The sound analysis team subsequently found a number of additional double raps, which seemed to occur either early or late in the day — the times when a woodpecker would be emerging from or entering its roost hole — so the sounds were very intriguing.

The problem for the searchers was the lag time. Here we were, a week into February, and we were listening to sounds that had been recorded at Christmas. It was no one's fault. We have numerous ARUs deployed in the Arkansas search areas, and they usually stay up for at least a couple of weeks. At any given time we have hundreds of hours of sound waiting to be analyzed and only a small number of sound technicians to go through them. But the sound-team leader, Russ Charif, decided to make a special effort to examine sounds recorded as recently as possible at the site where the other double raps occurred. The team soon found a couple more double raps, which were recorded on the morning of January 25. A lot of searchers headed up the bayou to stake out the area, but it was actually in a place well to the south that we had our next breakthrough.

February 14, 2005: Casey Taylor, one of the full-time searchers at Bayou de View, was stationed at the power-line cut near the south end of Stab Lake — the same place where Melanie Driscoll had seen an ivory-bill the previous April. At 3:57 in the afternoon, she heard a loud, distinct double rap coming from somewhere around the eastern end of the power line. She had listened to the double raps from the ARU as well as recordings of a powerful woodpecker and thought they sounded identical to what she had just heard. She pulled her canoe out and began making her way slowly and quietly southeast along the power line, with her camcorder running, trying to get closer to the source of the sound. In the next few minutes she heard an additional five or six double raps, and then she ran out of videotape. As she was rewinding it, she heard the noise again. She switched her camcorder back into record mode and continued trying to track down what was making the sound.

Casey sat still for about a half-hour without seeing or hearing anything of interest. She wrote up some notes and then started playing back her camcorder with the sound turned up, listening closely to see if she could hear the double raps.

At about five o'clock she noticed a group of about five crows chasing a large dark bird toward the southeast, parallel to the power-line cut, about sixty or seventy yards behind her. They were flying just above the forest canopy. Casey noticed that the bird being chased was not making deep wingbeats, and yet it was flying powerfully, easily keeping ahead of the crows. At first she thought it might be a hawk of some kind, but then it turned to cross the power-line cut just fifty yards in front of her, and she suddenly realized that this was no hawk. She saw the distinct shape of a large woodpecker, with a long straight bill and black-and-white plumage. Quickly raising her binoculars, Casey locked onto the bird for three or four seconds before it reached the trees. She plainly saw extensive areas of white on the bird's wings, running all the way to the trailing edge. She feels confident that the bird was an ivory-bill.

I have a copy of Casey's field notes on my desk, with a crude sketch of the bird she saw in the margin. It includes all the major field marks of an ivory-billed woodpecker.

That has been it for almost three weeks. Several people went to the area of Casey's sighting before dawn the following morning and were in place before the sun came up. Although three separate teams reported hearing some "interesting" sounds that morning, which may or may not have been *kent* calls, the faint recordings on their camcorders are inconclusive. Since then, the searchers have not seen or heard anything.

Many of us are resigned to the possibility that the evidence we have now might be all we have when we announce the ivory-bill's rediscovery, which is tentatively planned for May 2005. Consequently, the researchers are anticipating questions that will be raised by skeptics and attempting to determine whether anything but a *Campephilus* woodpecker could have produced the double raps and whether the bird in David Luneau's video could be anything but an ivory-bill. It's a difficult, complicated process. At the same time that the sound analysis team is searching through countless hours of recorded sound from the ARUs, they are examining recordings of all the other *Campephilus* woodpeckers, analyzing them in detail and comparing them with the double raps recorded at Bayou de View.

The video analysis is even more complicated. For months people have been trying to film pileated woodpeckers as they fly through the woods so we will have something to compare with David Luneau's video. David himself filmed one of the better segments of this species. Viewing this video, you can certainly see flashes of white as the pileated's underwing comes into view, but some black always seems to be visible at the trailing edge of the wing. And sometimes, when the bird's wings are in the full downstroke position, all you see is black.

David also went back to the tree the bird took off from and attached pieces of masking tape to mark where the top of the bird's head was visible as it peeked around the trunk and where its tail emerged as it flew, so he could measure the approximate size of the bird. Then he videotaped the tree again.

To take things one step further, Bobby Harrison — ever the artist — has created life-sized models of a pileated woodpecker and an ivory-bill with their wings outstretched. By moving a long dowel up and down, you can actually make the wings flap. This weekend, David and Martjan intend to take these models to the spot where David videotaped the bird on April 25, 2004, and try to recreate the bird's flight from the tree, using the models. The videos they shoot will be compared with each other and with the original video. Marc Dantzker at the Macaulay Library will then put these videos through all the same processes he used with the original film — breaking them down frame by frame, improving the sharpness and contrast — to see if there is any possible way that the bird in David's video could be a pileated woodpecker. I'm betting that David's video will stand the test.

So is John Fitzpatrick. "The bird captured on this video can be nothing other than an ivory-billed woodpecker," he said recently. "Besides studying and measuring the image frame by frame, we've shown the video to more than a dozen experienced ornithologists, and they've all come to the same conclusion. In combination with the series of credible sightings and our acoustic evidence of characteristic display drumming, I am convinced that at least one ivory-billed woodpecker is currently living in this portion of the Arkansas delta." He also suggested that perhaps during the years when the birds were being hunted extensively by collectors, only the quietest and wariest individuals in a few remnant forests survived to pass on their genes to future generations. This could explain why it is so difficult to find an ivory-bill and record its calls. Perhaps all the noisy and approachable ones were killed off a century ago.

Bobby called me from Bayou de View last Sunday just after lunch. It was 1:15 in the afternoon on February 27, 2005, a year to the minute since we had seen the ivory-bill fly past in front of us — a moment that changed both of our lives forever. I wish I could have been there to celebrate the anniversary in person. As we spoke, Bobby was sitting on a fallen log, eating tuna and crackers, with his feet ankle-deep in swamp water. From there he could see the exact spot where the bird had flown across the bayou. He had two camcorders aimed there, on the off chance that history might repeat itself. Of course, it didn't happen. It was a different day — a little cooler this time, overcast, with rain threatening, and the water was a couple of inches deeper.

It's been a long and amazing year. Somehow we have managed to keep the story quiet, hoping to complete a full field season before all the media hoopla begins and hordes of birders descend on this place. We've almost done it. Our field season is over at the end of April, just a few weeks away. Still, I can't help feeling a certain amount of dread. I have no idea what it will be like when the announcement is made. I suspect that for all of us who have been deeply involved in this search, our lives will never again be the same. And that may well be true for the ivory-bill as well. I hope that for the bird, the changes will be positive — that more habitat will be preserved, that a major bottomland swamp forest restoration process will begin. In some ways, I can't help hoping that after an initial flood of interest and new visitors to Bayou de View, the excitement will slowly peter out, as it did at the Pearl River, and only people who really care about the ivory-bill will come to this swamp. I know Bobby will be there, and so will David and Gene.

One thing that quickly became clear as I was writing this book is that this story has a timetable all its own. As I finished the last chapter, it was obvious that I would need an epilogue to bring readers up to date on everything that had happened in the field. But then, no sooner had I handed in the epilogue than the next major stage in the saga of the ivory-bill's rediscovery began to unfold, so I'm adding this postscript.

Late in the day last Thursday, March 3, 2005, Beth Howard was checking through ARU sounds that had been automatically flagged by a computer program designed to detect *kent* calls when she noticed a string of calls, lasting a minute or more, that were strikingly similar to those from the 1935 Cornell recordings. In fact, when Russ Charif told me about them the next day, he didn't want to make a big deal of it. He was afraid it would turn out that someone had been playing a recording of an ivory-bill and the ARU picked it up. This had already happened a couple of times earlier at Bayou de View, so he was justifiably cautious. But these new calls had been recorded at the White River refuge on January 17. I told him I was almost positive that no one had done any playbacks there that early. And then I listened to them and was astonished. They were a series of short toots, similar in pitch to the Allen recordings but different enough for me to be certain they could not have been a playback. And when we checked with Peter Wrege, he said his team had indeed not done any playbacks before January 20.

John Fitzpatrick was out of town, but as soon as he got back, he made arrangements with Russ, Ron Rohrbaugh, Ken Rosenberg, Marc Dantzker, and me to get together at the lab on Sunday at noon to review the material. We sat listening to the new sounds over and over again, and then to every existing ivory-bill call recorded on the 1935 expedition. The ARU calls were remarkably similar to the known ivory-bill calls. Could this be the audio smoking gun that we had all been dreaming about? No one would dare say.

What were the other possibilities? A blue jay doing an imitation? Perhaps. These birds are excellent mimics. I've heard them do great imitations of Cooper's and red-shouldered hawks, but just as soon as you start thinking you might be hearing a raptor, they always seem to throw in a typical jay call, as if to say, "Gotcha!" This bird made these calls for much longer than I've ever heard a jay do an imitation, and it never made a jay call.

Fitz immediately asked Russ to go through all the blue jay recordings at the lab and put them through a spectrographic analysis, comparing them with this new recording. He said that it is vitally important to eliminate any other possible sources for these calls if they are to be accepted by the scientific community as ivory-bill *kent* calls — the first recorded in decades.

One very interesting thing about these sounds is the place where they were recorded: within a mile of the spot where Mary Scott said she saw an ivory-bill, Bob Russell heard a *kent*like call, and David Luneau, Bobby, and I saw trees with significant bark peeling.

I have no idea what will happen next, but this is an exciting time. After the official announcement of the ivory-bill's rediscovery, updates on the search will be available on the Cornell Lab of Ornithology's Web site, www.birds.cornell.edu, and the Nature Conservancy's Web site, www.tnc.org.

AFTERWORD

I have just reread the epilogue of this book, and it put me right back where I was last March, when events in the ivory-bill project were unfolding so quickly I had to keep adding postscripts almost right to the end, as the press was running. What a crazy year it has been! As we neared our announcement date (which we had originally planned for May 18, 2005), everything started moving faster and faster, like an avalanche.

At Cornell we had to prepare reams of material about the history of the ivory-billed woodpecker: its ecology, its catastrophic decline, and its earthshaking rediscovery. We knew the public would want to know everything about this bird as quickly as possible, so we set out to provide copious quantities of in-depth information in print and on our Web sites. But our most important task was to analyze the data we had gathered and write a scientific article about the rediscovery.

Our decision to go public was a tough one. We had data to support our contention that the ivory-billed woodpecker still exists, but would it pass muster with a peer-reviewed journal? John Fitzpatrick made no bones about it: if the article was not accepted by a mainstream scientific journal, there would be no announcement. He had a couple of other caveats: the article had to come out simultaneously with our announcement, and it had to be published in *Science*, one of the most respected and prestigious journals in the world and one of the toughest in which to be published.

The article's title, "Ivory-billed Woodpecker (*Campephilus principalis*) Persists in Continental North America," was remarkably understated — a real sleeper title for one of the most exciting ornithological rediscoveries of our lifetime. And the list of authors was long, seventeen in all — John W. Fitzpatrick, Martjan Lammertink, M. David Luneau, Jr., Tim W. Gallagher, Bobby R. Harrison, Gene M. Sparling, Kenneth V. Rosenberg, Ronald W. Rohrbaugh, Elliott C. H. Swarthout, Peter H. Wrege, Sara Barker Swarthout, Marc S. Dantzker, Russell A. Charif, Timothy R. Barksdale, J. V. Remsen, Jr., Scott D. Simon, and Douglas Zollner — including nearly everyone who had taken part in our weekly conference calls for the previous fourteen months plus a few people who had helped with various aspects of the analysis.

The article appeared in *Science Express* (the online edition of *Science*) on April 28, 2005, the day we made our announcement in Washington, D.C. (It was the cover story in the print version of *Science* on June 3.) Although the article covered the sightings by Gene Sparling, Bobby and me, Jim Fitzpatrick, Mindy LeBranche, Melanie Driscoll, and Casey Taylor, David Luneau's video was the primary piece of evidence that we analyzed for the article. (In the interest of brevity, we reduced the list of sightings from eighteen to the seven that had the best documentation; Bobby was the only observer who had two sightings discussed in the article.)

The article focused on David's video, of course, because it was tangible, a piece of forensic evidence that could be analyzed endlessly, measuring the trees in the background, the bird's wrist-to-tail-tip length, wing-flap speed, and so on. Several of us wanted to include some of the ARU recordings of possible *kent* calls and *Campephilus*-like double raps, but we were working hard to achieve consensus in our group, and at least two key members of the team believed it was premature to include acoustic evidence. They insisted that the initial article should focus only on David's video, pointing out that we could present the sound analysis later, when we'd had time to study it more thoroughly. Their view won the day, and we didn't release the sounds recorded by our ARUs until late August, at the American Ornithologists' Union meeting in Santa Barbara.

The most fortunate aspect of David's video was that he knew
the exact tree from which the bird had flown, so we had something solid to measure. One day David, Bobby, Martjan, Utami
Setiorini, Tim Barksdale, and Nick Meyer revisited the spot to
try to recreate what had happened when the bird took off from
the tree. Bobby took all of his decoys plus two life-sized flapping
models, one of an ivory-bill, the other of a pileated woodpecker.
Some of the pictures taken that day were hilarious. One shot of
Tim, with his big white beard and his hair tucked into a wool hat,
looked like Santa Claus surrounded by his band of elves. The
group made extensive measurements of the tree and determined
exactly where the bird's back had been showing and where its tail
had flared out at takeoff. They took still photographs and videos
of the entire sequence.

Although I wasn't there for the reenactment, a couple of
weeks later Martjan and David came to Cornell and joined Fitz
and me to work on the analysis. We hid ourselves away in the
Kingfisher Room, a large conference room on the second floor of
the Lab of Ornithology, and projected the photographs on a
screen on the far wall. David had taped measurements on the
tree before photographing it, so we knew the exact diameter of
the tree at the place where the bird's back and tail were visible
just before it launched itself. We compared this to the length of
the bird from its wrist to the tip of its tail and were able to extrap-
olate its approximate length, which we compared with measurements from dozens of museum specimens of ivory-billed and
pileated woodpeckers. We also took measurements of ivory-bills
from the still photographs and motion pictures made by Arthur
Allen in 1935. Fortunately, Allen had cut down the nest tree and
brought a section of it back to Cornell, and we still had it, so we
were able to measure the entrance hole of the nest and compare
it with a photograph of a living ivory-bill clinging to the trunk
beside it.

We compared all of these measurements with those of the bird
David had videotaped, which turned out to be far larger than a
pileated and was actually at the upper end of the size range for an

ivory-bill. Moreover, although the video was blurry and out of focus, all the visible field marks said ivory-bill. At no time could any of us detect any black on the trailing edge of the bird's wings, top or bottom. We compared this with similar videos of pileated woodpeckers. Even when they were motion-blurred and out of focus, the black trailing edge of the pileated's wings was visible.

Even more persuasive were the reenactment videos and still images of Bobby's life-sized flapping models. Each model was mounted on a stick, and Bobby had designed a string-and-pulley system that moved the wings quickly up and down to simulate flying. David videotaped each of them in action, using a deliberately soft focus to recreate the situation in the original video. The thin black line in the center of the underside of the ivory-bill model's wings invariably disappeared, overwhelmed by the great expanse of white on either side. But the much wider band of black at the trailing edge of the pileated woodpecker's wings was always plainly visible in the videos.

During the reenactment, the crew also looked closely at an unusual black-and-white shape that had been visible on a tree in David's video just a few seconds before the bird launched itself. They located the tree, which no longer had a black-and-white shape on it, and Bobby attached one of his decoys at the spot where the object had been. They took an out-of-focus videotape of the decoy from the exact location of David's canoe. The result? On the reenactment video, the decoy became a blurry black-and-white object, strikingly similar to the one seen on the same tree in David's video.

For me the strongest evidence in David's video is what I see when it's played in real time without any enlargement. The bird in the video simply does not fly like any pileated woodpecker I've ever seen. It is far more ducklike, which is the way the ivory-bill's flight is consistently described in all the published literature on the species.

By the end of this exercise, we all felt confident in our analysis and ready to move ahead with writing the article. John Fitzpatrick drew illustrations depicting our interpretation of the bird while it was perched on the tree and also in several key frames of the video. And then we began the long process of passing the manuscript around by e-mail, sometimes working late into the night polishing the article and striving to reach consensus among all the authors on every point.

By late April the article had been peer-reviewed and accepted for publication, and we thought we might have a couple of weeks to catch our breath and prepare for our May 18 announcement, tentatively planned for Arkansas. But it was not to be.

On April 25, 2005, exactly one year after David Luneau shot his historic videotape, word of the rediscovery began leaking out — at first just a trickle, then an overwhelming dam burst as the news spread around the world on the Internet. The next morning we were still hoping that we might be able to contain the leak. But by the afternoon we knew it was all over, and we started planning a news conference, to take place on Thursday, April 28, in an auditorium at the Department of the Interior in Washington.

The morning of the press conference, National Public Radio was the first to break the story. The reporter, Christopher Joyce, had known about the rediscovery for several months but had kept our secret well. He had spent several days with us in the swamp earlier in the season, preparing a piece on the ivory-bill for *Radio Expeditions*. Before the story aired, a lot of Internet-savvy birders around the world had heard rumors that an ivory-bill had been found, but the general public had no clue. Bobby and I were sharing a hotel room, and we listened to Chris's radio piece together that morning. I choked up with emotion on hearing it, and apparently thousands of listeners, many of whom knew little about the ivory-billed woodpecker, had similar reactions. It was such a hopeful story, after so many years of dismal news about ecosystems wrecked and wildlife populations obliterated. I heard later that people all across the country, listening to Chris's story as they made their morning commute, had to pull over to the side of the road, their vision too blurred with tears to drive safely.

I suspect that the NPR story was what got the attention of the press corps. The auditorium was packed with reporters, photographers, and television crews as we got ready to announce the rediscovery of the ivory-bill. You'd think that Washington media people, who have seen every kind of corruption and scandal, would be jaded and cynical. But we were amazed to see how genuinely excited and enthusiastic they were.

We heard speeches from a number of dignitaries, including Secretary of the Interior Gale Norton and Secretary of Agriculture Mike Johanns, who pledged a combined total of $10 million to aid the recovery of the ivory-bill; Senator Blanche Lincoln, who spoke eloquently of visiting the swamps of eastern Arkansas with her father as a child; and John Fitzpatrick, who told of the importance of preserving and enhancing the Big Woods of Arkansas for the good of the ivory-bills as well as for the citizens of the world in the centuries ahead.

After all the dignitaries had spoken, the emcee invited members of the press to ask questions. The first person who came up to the microphone was a woman from Reuters, who asked, "Can't we hear from some of the people who actually saw the bird — like Tim and Bobby and Gene?" The three of us plus David Luneau made our way to the podium, and suddenly it was like being the Mercury astronauts in *The Right Stuff.* None of us had anything prepared to say. We all just stood there and babbled away, saying anything that popped into our heads as the reporters wrote feverishly on their notepads, hanging on every word we said. As soon as we stepped down, they were all over us, asking more questions, pulling us away to be on camera or inviting us to television studios for more interviews.

Bobby and I stayed up most of the night on Thursday, doing Internet searches to find out how far the news of the ivory-bill's rediscovery had spread. It was front-page news worldwide. We read articles from India, Turkey, Australia, Germany, Britain, and many other faraway places. Bobby had become instantly famous for breaking down and sobbing after seeing the bird. I remember thinking, *So this is our fifteen minutes of fame.* But it quickly stretched to *60 Minutes,* as Ed Bradley and his camera crew traveled to the swamp a short time later to film a television segment that would run the following October.

Within days of the announcement the bird had become part of Washington's political lexicon. On a television program a few days after the announcement, I heard a political pundit say, "Democrats who support President Bush's Social Security reforms are rarer than ivory-billed woodpeckers." And not long afterward I saw a political cartoon of an ivory-bill whacking its way through the trunk of a tree amid a forest of stumps. The bird's face was remarkably similar to the president's, and the caption read "The Ivory-billed Woods Wrecker."

It was enough to make us all giddy. But of course we knew that this unbridled euphoria could not last forever. Somewhere dark clouds were surely forming. Long before we wrote the paper for *Science* and announced to the world our rediscovery of the ivory-billed woodpecker, we knew that it would not all be smooth sailing. Somewhere, sometime, the doubters would emerge. For more than fifty years, every time someone reported a seemingly credible sighting of this species, the skeptics slammed it. This time would be no different. But I didn't think it would happen so quickly. Barely two months after our announcement, we got word that three ornithologists — Richard Prum of Yale, Mark Robbins of the University of Nebraska, and Jerome Jackson of Florida Gulf Coast University — had written a rebuttal article, which was slated to run in the Web-based scientific journal *Public Library of Science* (*PLOS*).

My immediate response was visceral anger. I remember thinking that we had taken fourteen months to evaluate our evidence before going public, while the rebutters didn't take even fourteen weeks. More than that, I thought, considering the impact their paper might have on our conservation initiative in the Arkansas swamps, it would have behooved the critics to make very sure that we were wrong — to have visited us at Cornell, viewed all our evidence, interviewed the people who had seen the bird, and perhaps even gone out and explored the swamps where the ivory-bill had been seen. But after a few days I cooled off. This is the scientific process: you publish a paper and people respond to it. As the mobsters in *The Godfather* said before bumping off a colleague, "It's nothing personal; it's just business." And so it was: an esoteric exercise, science in the abstract.

The premise of the rebuttal article was not that David's video depicted an unusually marked pileated — which we had all thought possible originally — but that it showed a completely normal pileated woodpecker and that we had misinterpreted its position and posture on the tree right before it took off, thus making all of our subsequent measurements incorrect. According to the rebutters, the white patch we had used to estimate the bird's size was too big, too broad, and too far forward to be the white wing patch on the back of an ivory-bill. The shape and size and the timing of this white patch as it came into view, they wrote, was consistent in every way with the underwing of a pileated woodpecker. The authors also took us to task for failing to obtain sound recordings of the birds, despite our intensive acoustic census of the search area. Of course, because the article did not discuss our acoustic evidence, they had no way of knowing how many recordings we had that were at least suggestive of the presence of ivory-bills.

One of the most interesting remarks made by the rebuttal authors was that the wing-flap speed of the bird in David's video — 8.4 flaps per second — was far too fast for an ivory-bill. They stated that the average wing-flap speed of a pileated woodpecker was 5.2 flaps per second. Because an ivory-billed woodpecker is larger, they reasoned, it should have a lower average wing-flap speed, which they estimated at approximately 4.6 flaps per second. They admitted that 8.7 wing flaps per second was exceptionally fast for a pileated woodpecker, but they believed it would be even more exceptional for an ivory-bill. From the start, our team of authors felt that the fast, direct flight of this bird actually bolstered our identification of it as an ivory-billed woodpecker because it so closely fit the anecdotal descriptions of the species in the scientific literature. We would soon have a chance to investigate this and other aspects of David's video again.

The editors at *PLOS* agreed to let us write a response to the rebuttal, which would run side by side with it on the publication's Web site. So once again we were in rush mode, frantically working to put together an article. But this process was useful, for it forced us to reevaluate our data and scrutinize it even more closely than before. We came away feeling that our views about the bird's identity were strongly vindicated.

The wing-flap speed turned out to be the easiest point in the rebuttal to shoot down. Amazingly, we had a sound recording at Cornell of an ivory-bill flying away from its nest tree, made by Arthur Allen and Peter Paul Kellogg in the Singer Tract in 1935. The wing flaps are clearly audible, and it was a simple matter for our acoustic analysts to look at a spectrograph of the sounds and measure the number of flaps the bird made in a second. The Singer Tract ivory-bill flapped its wings 8.4 times per second — exactly the same rate as the bird in David's video and far faster than any documented pileated-woodpecker flight.

We tried to address every point in the rebuttal in the limited amount of space available. The rebuttal authors had written that too much white was showing on the bird perched on the tree in David's video for it to be an ivory-bill; it must be the extended wing of a pileated woodpecker as it was taking off. But if that was the extended wing of a pileated, where was the band of black that should be distinctly visible on the left? It was just not there, no matter how I strained my eyes and squinted at the picture. We tried holding the wing of a pileated woodpecker in that position behind a tree and taking pictures of it, varying the focus. In every instance the wide black edge of the wing was visible.

Martjan photographed a number of ivory-bill museum specimens and found that the amount of white on their backs varied greatly. Moreover, if a mounted ivory-bill was photographed from slightly below as it was leaning away (as a bird would be if it were about to take off), the expanse of white seemed much larger. The capper, though, was Martjan's photograph of a mounted ivory-bill specimen taken from this lower angle and then spliced into a picture of the tree from which the bird in David's video had launched. We looked at this image beside the image from the video, and it was more than strikingly similar — it was almost identical.

At the end of this exercise, we certainly felt that we had made our case. Word of the rebuttal had already leaked, and articles had appeared in the *New York Times* and *Nature* and on NPR. We were eager to have the rebuttal and our response published to clear the air and dispel the rumors that were flying around. We sent a draft of our article to the authors of the rebuttal so that they could write a response to our response. (This process is endless.) We also sent them a CD containing a sampling of the sounds recorded by our ARUs in the Cache River and White River refuges.

At that point a remarkable thing happened. The lead author, Richard Prum, decided not to publish the rebuttal paper, and Mark Robbins joined him in this decision; the third author, Jerome Jackson, was out of the country.

Apparently, after hearing the sneak preview of our acoustic evidence, Prum and Robbins were completely convinced that there were ivory-bills in our Arkansas study area. "The thrilling new sound recordings provide clear and convincing evidence that the ivory-billed woodpecker is not extinct," Prum told the *New York Times.* He went on to say that he was "strongly convinced that there is at least one pair of ivory-bills out there." One of the recordings from the White River that we supplied to Prum and the others was of a distant double knock followed less than four seconds later by a closer one — exactly like two *Campephilus* woodpeckers signaling each other. This is the evidence that Prum and Robbins found most convincing. "We were astounded," Robbins told *CBS News.* "I totally believe, thank goodness, there are ivory-bills."

I spoke with Jerry Jackson a couple of times after this, at the American Ornithologists' Union meeting in August and at a large woodpecker symposium in Brinkley, Arkansas, in early November, at the beginning of the new search season. He told me that he had regrets about the paper being withdrawn from *PLOS,* for he felt that the rebuttal brought up some significant issues that should have been aired in a peer-reviewed journal. I tend to agree with him, particularly because a lot of tantalizing rumors came out in popular articles about the rebuttal, and there was no mechanism to respond to them. These rumors have since fueled a number of blogs and Web sites devoted to various conspiracy theories about the ivory-billed woodpecker rediscovery.

The conspiracy theorists range from people who think the rediscovery was something cooked up by scientists to get more funding for their pet projects to those who believe scientists have always known the bird existed and have kept it quiet for nefarious reasons — which sounds a bit like a plot from an episode of *The X Files.* It would have been far better to clear the air and publish the rebuttal and our response.

We do plan to present the full analysis of David Luneau's video on our Web site (www.birds.cornell.edu/ivory) for people who wish to view the information and images I've described here. It should be online by the time this new edition of *The Grail Bird* is published. Anyone who wants a copy of David's ivory-bill video can purchase a DVD of it through his Web site, ibwo.org. The DVD contains the video, shown at various speeds and magnifications, plus commentary and some selected still images. Another Web site of interest is bobbyharrison.com, which describes Bobby's latest adventures in the swamp and lists his upcoming appearances across the country.

On a positive note, I recently learned that the Arkansas Audubon Society's Bird Records Committee reviewed our evidence and voted to change the status of the ivory-billed woodpecker from "extirpated" to "present" in the state. This committee has been responsible for reviewing all unusual or exceptional bird sightings since 1955, when Arkansas Audubon was founded. All five committee members must study the documentation of a bird sighting in great detail and at least four of them must vote in favor of accepting it before it becomes official, so this is a strong affirmation of the ivory-bill's rediscovery.

When I started this project, I never imagined where it would lead me. I began with the simple desire to record the recollections of as many people as possible who had seen ivory-billed woodpeckers. I didn't know if the ivory-bill still existed; I just knew that many living witnesses to this spectacular bird were getting older, and many were passing away. I knew that if the birds really were extinct, the knowledge that would be lost with the deaths of these human witnesses could never be duplicated.

I came to this project not as a scientist but as a naturalist and journalist with a deep love of history. Also, I have always enjoyed the challenge of trying to sort out a mystery. The quest for the ivory-bill had everything. What I brought to the search was an open mind and a willingness to hear people out if they had a compelling story to tell. As I traveled and spoke about the ivory-bill, I kept finding out about people who'd had possible sightings long after the bird was supposed to be extinct, and some of them seemed entirely credible. There was Larry Wright, a forester, who in the mid-1980s was walking a transect through a stand of timber in eastern Arkansas, evaluating the trees for a lumber company, when he saw a large black-and-white woodpecker drop down from above the canopy and land on the trunk of a huge cypress tree. He raised the binoculars he always carried with him and studied the field marks of the bird, a species he was certain he'd never seen before. When he looked it up in his field guide, he was stunned to see that it exactly fit the description of an ivory-bill. And there was Mary Scott, whose sighting in the White River refuge is covered in detail in Chapter 4. And of course there was Gene Sparling, whose amazing sighting in Bayou de View (forwarded to me by Mary Scott), made possible everything that followed. I think my role, and Bobby's, was to connect the dots between these sightings and provide the strong visual confirmation of the ivory-bill's continued existence that launched the massive research effort.

I recently learned that Bobby Harrison, Gene Sparling, and I will receive the Explorers Club President's Conservation Award in March 2006 at the group's annual banquet at the Waldorf Astoria. It's a black-tie affair featuring famous explorers and exotic foods. I can't wait; it will be worth going just to see Bobby and Gene dressed in tuxedos. My only regret is that Mary Scott won't be there. She played a vital role in the rediscovery of the ivory-bill and has not received the recognition she deserves.

Down in Arkansas the search is under way once again. Our ivory-billed woodpecker research team is already there in force, fanning out across the swamps and bottomland forests to find out more about this elusive species, including where the birds roost and if and where they are nesting. It is unbelievably grueling to scour more than half a million acres of woodlands for a species whose numbers are undoubtedly extremely small.

I went to Arkansas for a few days in early November to meet the new full-time searchers. Many of them are young; all are idealistic and passionate about the ivory-billed woodpecker. Their excitement was palpable as they went through the training sessions and got ready to hit the swamp. They will all stay there for a full six months. I admire their dedication.

The full-time searchers have been joined by about one hundred volunteers, each of whom has agreed to spend a minimum of two weeks searching the swamps in groups of fourteen. The volunteers were chosen from hundreds of people who contacted us, eager to help with the search.

I returned to the swamp again briefly in mid-December — just last week — and spent three days exploring Bayou de View. I find it hard to get back to Arkansas as frequently as I would like because I spend so much time traveling across the country now, speaking to enthusiastic audiences about the ivory-bill. Although I enjoy giving talks, I would far rather be out in the swamp, searching for this bird. I am reminded of something John Fitzpatrick said to me the morning I first told him about seeing the ivory-bill in Arkansas. "Our lives will never be the same again," he said. That has certainly been true for me.

I felt wistful last week as I paddled up Bayou de View in a canoe with David Luneau. It was so peaceful and still, and the trees arching above us seemed so stately, with a scattering of massive cypresses adding depth and age to this shadow forest. I thought of all the people I'd encountered during the course of this search, all the friends I'd made, including some who have since passed away. And I thought of John Dennis and George Lowery and the many others who were scorned for daring to believe that the ivory-billed woodpecker still lived. Surely the work we have done in Arkansas, the rediscovery of the species, has vindicated them, I thought. Or has it? Who knows? If no additional evidence of the ivory-bill is found this field season, we may well join the ranks of ornithological pariahs. As I paddled the canoe slowly through the bayou, though, I really didn't care. It was just great to be in that special place once again, a place that will always be close to my heart.

ACKNOWLEDGMENTS
AND SOURCES

I owe a debt of gratitude to dozens of people who helped and encouraged me or provided vital information as I worked on this book. I especially thank Bobby Ray Harrison, a constant companion during most of my travels through the trackless swamps of the South, for his boundless enthusiasm and ingenuity and his unwavering belief in the continued existence of the ivory-bill. Oakwood College, where Bobby teaches, also deserves recognition. It is a wonderful part of this story that a small institution like Oakwood has supported one of its faculty members in a quest of this kind.

I also thank David Luneau. His steadfast determination — sustained for several years now — to see and document this species is truly impressive. I wasn't surprised at all that he was the first person to capture the bird on videotape.

Of course, the rediscovery would have been impossible without Gene Sparling's initial sighting of a mystery woodpecker at Bayou de View. I'm still absolutely amazed by Gene's ability to move silently through the swamp in his kayak, largely unnoticed by the wildlife he encounters.

I thank Mary Scott for passing along to me any promising ivory-bill reports — including Gene Sparling's — that she received through her Web site. And her own sighting at White River a year earlier is what originally got Bobby and me interested in searching for the bird in Arkansas.

I am grateful to all my friends at the Cornell Lab of Ornithology, especially the lab's director, John Fitzpatrick, who had the courage to believe my story and act on it when I emerged wild-eyed and shaggy-haired from the swamp with a tale that many scientists would have laughed at. I also salute the sound technicians in the lab's Bioacoustics Research Program and Macaulay Library. Although my book focuses mostly on the field biologists searching the swamps of Arkansas, the crew back home did equally important work, searching through hundreds of hours of recordings for the calls and double raps of ivory-bills. Led by Russ Charif, the sound analysis team included Ann Warde, Dimitri Ponirakis, Melissa Fowler, Chris Tessaglia-Hymes, Mike Powers, Beth Howard, Mike Pitzrick, and Mickey Scilingo.

I thank the staff of the Division of Rare and Manuscript Collections at Cornell's Kroch Library for sharing their treasure trove of books (some centuries old), field notebooks, obscure letters, and manuscripts. I especially thank Laura Linke for her help and guidance in my searches over the years.

I am grateful for the ongoing work of the Arkansas chapter of the Nature Conservancy, which has played a major role in saving thousands of acres of bottomland swamp forest in Arkansas. The state director, Scott Simon, used his considerable people skills to keep our team of researchers and ivory-bill enthusiasts dedicated to the task and working together.

I am forever indebted to Nancy Tanner for her insights into her husband, Jim Tanner's, ivory-billed woodpecker research and for her own observations of the birds in the early 1940s. In our conversations, her descriptions were as vivid as though she had seen the birds the day before. I also thank Nancy's son, David, for talking with me about trips he took with his father in search of ivory-bills in Georgia and imperial woodpeckers in Mexico.

David G. Allen, the son of the famed ornithologist Arthur A. Allen, who founded the Cornell Lab of Ornithology and led the 1935 expedition to the Singer Tract, shared with me a wealth of knowledge about his father's work with the ivory-bill and other birds.

During the course of my research, I got to know John Dennis, Jr., whose late father figures prominently in several sections of this book. I greatly appreciate the time he took searching through boxes of his father's papers and correspondence for references to ivory-bills.

I thank Van Remsen, the curator of birds at Louisiana State University's Museum of Natural Science, for sharing his deep knowledge of ivory-bill lore and for his help in tracking down key people to interview for this book.

I am indebted to my literary agent, Maria Carvainis, for her expert advice and encouragement through every phase of this project. Her boundless enthusiasm for the book kept me going month after month until the job was done.

And I thank everyone at Houghton Mifflin who helped to make *The Grail Bird* a success, especially my editor, Lisa White, who took on the project and worked with me from the beginning. She and the production editor, Liz Duvall, did a masterful job of editing the morass of words I turned in, as winding and tangled as any bayou. Thanks also to my publicist, Taryn Roeder, for getting out the word about this book.

Above all I thank my wife, Rachel Dickinson, and my children, Railey, Clara, Jack, and Gwendolyn, for putting up with months of neglect as I sealed myself away night after night to work on this project. Without their support and encouragement, none of this would have been possible.

In the course of writing this book, I read everything I could find about the ivory-billed woodpecker. I dug through huge ornithological tomes; bird field guides, new and old; scientific journals; features in popular magazines and newspapers; fictional accounts; children's books; and short notes in obscure nineteenth-century publications long defunct. And I sifted through reams of correspondence and unpublished manuscripts and the field notebooks of earlier researchers. A few of these sources really stood out, providing vital insights into the behavior and natural history of this rarest of birds.

For me, the oldest books are the most interesting — those

written when the great primeval swamp forests still spread across the South, by authors who had seen numerous ivory-bills. I was fortunate enough to be able to look through original copies of these works, with their hand-colored engravings, at Cornell, but some are available in smaller reprinted editions. Mark Catesby's *A Natural History of Carolina, Florida, and the Bahama Islands* (London, 1731) is wonderful from a historical perspective, with rich illustrations and Catesby's colorful prose. But a more recent book, *Catesby's Birds of Colonial America,* edited by Alan Feduccia (Chapel Hill: University of North Carolina Press, 1985), was more useful to me, having all of Catesby's text as well as biographical information. Another excellent source was *Mark Catesby, the Colonial Audubon* (Urbana: University of Illinois Press, 1961), by G. F. Frick and R. P. Stearns.

Alexander Wilson is one of my favorite characters from colonial America. Many call him "the father of American ornithology," though some might argue that Catesby is more deserving of that title. Wilson's ten-volume *American Ornithology* (Philadelphia, 1811) was certainly the most ambitious work of its kind ever attempted at that time. What I like about it is that the natural history accounts are so full of personal anecdotes. The wonderful quote about Wilson weeping copious tears over the grave of his friend Meriwether Lewis came from the species account for the Lewis's woodpecker. (Captain Lewis collected the first specimens of this species during his epic journey with the Corps of Discovery.) The story about the ivory-bill destroying the mahogany table and the wall at the inn came from the ivory-billed woodpecker species account. Clark Hunter's *The Life and Letters of Alexander Wilson* (Philadelphia: American Philosophical Society, 1983) has useful biographical information on Wilson.

Volume 4 of John James Audubon's classic *Birds of America* (Philadelphia: J. B. Chevalier, 1842), with its stunning full-sized portrait of a group of three ivory-bills, has excellent information on the natural history of this species, from numerous firsthand observations made by Audubon.

The wonderful material about Theodore Roosevelt's 1907 visit to the Tensas River area of northeastern Louisiana came from a lengthy article he wrote entitled "In the Louisiana Canebrakes," which was published the following year in *Scribner's Magazine* (vol. 43, no. 1, pages 47–60).

James T. Tanner's *The Ivory-billed Woodpecker* (New York: National Audubon Society, 1942) is still the bible for those who search for this bird. Other books may be more entertaining, but this has the solid facts based on more than two years of observation. I still refer to it constantly. But far more interesting to me than Tanner's book are his personal papers at Cornell's Kroch Library. I spent many hours going through his correspondence. It was here that we found a copy of John V. Dennis's ivory-bill recording that he had made in Texas in the late 1960s, as well as some interesting letters from George Lowery about the two mystery snapshots taken in the Atchafalaya Swamp in 1971. Nancy Tanner gave me copies of two unpublished essays from which I have drawn — one about the Singer Tract, titled "A Forest Alive," the other about a Florida river, titled "The Suwanee River, 1890–1973."

Arthur A. Allen wrote several articles about ivory-bills in the course of his life. "Vacationing with Birds" ran in *Bird-Lore* (precursor to *Audubon* magazine) in 1924 and told of his and his wife's experience finding an ivory-bill nest in Florida. (The birds ended up being shot by collectors, to Allen's chagrin.) Allen and Peter Paul Kellogg co-wrote a scientific article in 1937 titled "Recent Observations on the Ivory-billed Woodpecker" (*Auk* 54: 164–84), presenting an in-depth account of the birds they had seen in the Singer Tract two years earlier as well as more information about the 1924 Florida nest. Allen also wrote much of the ivory-billed woodpecker species account in *Life Histories of North American Woodpeckers* (U.S. National Museum Bulletin 174, 1937), edited by A. C. Bent.

But my favorite version of the story of the Cornell expedition to the Singer Tract was told in George Miksch Sutton's *Birds in the Wilderness* (New York: Macmillan, 1936). Sutton's essay "Kints" is a classic. I relied heavily on his vivid descriptions of the people and their conversations when I was writing Chapter 1. George Lowery's *Louisiana Birds* (Baton Rouge: Louisiana State University Press, 1974) also has some interesting details about the Singer Tract in the early 1930s. I also drew from Michael Harwood's excellent 1986 article, "You Can't Protect What Isn't There" (*Audubon* 88, no. 6), for more information about Mason Spencer, the Singer Tract, and a later search for the ivory-bill in the Atchafalaya.

Most of the information about Richard Pough is from conversations I had with him during a four-day visit in 2003. I also quote from two articles: "Richard Pough: Man of Action" (*Audubon* 105, no. 3, September 2003), and "DDT," a Talk of the Town piece that appeared in *The New Yorker* (vol. 21, no. 18, May 26, 1945).

I used several sources for my material about John V. Dennis. Especially useful was "The Ivory-billed Woodpecker," a lengthy article Dennis wrote for *Avicultural Magazine* in 1979, which had extensive information about his own sightings plus those of several other people. His son, John V. Dennis, Jr., also provided copies of two unpublished manuscripts and numerous letters and notes from his father's personal papers. The following sources were also helpful in piecing together John Dennis's experiences with ivory-bills:

Dennis, John V. 1948. "A Last Remnant of Ivory-billed Wood-
    peckers in Cuba." *Auk* 65: 497–507.
———. 1967. "The Ivory-bill Still Flies." *Audubon* 69 (6): 38–44.
———. 1984. "A Tale of Two Woodpeckers." *Living Bird Quarterly*
    3: 18–21.
———. 1987. "Davis Crompton and the Cuban Ivory-billed Wood-
    pecker." *Bird Watcher's Digest* 9 (4): 18–25.
Moser, Don. 1972. "The Last Ivory-bill." *Life* 72 (13): 52–62.
Nevin, David. 1974. "The Irresistible, Elusive Allure of the Ivory-
    bill." *Smithsonian* 4 (11): 72–81.

I based the chapter "Mary, Mary" on information from Mary Scott's Web site, www.birdingamerica.com, and on several conversations with her and with Bob Russell.

Of the more recent books with ivory-bill information, Christopher Cokinos's *Hope Is the Thing with Feathers* (New York: Tarcher/Putnam, 2000) was the most interesting and was one of my major sources for details about the 1943 meeting between Audubon's executive director, John Baker, James E. Griswold, and others over the fate of the remaining Singer Tract.

Jerome Jackson's recent book *In Search of the Ivory-billed Woodpecker* (Washington, D.C.: Smithsonian Press, 2004) is a useful compendium of the science and lore of this bird, written by someone who has spent a good part of his life looking for this bird. Jerry also wrote the species account for the ivory-bill in the *Birds of North America* series.

Phillip Hoose also came out with a book on the ivory-bill in 2004: *The Race to Save the Lord God Bird* (New York: Farrar, Straus & Giroux/Melanie Kroupa). Although Phil began this book with adolescents in mind, it's an enjoyable read for anyone and lays out the grim history of the Singer Tract's demise better than anything else I've read.

I also found the following books and articles useful in writing *The Grail Bird:*

Agey, H. N., G. M. Heinzmann. 1971. "The Ivory-billed Woodpecker Found in Central Florida." *Florida Naturalist* 44 (3): 46–47, 64.

———. 1971. "Ivory-billed Woodpeckers in Florida." *Birding* 3: 43.

Barrow, Mark V., Jr. 1998. *A Passion for Birds*. Princeton, N.J.: Princeton University Press.

Christy, B. 1943. "The Vanishing Ivory-bill." *Audubon* 45 (2): 99–102.

Eckelberry, Donald. 1961. "Search for the Rare Ivorybill." In *Discovery: Great Moments in the Lives of Outstanding Naturalists*. J. K. Terres, ed. Philadelphia: Lippincott, pp. 195–207.

Hardy, J. W. 1975. "A Tape Recording of a Possible Ivory-billed Woodpecker Call." *American Birds* 29: 647–51.

Jackson, Jerome A. 1991. "Will-o'-the-wisp." *Living Bird Quarterly* 10 (1): 29–32.

———. 2002. "The Truth Is Out There." *Birder's World* 16 (3): 40–47.

Lamb, George R. 1957. "The Ivory-billed Woodpecker in Cuba." Pan-American Section, International Committee for Bird Preservation, Res. Rep. no. 1.

Lammertink, Martjan. 1992. "Search for Ivory-billed Woodpecker in Cuba." *Dutch Birding* 14: 170–73.

———. 1995. "No More Hope for the Ivory-billed Woodpecker." *Cotinga* 3: 45–47.

Lammertink, M., A. R. Estrada. 1995. "Status of the Ivory-billed Woodpecker in Cuba: Almost Certainly Extinct." *Bird Conservation International* 5: 53–59.

Lewis, Fielding. 1988. *Tales of a Louisiana Duck Hunter.* Franklin, La.: Little Atakepis.

Peterson, Roger T., James Fisher. 1955. "Ivory-bill Quest." *Wild America.* Boston: Houghton Mifflin.

Short, Lester L. 1985. "Last Chance for the Ivory-bill." *Natural History* 94 (8): 66–68.

Short, Lester L., J.F.M. Horne. 1986. "The Ivorybill Still Lives." *Natural History* 95 (7): 26–28.

Snyder, N.F.R., K. Russell. 2002. "Carolina Parakeet." *The Birds of North America,* no. 675. A. Poole and F. Gill, eds. Philadelphia: The Birds of North America, Inc.

Stoddard, Herbert L. 1969. *Memoirs of a Naturalist.* Norman: University of Oklahoma Press.

Tanner, James T. 1941. "Three Years with the Ivory-billed Woodpecker, America's Rarest Bird." *Audubon* 43 (1): 5–14.

———. 1942. "Present Status of the Ivory-billed Woodpecker." *Wilson Bulletin* 54: 57–58.

Weidensaul, Scott. 2002. *The Ghost with Trembling Wings.* New York: North Point Press.

Williams, J. J. 2001. "Ivory-billed Dreams, Ivory-billed Reality." *Birding* 33: 514–522.

INDEX